W9-BBR-803

The
OLD MAN
and the TEE

Also by Turk Pipkin

Fast Greens
When Angels Sing

The
OLD MAN
and the TEE

How I Took Ten Strokes Off My Game and
Learned to Love Golf All Over Again

TURK PIPKIN

St. Martin's Press ❦ New York

THE OLD MAN AND THE TEE. Copyright © 2004 by Turk Pipkin. Foreword copyright © 2004 by David Leadbetter. All rights reserved. Printed in the United States of America. No part of this book may be used or reproduced in any manner whatsoever without written permission except in the case of brief quotations embodied in critical articles or reviews. For information, address St. Martin's Press, 175 Fifth Avenue, New York, N.Y. 10010.

www.stmartins.com

Design by Phil Mazzone

"I'd Have to Be Crazy" written by Steve Fromholz
© 1973, 2001 Bughouse (ASCAP) / Prophecy Publishing (ASCAP)
All Rights Reserved. Used by permission.

"Straight Down the Middle" by Sammy Cahn and James Van Heusen
© 1957 by Mayfair Music Corp.
Copyright renewed and assigned to Cahn Music Company, Van Heusen Music Corp. and Edwin H. Morris & Co., Inc.
All Rights Reserved. Used by permission.
Warner Bros. Publications U.S. Inc., Miami, FL 33014

Golf's Biggest Myths, adapted from:
What You Know Can Hurt You, by Kip Puterbaugh, Lowell Publishing, 2002.
All Rights Reserved. Used by permission.

Library of Congress Cataloging-in-Publication Data

Pipkin, Turk.
    The old man and the tee: how I took ten strokes off my game and learned to love golf all over again / Turk Pipkin.—1st ed.
        p. cm.
    ISBN 0-312-32084-1
    EAN 978-0312-32084-3
    1. Pipkin, Turk. 2. Golfers—United States—Biography. 3. Golf—Anecdotes. I. Title.
GV964.P53A3 2004
796.352'092—dc22
[B]   2004048177

First Edition: September 2004

10   9   8   7   6   5   4   3   2   1

To Pip

And to old men everywhere

Contents

Contents

FOREWORD

When Turk Pipkin asked me to help him drop ten shots off his game in one year, with his final exam being a round at none other than Pebble Beach, I knew only a Texan could think so big! Having spent twenty-five-plus years teaching some of the best players in the world, I knew we had our work cut out—but it is, after all, only a game.

As with any player I work with, from major winners to weekend warriors, I've always felt the first step toward improvement is having a clear understanding of one's game, a "blueprint" for improvement if you will. At six feet seven inches tall, Turk looked like he was trying to swing the golf club like that other Texan, Ben Hogan, who was considerably smaller at five feet seven. In short, his swing did not fit his posture.

Armed with a clear concept of how he needed to swing the club, Turk was able to apply the aspects of sound technique to his taller frame using visual feedback and some simple drills. With a purposeful practice plan and a willingness to stay the course, Turk demonstrates how much enjoyment one can have while chasing a lifelong dream.

Ultimately *The Old Man and the Tee* is a very humorous account of Turk Pipkin's goal to become a better golfer. Turk's quest is filled with entertaining experiences and encounters reminding us of just how challenging and fun this game can be. Whether you've played the game for a lifetime or you're just starting out, this book will certainly make you laugh and might even inspire you to find out how good you really are!

—David Leadbetter

"Fish," he said softly and aloud,
"I'll stay with you until I am dead."

—Ernest Hemingway,
The Old Man and the Sea

The
OLD MAN
and the TEE

CHAPTER 1

The Beginning of the End

That last perfect moment is frozen in my mind, a crystalline memory of how the world would never be again—the rising sun painting halos on the treetops, the spray of morning dew as a ball came rolling through the fringe, the scent of pine trees and sea air on the day's first breeze.

It's tournament week at Pebble Beach and life is good. A smile on my face, I'm on the putting green trading jokes with players and caddies alike. Since I was a scrawny kid learning to play golf in bone-dry West Texas, I've longed to be here for the Crosby Clambake. My dad loved Bing, Bob, and Arnie, and the two of us always tuned in for the broadcast.

I was seven or eight, watching the Crosby on TV, when Bob Hope told the first golf joke I ever heard.

"How come a golfer wears two pairs of socks?"

"In case he gets a hole in one."

Okay, it's not much of a joke, but to an entertainment-deprived kid in Hicksville, it was practically hilarious. I told that joke to everyone I knew, starting with my dad, who'd missed it on TV, and I've never forgotten that he actually laughed. Who knows? Maybe that first laugh from my father was part of why I would later spend a decade of my life telling jokes in comedy clubs.

Even though the tournament name has long since changed to the AT&T Pebble Beach Pro-Am, I still feel like a big kid in a dream as I walk the putting green with Furyk and Fluff. I've got a rented red convertible, a press pass for the week, and an assignment to write a story about—and this is almost too good to be true—those age-old nuggets called golf jokes.

So what if the jokes I'm hearing are lamer than a one-legged kickboxer? Jokes aren't about setups and punch lines; jokes are about the people who tell them. For the next four days, the people telling them to me will be Bill Murray, Ray Romano, and just about everyone else who knows how to skate into a big-time golf tournament on a good laugh.

Perhaps it is too perfect. Or perhaps the golf gods simply have other plans for me, because just as Fluff starts to tell me a joke, the cell phone in my pocket vibrates its silent ring. I ignore it, but in a few moments the phone begins to vibrate again. Stepping to one side, I answer the call, listen a moment, and then I'm gone.

I don't even say good-bye.

Five minutes later I'm driving like a madman, doing seventy in a forty-five zone as I race toward the airport, hoping to make the next plane to Texas and praying my father will live long enough for me to see him again.

I didn't have any idea how much that morning would change my life. I'd never known the kind of loss I faced that day, didn't have a clue how lucky I'd been so far or how determined I could become.

I certainly didn't know that phone call would lead me to the doorsteps of golf's greatest teachers, or that I would throw myself upon their mercy, saying, "Help me become a golfer my father would have been proud of."

The Beginning of the End

I didn't know I'd dream up the crazy idea of trying to take ten strokes off my game in just a year, that I'd ignore my kids in order to hit practice balls in the hot Texas sun until my lips bled, that I'd become so obsessed that my wife would wonder if she even knew me. I didn't know that I'd come to doubt who I was and what my life had been about. All I knew was I had to go fast.

This is a story about the love for your father that is inherent in all of us who are lucky enough to have known a father's love. It's a story about the love of a game that seems to have an almost mystical hold on those who come under its spell. It's a story about repaying love that can never be repaid, about forgiving a broken mind and mending a broken heart. It's a story about turning a broken machine that was flawed in the first place into a thing of occasional beauty, then laying it all on the line for no particular reason other than to say, "Thanks, Dad. Wish you were here."

Ultimately, it's the story of what it takes to hit the ball in the sweet spot and launch it with a perfect rising arc toward a distant flag. A story about how to hit the right shots at the right times, and the wrong shots when they won't hurt you.

Though I'm hardly qualified to preach or teach the gospel known as golf lessons, it's also quite possible that this story may teach you what you've always wanted to know about man's most exquisite game.

Considering all that, I suppose I should start at the beginning.

I was just a short-stuff when my father first took me to the sunburned links of West Texas and taught me how to carry a bag and tend a pin. I was too young for the work, and I think he knew it, but I was determined to give it a try, and he gave in to my pleas.

Even though his bag occasionally dragged the ground that day, I still managed to slog around eighteen holes without falling too far behind. That night, completely exhausted, I fell asleep dreaming of my day in the company of men as we walked on playing fields of green. Who knows, perhaps I've never stopped dreaming of that day.

The Old Man and the Tee

How else can you explain that forty years later—though still not much of a player—I was more obsessed with golf than ever? Having given up the world of stand-up comedy, I'd started writing for a living, turning out books, scripts, and magazine stories. Somehow I'd managed to write about whatever I wanted, and the subject I most often chose to write about was golf.

I'd written about golf in the pastures of Texas and on the links of Scotland, about greens made of sand and greens mowed by sheep, about night golf played by the light of the moon or the glow of a cigarette. I'd even written a novel called *Fast Greens* about a young caddie in search of a father, and because I didn't want my dad to take the story personally, I'd also written about the joy of caddying for and playing with my old man.

But with my father dying, golf suddenly seemed devoid of meaning. All of my golf stories had been written for him. What would I write without him there to read them? What would I be without my father?

His name was Raymond Pipkin, but everyone knew him as Pip. His goals in life were simple, and none of them involved work. What Pip wanted to do was hunt, fish, play golf, and be a good father to his five children. He was skilled at all of these, and loved by just about everyone who met him in ways that were impossible for my mother to understand, for she had to bear the burden of practicality.

Things had started to go wrong long before my emergency call at Pebble Beach. At age seventy-five, Pip finally had to admit that his knees would no longer support him on the links or in the field. The choice he faced was to sit down and stay down or to have a knee replacement operation. Unfortunately, a lifetime of chicken fried steaks, enchilada plates, and way too many cocktails had put as much strain on his arteries as it had on his knees. The stroke he suffered while under sedation for the surgery wasn't discovered for days, and he subsequently spent eight long years in a nursing home.

The Beginning of the End

Confined to a wheelchair and generally unable to remember the names of his children, he was still the life of the party, he could still beat me at checkers, and everyone loved him as they always had. In some ways, it was a miracle he lived as long as he did. Knowing that would not make losing him any easier.

From Pebble Beach, I made it back to West Texas to find Pip propped up in a hospital bed, a smile on his face as his family gathered round to enjoy his miraculous recovery. Just like old times, he and I turned on the TV and watched the broadcast of the golf tournament. The only difference was, instead of Bob Hope, it was Bill Murray cracking everyone up at Pebble. Instead of Arnie, the crowd favorite was Tiger.

"That's a beautiful place," Pip told me as the camera panned over the ocean and Pebble's eighteenth hole. "We should have played there."

Though he had a gentle smile on his face, a pang of regret stabbed at my heart. He was absolutely right. We should have played there, a father and his youngest son at a place they'd long loved. If only I'd made the effort while there was till time.

When I left the hospital with my brothers and sisters that evening, Pip was still smiling, but somehow we knew we'd never see him again. Though I'd been careful to take advantage of that final opportunity to tell my father that I loved him, in the weeks following his funeral, I could not shake his passing. Pip was gone—and with me sneaking up on the fifty-year mark myself, I suddenly realized that I was next. Suddenly I was the Old Man.

Playing golf was unthinkable, and finishing that golf joke story was no picnic, either. Jokes that once seemed mildly amusing now were mostly annoying.

"Bad day at the course," a guy tells his wife. "Charlie had a heart attack on the third hole."

"That's terrible!" she says.

"You're telling me. All day long, it was hit the ball, drag Charlie."

You'd be amazed how many golf jokes are about dead golfers.

The Old Man and the Tee

I was half asleep one night when one of my dad's old golf buddies popped into my head. I'd hardly thought of Marshall Jones since the days when I caddied for him in my youth, certainly not since he passed away several years ago. But now Marshall was clear in my mind as he descended to my father's hospital bed with one final golf joke.

"There's good news and there's bad news," Marshall told my dad.

"Good news first," Pip replied.

"Well, it turns out there's golf in heaven. We've got a beautiful track just like Pebble Beach."

"That's great," my dad said with a smile. "So what's the bad news?"

"You and I are playing Hogan and Snead at eight A.M."

Well, let me tell you, I laughed and I cried, and I mean for the rest of the night. The next morning, I called Pebble Beach and booked a tee time to play the round of golf that I should have played with my father. With Pip in my heart, but not at my side, my intention was to play eighteen holes at Pebble that would have made him proud.

All through my teens, I'd felt that Pip wanted me to be a solid golfer. My brothers, John and Marvin, had always been better, more gifted golfers than me. They'd played on the high school golf team, and John had played on the team at the University of Texas. I, on the other hand, had only played. Even at my best, I still suspected that my game fell short of Pip's hopes. To complicate matters, for the last couple of years, my swing had become insanely unpredictable. My apathetic drives were both short and crooked; my bipolar irons were divided between life-threatening hooks and knifing slices, and so many of my putts spun out of the hole, my friends were calling me "Hairlip."

In short, I sucked! And after half a lifetime of flirting with the idea of being a good golfer, it is not a pretty feeling to discover the simple truth that your golf game sucks.

To notch a reasonably good score at Pebble, I figured I just needed fewer distractions from work and family, and a little more play. I'd practice a few weeks, straighten out my drives, gather my wits, and throw a nice score up on the board.

The Beginning of the End

Maybe that would help me miss my father less. Maybe it would help me ease the regret of how little time I'd given him. If nothing else, I figured it would be a lot healthier than drinking nightly to his memory.

A year later, as I look back on my preparations for that first round at Pebble, I realize just how wrong I was to think everything could be so simple.

CHAPTER 2

A Monkey Humping a Football

"It's the only sport that every player, no matter their ability, can hit a shot that even the best player in the world would be proud of. That's the beauty of the game—the magnet."

—David Leadbetter

Before I took an emotional swan dive off the high board at Pebble Beach, I figured I better tune up my game. My preparations were pretty straightforward. In the evenings, I was rereading the golf books that once helped hone my swing. Ben Hogan's *Five Lessons: The Modern Fundamentals of Golf* and *Power Golf* were pretty much the Old and New Testaments of my game.

I hadn't spent much time on the practice tee as a kid. Range balls cost money that we didn't have to spend.

"Just get out there and play" was Pip's solution to any golf problem.

Pip also had little faith in taking lessons, most likely for the same reason he didn't believe in hitting practice balls—cash.

"Lessons will just screw you up," he'd say, an opinion I've continued to hear throughout my life.

With a little more fold in my pocket than in my childhood, I figured a few large buckets of balls would straighten out my flagging game, but then I heard that David Leadbetter—the most celebrated instructor in golf—was coming to Austin to open a new Leadbetter Academy at Barton Creek. That was too good to miss.

Joining the crowd on the practice tee at Barton Creek's Fazio Canyons course, I was primed to hear the gospel according to David.

"It's funny talking theory about a swing," Leadbetter told the crowd. "The problem is what we *feel* we do and what we *actually* do are totally different. They're miles apart. But no matter how you swing, it all comes down to getting the clubface square on the ball, traveling at maximum speed down your target line. There are various ways to do that—a lot of different ways of skinning a cat."

If there's more than one way to skin a cat, I thought, then I don't want to know about it.

"No two golf swings are alike," David continued. "There are certain actions we all try to create through a repeating-type motion, but it still boils down to the fact that we're individuals, each with our own swings. And everybody's swing is like a fingerprint."

Back in the dark recesses of my mind, a light was starting to switch on. I'd spent my whole life trying to copy Hogan's swing, but I'm six-foot-seven in old socks; Hogan was five-nine in new spikes on concrete.

As he spoke, Leadbetter began to swing an iron back and forth with ease, his movements the perfect illustration of his words.

"Most golfers don't understand," David told us, "that the golf swing involves both a swinging motion of the club and a turning movement of the body. The most common errors arise from people misinterpreting how to actually get that club moving from a stationary position. There's also a sort of *Hit!* syndrome that creates habits—from snatching it away, or taking it inside, or coming over the top, or getting steep."

Snatching it inside and coming steep over the top—Leadbetter was describing everything wrong with my own swing.

"Almost every poor player gets too steep," David continued. "As they swing back to the ball, the club is coming down on too vertical an angle. It looks like an outside-to-inside swing, but the real problem is the steepness."

"But if you do certain things correctly," he added, "the club almost swings itself."

Now David gripped the club with the thumb and two fingers of his right hand, and demonstrated the simplicity of the golf swing, the club swinging back and hinging up naturally, then reversing and swinging through to the target. This near-perfect, one-handed swing was accomplished with almost zero effort as long as David kept the club moving on the same swing plane or angle at which he'd started. If he moved the club off line—taking it back inside his target line, for instance—gravity would compound his errors, and the easy swing was almost instantly lost. But when he put the club back on plane, the three-finger swing became smooth again.

As the club metronomed back and forth, I began to fall under Leadbetter's spell. A rare combination of master and teacher, Leadbetter combines a deep understanding of golf mechanics with an intuitive ability to communicate what he knows. He also puts the icing on the cake by being almost constantly entertaining. Whenever our brains began to freeze up from too much technical talk, Leadbetter would toss out a golf joke or a story.

"Faldo has this caddie from Ireland," David told us, "and the sole of the caddie's shoe is separated from the upper and it's flopping and flopping and driving Faldo crazy. Finally, Nick can't take it anymore. 'You're not gonna wear that during the tournament, are you?' he asks. The caddie explains that he's just arrived from Ireland and is a little short of money. So Faldo takes out a huge roll of bills, and the caddie's eyes are bugging out. Nick takes the rubber band off the roll . . . then tosses the rubber band to the caddie and says, "Here, this ought to take care of it."

Along with the other golf writers at the event, I'd been invited to take a quick private lesson with the man himself. At the opposite end of the Canyons range, where the new school would be located, we lined up and began hitting our seven-irons while David walked down the row and offered a little personal guidance to each player.

By the time David arrived at my station, having simply watched him swing the club earlier already had me hitting the purest iron shots I'd struck in months. One swing after another, I was hitting crisp fades that I felt sure David would compliment. Sure, my divots were pointing too far left, but the results were still good.

After watching me hit a few, David definitely had things to say.

"One of the best examples of *that* swing I've ever seen," he told me. "However, you may want to try this."

We only had a few minutes together, so he didn't change much— just my stance, posture, takeaway, swing plane, ball-strike, and finish.

His first and most often repeated advice was that I should "swing the handle," letting my hands initiate the swing with the clubhead following, instead of the other way around.

Adopting as much of his advice as I could, I took a few practice swings and felt like a stranger in a strange land.

"For a guy your height, your stance is way too narrow," David told me. "You have to get down to your work. Did you ever see a giraffe take a drink without spreading his legs?"

Widening my stance considerably, I tried again.

My old swing was comfortable as a worn shoe. Now I felt like a monkey humping a football. Like a polo player without a horse, as Bob Hope used to say. I took another swing and topped a ball that dribbled off the front of the tee.

"Trust it," Leadbetter told me.

With all his advice ringing in my ear, I took another swing and this time I caught one pure. The ball leapt off the clubface and soared up against the blue sky, a tiny rocket in flight. Drawing a little to the left, the ball sailed thirty yards past my previous shots and plugged in its own divot.

"How'd that feel?" he asked.

Stunned, I think I said, "Wow!"

After watching me hit a few more rockets, David moved on down the line, leaving another satisfied customer in his wake. But ten minutes later, with his words floating away, my perfectly aligned divots began to point further and further left, and my weak shots again began to slice as in days of old. That's how it goes with golf instruction: you learn something new, then you forget it. Then you learn something else to forget tomorrow.

With Nick Price waiting in Florida for a tune-up, David couldn't linger long at Barton Creek, but as Leadbetter was leaving, he walked by and saw that I was struggling again.

"The things we talked about are all good for you to work on," he told me, "but you can't turn into a solid player with a few golf tips. Tips are for horse races. At the end of the race, you need a new tip."

"So what *will* make me better?" I asked.

"You need the tools to be able to help yourself—a better understanding of the swing, a picture of what you want to accomplish, and some drills to help you find and maintain your swing."

Somehow I couldn't see myself repeating all kinds of golf drills over and over and over.

"You could be a lot better," David concluded. "But you'd have to work at it."

CHAPTER 3

Pebble

"It took me seventeen years to get 3,000 hits in baseball; I did it in one afternoon on the golf course."

—Hank Aaron

For the next month, I kept searching for my game, both on the range and on the course with some Austin golf buddies. When I left for Pebble Beach in June for my round in tribute to my dad—despite Leadbetter's words of wisdom, my USGA handicap index was sitting at 15.9, the worst official handicap of my life. And since the handicap system automatically chooses your best ten scores from your most recent twenty posted, I was in danger of going higher with every new round. In other words, I sucked even more than before.

To make matters worse, Pebble was waiting for me, lurking in the shadows of my dreams for a chance to pounce on my pitiful game. What scared me most was my random mix of seemingly opposite results: the power pull and the feeble fade. A golfer who slices every shot can at least aim left and let his shots drift back to the fairway. But if you're spraying the ball right and left, it's impossible to aim anywhere with confidence. Even Stephen King couldn't dream up a worse golfer's nightmare.

As I turned onto 17-Mile Drive and stopped at the guardhouse, I could already feel the first-tee jitters rising up inside me.

"I have a tee time at Pebble," I told the guard, trying to sound as if I really did belong there in golf's Garden of Eden, not as a writer with a reporter's notebook in hand, but as a player with a bag of clubs in the trunk and a lump in his throat. When the guard waved me on, I was almost surprised.

Driving down the hill to the ocean, I thought about my previous trip on this road, headed *up* the hill, going way too fast, flashing my lights at anyone who looked like they might slow me down. Now I couldn't go slow enough. In my rearview mirror, I noticed the traffic stacking up behind me.

Why was I going so slow? I wondered. Sure, I had swing problems, but that was nothing new. And Pebble's plenty tough, but I've also played my share of hard courses.

No, the problem, I realized, was that I didn't have a plan B. I'd watched enough old caper movies to know you should always have a plan B, but for the first time it was dawning on me that I might *not* play the kind of round that would make my father proud. What then?

As I took my clubs out of the trunk, my throat was dry as the Sahara and my heart was pounding to beat the band.

The first-tee jitters did not subside as I stepped onto the first tee. Taking a deep breath, I smacked a three-wood and somehow avoided the bunker on the left and Pebble's high-dollar lodgings, Casa Palmero, on the right. Not too bad. But the next thing I knew, I'd hit into the bunker right of the green, blasted over, chipped on, and two-putted for a double bogey six.

A string of bogeys followed for the entire front nine, and some of these were brilliant bogeys. On the short par-four fourth, I hit my tee shot over the bluff to the shores of Stillwater Cove. Seeing the ball on the beach, I shrugged my shoulders and climbed down the cliff with wedge in hand, then knocked my ball back into the fairway. Several sunbathers applauded my shot.

On the eighth, perhaps the most beautiful and intimidating par four in all of golf, I hit a big drive up the steep hill, but my four-iron over the ocean drifted right of the green and flew into the face of the grass-covered bluff. My playing partners could hardly watch as I risked life and limb and climbed precariously down to the ball from where I knocked it on the green and again saved bogey. At least I was showing some spunk.

I'd never set a specific goal for my round; the idea was simply to strike crisp shots and walk proudly with my club at my side. Up and down for par at ten and an easy birdie on eleven, and that's just what I was doing. With my nerves conquered, I'd soon be in the clubhouse with a score in the mideighties, not bad for Pebble Beach. In the Tap Room, I'd raise a toast—or two or three—to Pip, then I'd go home to my family and the screenplay I'd set aside to prepare for this day.

Even a careless double bogey on fourteen doesn't spoil my mood.

"If I par in," I think, "I can still shoot 84."

For me, 84 at Pebble was the kind of score that would've once prompted me to call Pip and brag about my round. But instead of parring in, I begin to fall apart, making careless mistakes, then compounding them with bad chips and an inability to make any putt over two feet.

The last group off the tee for the day, my foursome is barely going to finish before darkness sets in. With a glorious red-streaked sky spreading out above us, at the infamous par-three seventeenth, I top a shot that bobbles halfway to the green. As I look up in disbelief, I see the color drain from the sky as I suddenly imagined it must have drained from my father's beautiful face in his final moments.

This is not what I intended.

Walking to the ball in disgust, I pull my sand wedge, then hit into one of the pot bunkers behind the green.

"You idiot!" I shout at myself. "You freaking moron!"

The Old Man and the Tee

Suddenly I realize what Pip would have thought about me talking and acting this way on a golf course. I was failing at everything I set out to do. Instead of a proud round for my father, I was simply embarrassing myself in front of three other golfers who also wanted great things from their rounds at Pebble.

Eighteen turns out no better. Tee shot in the ocean, and I'm suddenly wondering if I'll even break ninety. Adding a penalty stroke, I hit my third from the tee, sending the ball so far right that we all yell, "Fore!" to a couple walking all the way over at the seventeenth tee.

As I walk to the ball with shoulders sagging, a terrible thought comes to me. After forty years of golf, exactly what is the point? Why do I even play? Why not finish this one final hole with the eight or nine that I'm headed toward like a runaway freight train, then simply walk over to the edge of the bluff by the green and hurl my sticks out into the ocean? Why not make this the last frustrating round of my life? In the darkness, no one would even see me.

And what would I do without my clubs? The possibilities are endless. I'd spend weekends with my kids; I'd have extra time to write and read and do a hundred great things I rarely have time for. I'd do everything *except* spend all my spare time on the course.

Freed of the lifelong burden called golf, I hit a solid three-wood toward the green. When I arrive at the ball, it's trickled into the long bunker alongside the ocean, but I don't even care. I'm done with the game. Looking up to the green from a hundred yards out in the bunker, I make one last hard swing, and the ball moves about three feet. Screw it, I think, chopping at the ball without even looking.

"Nice shot," one of my playing partners calls to me.

Looking up in surprise, I see that I'm on the green. A glimmer of light still shows in the sky. I have a thirty-foot putt for double bogey. If I make it for seven, I still break ninety. Not much pride in that, but it'd be better than closing my career with a snowman . . . or worse.

Barely able to see the hole in the remaining light, all I'm really thinking about is whether this will be the last long putt of my life. Giving the ball a solid rap, I watch it climb the slope, turn to the left, then dive straight into the cup!

In a heartbeat, everything changes. Suddenly my playing partners are giving me high fives, for I've made an improbable double bogey— a tough par on my second ball, and done it in the near darkness, all of which they see as cause for celebration. Five hours ago, we were strangers, but now we're golf buddies talking about playing again someday.

Whether it's making that putt or simply their reaction, the idea of tossing my clubs into the Pacific has vanished. In its place, another idea begins to form. I've shot 89 at Pebble, not great, but good enough to know I can do better.

What if I dedicate, not a round to my father and to the game that we loved, but a year? What if I started all over and learned to play golf properly? In my imagination, I can see my father smiling at the very idea.

"You could be good," Leadbetter had told me back at Barton Creek. "But you'd have to work at it."

What if I went back to Leadbetter, laid out my tale of woe, and persuaded him to take me on? I could also go to fellow Austinite Dave Pelz and ask him to teach me the short game the same way he teaches the pros. I've known Ben Crenshaw since we were at the University of Texas together in the early seventies. What if I asked Ben to teach me to putt? All of a sudden, the ideas are flying around my head like cartoon stars.

I wouldn't make big progress immediately, but if I worked on my game every day, there was no reason why I couldn't become a real golfer with a smooth backswing and a single-digit handicap. I'd once been better than the golfer I'd slipped to; perhaps I could gain that back and much more.

Then I could return to Pebble and serve up a proper tribute to my father. To break 80, I'd have to take ten strokes off my game. Ten strokes in a year——an insane idea, but it did have a nice ring to it. Even better, my fiftieth birthday was one year and a few days away. Breaking 80 at Pebble Beach on my fiftieth would be almost epic.

So instead of tossing my clubs into the ocean, I picture myself throwing my worthless, worn-out, over-the-top swing far out into the rolling waves.

Sharing a beer with my new golf buddies in Pebble's famous Tap Room, I thank them for the round and tell them my plan.

"I'll be back in one year," I say. "New clubs, new swing, new attitude . . . and I'm gonna tear this sucker up."

We all drink a toast to the idea, but when I glance up at them, I can see they think I'm crazy.

CHAPTER 4

ERC

---

*"If our clubs don't assist the average golfer in hitting more pleasing
shots, then why do we sell as many as we do?"*

—Ely Reeves Callaway

I'd never heard of a longtime golfer who'd taken anywhere
close to ten strokes off his game. The nature of the beast is that most
new players make quick strides their first few years, then reach a
plateau that's incredibly difficult to get beyond. Ten strokes would be
huge, and I knew I'd need every possible edge to pull it off. Working
from the ground up, the logical place to start was new and better
clubs.

Like my dad, I'd never been one to constantly switch clubs. He'd
always played Hogans and saw no reason to change them. Even with
the coming of all kinds of new golf technologies, in the forty years
I'd played the game, I'd owned just three complete sets of irons. I
played the Wilson X-31's Pip gave me on my thirteenth birthday for a
total of twenty-six years, not replacing them until my wife gave me a
set of Cobra irons on my fortieth birthday. As part of a story I'd
written a few years later on Austin golf guru Harvey Penick, I'd also

purchased a set of Penick irons, a fine club manufactured by Austin-based retailer and club-maker Golfsmith.

But neither the Cobras nor the Penicks seemed to be working for me anymore, so the questions before me were the same questions that face most players in the modern golf era. What equipment will give me the biggest advantage? And what can I afford? On a limited budget that would be mightily strained by blowing off much of my work for a year, what I needed was a connection to the good stuff.

In 1997, Ely Callaway—head of the most successful golf company in history—convinced my friend Larry Dorman to quit his job as lead golf writer for the *New York Times* and become the vice president of Callaway Golf's media and public relations.

With Callaway having practically patented the idea of game-improvement equipment, Dorman seemed like a good place for me to start. So the question I put to Larry was "Does Callaway want to be known as the golf club that can take ten strokes off your game?"

Dorman's response was to invite me out to Callaway's headquarters in Carlsbad, California, where I could undergo the same custom club fitting used by numerous pros and a growing number of amateurs, then tour Callaway's research and development facilities to see what makes this stuff tick. A week or so later, I'd also be receiving a new set of custom Callaways, tailor-made to my swing specifications.

This was not an offer I was inclined to refuse.

There are apparently a lot of golfers in America whose tendency to buy new equipment has run roughly parallel with my own. A good set of clubs was once thought to last decades, but Ely Callaway changed that notion and revolutionized the golf business by convincing golfers that equipment could help them hit the ball longer and straighter.

Thanks to Ely, the new buzzwords of golf became perimeter weighting, cavity backs, larger sweet spots, greater accuracy, and increased forgiveness.

Sounds sexy, doesn't it? We should all have lovers with larger sweet spots, greater accuracy, and increased forgiveness.

If you have any doubt that golfers are obsessed with equipment, consider my sometime golf pal Jerry Jeff Walker, the guy who wrote "Mr. Bojangles," and an entertainer with one of the largest fan clubs in music. One day at Barton Creek's Crenshaw Course, Jerry Jeff stepped up to the par-three eleventh and made a smooth-swinging hole-in-one. Cause for celebration, right? But even though J.J. high-fived everyone in the group, as he walked off the green, he turned on his cell phone, called the pro shop, and ordered a new set of irons. My god, the man had just made a hole-in-one! What could possibly be the problem with his sticks?

The answer was that J.J. had hit a longer club into the green than the others in his group. Never mind that his ball had gone in the hole, Jerry Jeff didn't like to think of himself as a short-knocker. Now that's a golfer who's hooked on gear.

And though Jerry Jeff may be the only player in history who discarded his irons immediately after making an ace, he is just one of millions who have bought multiple sets of irons and woods in the twenty years since Ely Callaway started building clubs that were designed to help us hit it longer and straighter.

I never met Ely Callaway, but he was born in 1919—the same year as my dad. Like my father, Callaway learned golf at an early age, he was a salesman, and he was well liked by a countless number of people. Unlike my father—whose main success in life was his children—Ely Callaway enjoyed remarkable success in practically every endeavor of his life.

By the time he left the textile industry with a big chunk of change at age fifty-four, Callaway had already started a vineyard in Temecula, California, where conventional wisdom said it was too hot to make good wines. I'd never heard of Ely Callaway at the time, but my wife and I chose his wines for our wedding reception, and Pip seemed to enjoy them immensely.

After selling his award-winning vineyard for a tasty $9 million in profit, in 1984 Ely plunked down $400,000 for an upstart golf company called Hickory Stick. A small manufacturer of clubs with hickory wood wrapped around a steel shaft, Hickory Stick's clubs sold primarily to golfers with a fondness for tradition because a golfer needed some special inducement to overcome the fact that they weighed too much and played too poorly.

Determined to create a demand for his product, Callaway sought out Chi Chi Rodriguez, then one of the hottest golfers in the world, and offered Chi Chi a quarter of a million dollars to play Hickory Stick wedges on tour.

Chi Chi's response: "I wouldn't play them for one million dollars."

Manufacturing an inferior and little-known product made the odds against Callaway's success phenomenal. The great majority of clubs sold in the previous thirty years were the product of a few name brands like Titleist and Hogan, and though there were an estimated 25 million occasional golfers in the United States, most of them felt little or no need for new equipment.

Twenty years later, despite the reported Tiger Woods boom, there are still an estimated 25 million occasional golfers in the United States, but for many golfers the interval between buying clubs is measured in months rather than decades, and Callaway Golf has now sold a total of over $5 billion in golf equipment.

So how did he do it?

Critics of Ely Callaway and the equipment that bears his name sometimes claimed that the success and growth of his company were mostly due to good salesmanship, but the truth is that Callaway Golf led the way toward innovation in golf clubs that hadn't changed all that much since the introduction of steel shafts half a century earlier. (For the record, Taylor Made introduced the first "metal" woods, an innovation that did not go unnoticed by Ely.)

Callaway's first game improvement clubs, the s2h2 (for short straight hollow hosel), sold well enough for Ely to bet the company's future on a new driver called the Big Bertha. Named for a World War I long-range German cannon—a name that almost no one in the company besides Ely liked—the Bertha was introduced in 1991, and played on the Senior PGA Tour by none other than Chi Chi Rodriguez, who began to win with it almost immediately. The Big Bertha retailed for twice as much as most other drivers, but it was the first club in the history of the game that golfers felt they *had* to have. Suddenly, everyone in the game was looking for an equipment edge.

By 1998—just seven years after the introduction of the first Big Bertha—Callaway drivers were played by 69 percent of all professional golfers on all tours worldwide. Among those who benefited most from this success was Chi Chi Rodriguez, who made millions—perhaps tens of millions—on the Callaway stock options he received for his endorsement of the Bertha.

Being both stubborn and old-fashioned, neither my dad nor I embraced the mad dash for length off the tee. In his later years on the course, Pip was happy just to play. As for me, I was long enough to get around most courses, and I could beat most of the guys I played with. Let them fart around with expensive new clubs and a million swing tips, I thought, and I'll just play golf.

In time, however, I began to realize just how much my stubborn traditions had cost me. I was in Cabo San Lucas a few years ago playing Jack Nicklaus's oceanside masterpiece, Cabo del Sol. By chance, I was matched up with San Diego Chargers quarterback Gayle Gilbert and two of his buddies from Austin. Well-oiled by a local aiming fluid called Pacifico Beer, we were betting high (by my standards) and pressing right and left. This was not a wise move on my part, for the other guys—all jocks fifteen years younger than me—were using Big Berthas and Taylor Made's new Bubble Burner driver. In my bag was a Wilson persimmon driver which had limited carry but pretty good roll, a terrible combination for Cabo del Sol, where the forced carries from the black tees are frequent and long.

"If I'm gonna stay in the game," I said when I got to sixty or eighty bucks down, "I've got to hit one of your drivers."

The combination of hitting Gilbert's Bubble Burner driver, plus the fact that I probably only drank ten beers instead of the fifteen that everyone else quaffed, put me in the winners column at the end of the day.

Since that day, I've never hit another ball with a persimmon driver. I had embraced the long. The question remained, though, would Callaway clubs really help me turn my game around?

Ely Callaway died of a heart attack in 2001—just months before my dad's heart failed him—so I took my equipment questions to the man who invented the Big Bertha, Richard C. Helmstetter, whose initials, RCH, appear on a number of Callaway products. Those same initials were embroidered on Helmstetter's claret-colored windbreaker as he sat behind his neatly organized desk. In 1985, Helmstetter was designing and manufacturing high-quality cue sticks in Japan when Ely persuaded him to return to America as the chief club designer for Callaway Golf. If Ely had a vision for his new clubs, it was Helmstetter who made that vision a reality.

"What's the secret?" I asked RCH. "How have you guys been so successful with pros and amateurs alike?"

As he pondered my question, a vintage red biplane suddenly flew out of Helmstetter's head, which, as you can imagine, really captured my attention.

"We spend more on R&D than our next three competitors combined," Helmstetter said, as if nothing had happened. "And we do that because we know if you're going to succeed in this business, you've got to come up with new and better products. One reason there are so may new products is because we contributed to this pace of new production. That's why we now feel the future of sales is in fitting and customized equipment."

All of a sudden, there it was again—a red biplane flying out of Helmstetter's head, though to be perfectly honest, I believe the plane was over the private airstrip across from RCH's office window and only appeared to be flying out of his head. But with Helmstetter choosing his words carefully and speaking so passionately about the game, it seemed like I was seeing some literal version of his mind doing touch-and-go landings.

"We spend a lot on biomechanical research, plus we bring in teachers to help us learn to teach," RCH continued. "One of the things we've learned is that we *cannot* substantially increase the swing speed of experienced golfers. Despite that limitation, we *can* still make them better players."

"How much better?" I asked. "A lot of people might think a thousand dollars is too much to spend to gain one stroke. Others would pay ten times that much."

"If your clubs really don't fit," RCH elaborated, "say your driver shaft is too stiff or loft too strong, you could easily gain two or more strokes with properly fitted equipment. Just knowing you have a club that suits you is invaluable to your confidence."

Confidence. That was always the catch. Somehow it seemed that the more I'd learned about the swing over the years, the less confident I'd become. If custom-fitted clubs would boost my confidence, I was all for them.

Just down the road from Callaway's corporate headquarters is the Richard C. Helmstetter Test Center, which houses forty of Callaway's one hundred and forty R&D employees. This is the place where great clubs are born and bad clubs are broken in very expensive ways.

What I was expecting to find there was a bunch of computer nerds gathered around Iron Byron, the ball-hitting robot named for the perfectly repeatable swing of Texas golf legend Byron Nelson. And I found Iron Byon all right, sitting on the shelf waiting to be refurbished for display as a museum relic.

Iron Byron had long since been replaced by better hitting robots, most recently by a computer-controlled model from Carlsbad-based GolfLabs that looks like it could put a ball on the moon. Standing proudly by his new baby was one of Callaway's technical specialists, Greg Dosch.

"Iron Byron had one swing and one swing only," Bosch told me. "But this new model can be set for a lot of different swing parameters, like shoulder angles, attack angles, and length of backswing. The ball position can be adjusted to create toe and heel strikes, while clubhead speed is variable from one to one hundred fifty miles per hour."

"How far does it hit the ball at one-fifty?" I asked.

"We've only done that once," said Dosch. "And the ball cleared the trees on the hill at the end of the range. That's four hundred yards away."

"Not bad," I said. "But Iron Byron had a better name."

The test range also has two pattern-tilt cameras that use missile tracking technology to record ball flight. What all this high-tech gear does is let Callaway's design engineers determine exactly what makes for best ball flight. Questions they answer here include such valuable ditties as: whether a drive should be caught with the clubhead coming up on the ball (yes); what swing characteristics and lofts will create the optimum apex or peak of ball flight (this is where my eyes started to glaze over); and even how to determine loft progressions so your new Callaway irons have uniform gaps between the distances you hit each club (and apparently they do).

These brainiacs are even developing something called on-board diagnostics. That's a golf club with electronics built into the shaft. When you swing the club, a computer gathers data from the test club, then automatically determines the golf club specs you need. On-board diagnostics—or OBD-One Kenobi, as I call it—is the light saber of golf. And its name is just as cool as Iron Byron.

Examining all these wonders, I could feel my confidence growing. This kind of dedication to details was bound to help me improve. Somehow, though, I couldn't help but wonder why—in spite of all the technological advances—golf scores haven't really improved on the PGA tour or among amateur golfers, whose average handicaps have failed to move lower in the past twenty-five years.

ERC

Ask almost any player, good or bad, whether the latest gargantuan metal woods are easier to hit straight and long than their old persimmon clubs, and you'll probably receive a resounding yes. So why are our scores only treading water? Is the game really that hard?

The answer, unfortunately, is yes, it really is.

What I needed, I decided, is a club with OBS—on-board skills. A computer-controlled club that swings itself. Now *that* would be a big seller.

CHAPTER 5

Fit to a Tee

————

"If the shoe fits . . . get another one just like it."

—Graffito

Like most kids who learned to play golf in the sixties, my first golf club was a hand-me-down. Today, a number of manufacturers produce clubs for juniors, but back then, the best a kid could hope for was an adult's five- or seven-iron with the shaft cut down to hopefully fit your size.

I don't even know the brand of that first five-iron my father gave me; I just remember that it felt really heavy when I swung it, and I had a hard time getting the ball airborne. That meant I hit a lot of worm burners, bug fruggers, grain reapers . . . We had lots of names for the shot.

Looking back, I realize that every time I swung that five-iron, gravity was working hard to pull that heavy clubhead off track, and my muscles weren't strong enough, or my swing sweet enough, for me to consistently return the clubhead to the ball.

What I needed was a five-iron that fit me.

The goal of custom club fitting is to insure you have the right equipment to return the clubhead to the ball on the best track and with optimal clubhead speed. It's an obvious idea, though most players consider it something best accomplished the way a tailor fits clothes by looking at your height or weight, or at the length and strength of your arms.

You're not, unfortunately, going to learn much with a tailor's tape measure. You can, on the other hand, learn everything you need to know at the world's most technologically advanced center for testing golf swings. And though few recreational golfers seem to know it— just like the pros—they can set up their own private custom fitting appointment at Callaway's Virtual Test Center. Even better, this fitting costs just fifty dollars, which is refunded with the purchase of any club, making it, perhaps, the greatest value in all of golf.

"Seventy-five percent of the players who come through here are playing with the wrong clubs," I was told on arrival by John Degen, the club-fitting pro who'd been assigned to size me up and put my swing through the works.

"I hope I'm one of them," I replied. "Otherwise I'm wasting my time."

Degen just smiled. The customer is always right, even when he sounds like he's gonna be a pain in the ass.

You may have teed up a few balls on one of the standard swing analyzers, which use a combination of video and computer to chart your swing speed and launch angles, but what Callaway's engineers have put together in their flight simulator just blows my mind.

The video cameras and the computer are still here; they're just more complex. In order to measure clubhead speed, attack angles, and swing path, reflective dots have been added to the shafts and heads of all the test clubs. The balls have been triple-striped in a perfect pattern of crossing circles to aid in measuring ball speed, launch angle, and degrees of back- and sidespin.

"Okay, I'll bite." I said. "How does it work?"

Placing one of the striped balls on the tee, Degen pointed to a small hole in the hitting mat. "When you swing, just before you make contact, the clubhead's shadow passes over this hole and a sensor triggers digital cameras that take twenty-five hundred pictures per second."

Twenty-five hundred frames a second? I thought. My swing looks bad in a snapshot.

Hoping not to embarrass myself, I took the driver Degen offered and made a big cut at the ball, which launched forward and slammed against a video projection screen showing the eighteenth hole at Pebble Beach. Almost immediately, the results of my swing were displayed in two different ways. First, the ball continued in virtual reality on the projection screen, sailing over the fairway of Pebble's tenth. And second, a vast array of technical data appeared at one corner of the screen.

The specs displayed included everything from clubhead measurements like trajectory, attack, lie angles, side angles, and clubhead speed to ball flight measurements, including ball speed, launch angle, side- and backspins. I believe there were several other measurements, but I stopped reading when my head swelled to such dangerous proportions that it was about to explode from excess activity.

"Warning! Warning!" my brain called out. "Information overload!" Over the sounds of air raid sirens in my frontal lobes, I could dimly hear my brain trying to talk me down. "Uploading images of bunny rabbits and beautiful breasts," my brain said in a soothing tone. "Do not access any more technical info."

Luckily, the main information I needed was right there in the middle of the screen in the form of my virtual ball flight. The ball had sliced—big-time! Teeing up another striped ball, I swung harder this time and managed to hit a slice that would have made Oscar Meyer proud. By the looks of the screen, the ball was headed in the general direction of Pebble's seventeenth tee, a shot with which I was already familiar.

"Fore!" I yelled to the virtual reality couple in my brain.

Not knowing what caused my giant slice, I decided to risk a brain embolism and glanced at the technical data on the screen. This time I went straight for the golfer's electronic G-spot—the clubhead speed!

"Ninety-six miles per hour," I read. "Not bad. But I bet I can do better."

Of course, I'd already forgotten that I'd sliced the ball. I just wanted to see how fast I could swing it. Call it a guy thing.

Tightening my grip—which nearly every instructor I'd see for the next year would say was a counterproductive move—I swung harder. In fact, I swung so hard that I made myself dizzy. When my head had cleared, I saw that—despite my Herculean effort—I'd only upped my clubhead speed from 96 to 98 mph, while the ball had actually gone shorter, not longer.

"Stupid machine!" I heard my brain say.

Instead of apologizing to Degen for my brain's stupidity, I cranked up my testosterone level and swung so hard I nearly passed out. When my eyes could focus again, I checked the clubhead speed: 95 miles per hour. I was going backward. And I was still slicing.

While I was doing my best Homer Simpson impression, Degen was studying both my swing and my stats, and verifying whatever conclusions he was coming to by checking out the wear marks on my old five-iron and driver, which I'd been told to bring along.

I'd just decided to swing so hard I'd throw up, when Degen handed me a different driver that was one degree upright and also had more loft than the first one. Each of the drivers and five irons in the fitting bay—and there are a lot of them—have different shafts, swing weights, lofts, or lie elevations.

The lie of the club, in case you, too, begin to develop an aneurysm when the talk gets technical, relates to the angle between the shaft and the clubhead. When you swing, the sole of the club should move into the ball without the toe or heel digging deeper than the other, either of which can cause you numerous problems. If the toe is consistently down, for instance, then you need a more upright lie to your club.

Since it's almost impossible to see many of these differences in the various test clubs by simply looking, each of the clubs in the test bay has a bar-code sticker, which is scanned into the computer before it is hit, presumably so you won't later spend thirty minutes saying, "This was the long one, right? Or was it this one? Doh!"

As Degen scanned a driver with ten-degree loft and a less stiff shaft into the computer, he filled me in on what he calls the three great mistakes in most player's equipment.

"The first big mistake," he tells me, "is that a lot of players think they'll get more distance out of lower-lofted drivers. They're trying for more roll, but they actually carry the ball shorter and have less control. What they really need is a higher launch angle with a flatter, penetrating ball flight."

In other words, when I switched from the nine- to the ten-degree driver, I was suddenly bombing it twenty yards farther. The fact that the virtual balls were still going virtually sideways led us to the second great problem of the great majority of the twenty thousand amateur golfers who've been through the same club-fitting process at Callaway.

"Ninety-five percent of slicers," Degen says about the second most common mistake, "set up to the ball with their shoulders open, which compounds their outside-to-in swing path."

Two items of on-screen data—swing path and face angle—are pretty solid indicators of that slice. Most of my driver swings showed me coming at the ball from two degrees outside the target line with an even larger side-angle to my face. In English, that means I was cutting across the face of the ball with an open clubface and hitting banana balls into the right rough.

Closing my shoulders a bit at address, I gave a ball a ride. And then another. Suddenly I was ripping long drives down the middle of the eighteenth fairway at Pebble. Though I was essentially using the same swing as before, closing my shoulders seemed to have put my clubhead on a better path to the target, improved my overall launch conditions, and cured my slice. Could it possibly be this easy? I wondered.

And though I was no longer trying to swing harder, my swing speed was starting to creep up—98 mph, 99, 100! This was fantastic! A little scientific feedback and I was hooked like a fat kid on chocolate.

"Warning! Warning!" my brain began to scream. "Addictive activity! Step away from the testing tee before you need this fix every day!"

But Degen had other plans for me—a ten-degree ERC II driver with a firm-flex shaft. (ERC, in case you've wondered, stands for Ely Reeves Callaway.) For the past few months, the USGA had been beefing about the ERC driver being too "hot," but as I tested the club in the summer of 2002, it appeared that the ruling body of American golf was going to work out a compromise allowing continued play with the club. As for me, I didn't know hot from potatoes, all I knew was the club looked and felt good in my hands.

The first swing with the new driver was 103 mph. The second dropped back to 98, but my launch angle was 12.9 degrees— "almost perfect," Degen told me. My swing path was straight, my backspin low, my sidespin practically nonexistent. In twenty minutes, I'd found my driver.

We were taking a short break when I remembered that Degen hadn't told me the third most common equipment-swing fault. And though this one didn't apply to my game, it did help my understanding of the swing.

"Players that fight the hook generally think the problem lies in their shaft," he told me, "but their shaft is probably fine. The problem is they have too much of an inside-to-out swing path."

Chances are Degen could help that hooker with a clubface that's more open, but I got the sense that he'd just as soon they opened their shoulders or stance, or whatever else it took to correct their swing path.

Because my five-iron swing is even more inconsistent than my driver swing, it took a bit longer to come up with irons that fit me, but soon enough I was walking out of the test bay with a full set of club specs in hand. Within two weeks, I'd be receiving Callaway's X-14 irons, an inch longer than standard to match my six-foot seven-inch height and swing posture, one degree upright, a two-degree lie angle, and midsize tour wrap grips to fit my big hands.

With them would be an ERC II driver, three-wood, and five-wood, all to match that last perfect swing.

It'd been a good day. For the first time, I had the feeling that maybe ten strokes wasn't such a crazy goal after all. I was halfway to the parking lot when John Degen came running after me with my old five-iron and driver.

"You may need these," he said.

"I doubt it," I told him. "I really doubt it."

CHAPTER 6

Bad Medicine

"A six-year-old knows nothing about lag, yet achieves it by swinging the club freely."

—Kip Puterbaugh

If spending my days scanning the brains of Callaway's technical geniuses wasn't fine enough, I was spending my nights at the nearby Four Seasons Aviara, not because I was addicted to luxurious accommodations—that wouldn't happen until later in my yearlong golf fantasy—but because the Four Seasons is also the home of Kip Puterbaugh's Aviara Golf Academy.

The day before I received the emergency call about my dad at Pebble Beach, I'd had a few minutes to talk with Bill Murray out on the course at Pebble's nine-hole Celebrity Shoot-out. Now I'm aware that bringing up a personal conversation with Bill "Cinderella Story" Murray sounds like major-league name-dropping, so let me just add that Bill and I were talking about that same irritating habit with Clint and Kevin—you know, as in Eastwood and Costner.

A short time later, I was seated on the eighteenth tee next to Bill as his partner prepared to hit the team's final drive in the day's alternate shot format. The reason I was able to sit next to Bill on the eighteenth tee at Pebble had to do with the fact that he'd called my home a few months earlier to tell me how much he liked *Fast Greens*. Whether he was referring to my novel, the screenplay of the same name, or just liked quick putts, I never discovered, because I wasn't home at the time. Instead, my *wife* had a nice conversation with Bill. I, on the other hand, had never spoken with him until that day at Pebble.

While we were on the eighteenth tee, I asked Bill how he'd managed to perfect his game to the point that he could clown around with the crowd and play golf at the same time, which is no mean feat. I'm frequently expected to accomplish both at various charity tournaments and find it darn near impossible. Whether it's the funny or the golf, something has to give. Bill was just telling me about his ace number one instructor, Kip Puterbaugh at the Aviara Golf Academy, when his partner duck-hooked his drive into the ocean. In a flash, Bill realized *he* now had to hit a drive from one of golf's most intimidating tees in front of a big gallery, then did it with ease.

"Hope I can do that when the chips are down," I thought, not realizing that all too soon the chips would be down, that I *would* have to hit that shot in a clutch situation, and that my result would be considerably less impressive.

To make a long story slightly longer, on Bill Murray's recommendation I ended up at the Four Seasons Aviara, where a long day of golf talk at Callaway sent me to the hotel restaurant for their weekly French buffet, where I ordered a bottle of Bertrand-Berge Fitou, an excellent wine made from the grapes of sixty-year-old vines, or so my waiter told me.

Just as Bill Murray led me to the Four Seasons, my wine led a neighboring group of Frenchmen to my table to congratulate me on my fine taste and offer a taste of their own favorite French vintages. Seventy-one glasses of wine later—at least it appears that way by the illegible scrawl of the notes in my wine-stained notebook—the conversation had descended to the lowest level of human communication.

In other words, we were talking about golf.

To be more specific, we were talking about my impossible dream of taking ten strokes off my game in a year. The fact that we were speaking in French—a language I haven't used much in twenty-five years—rendered most of my otherwise illegible notes of this conversation completely unreadable, but there in quotes—in French—I wrote, *"Impossible!"* And please don't ask how I know it was French because the word is spelled the same in both of the languages I was slaughtering at the time.

After a lengthy exchange that I didn't understand at all, one of the snail-eaters—and I hope they'll take that description in the best way, as each of them was consuming large numbers of snails at the time— one of the snail-eaters summed up their doubt of my ability to fulfill my quest in heavily accented English.

"You cannot learn to run," he said, "when you already know the wrong way to walk."

"Hunh?!" I said loudly, though my query was pretty much drowned out by light applause from the rest of the group.

After another bottle of Fitou all around, it finally occurred to me that what the fromage-muncher meant was that the alchemy of even the greatest golf wizards on earth could not convert my deeply tarnished Tinman swing into burnished gold. As Hitchcock might have put it, I had long ago become the man who knew too much.

With French chefs now joining the table's raucous discussion of what everyone seemed to feel was Jean Van der Velde's undeserved bad luck at Carnoustie at the '99 British Open, I declared it was time to cut my losses and get some sleep. After being kissed several thousand times on both cheeks, I made a mental note to never go to jail for any hard time with a French cellmate and said good night with a loud, "Bon knee!"

By coincidence, I discovered the next morning that I no longer knew too much about golf or anything else other than my need for vast quantities of Motrin and water. That put me in the perfect frame of mind for the golf school's opening discussion by Kip Puterbaugh, who, in a brilliant stroke of coincidence, had recently published an excellent book titled *What You Know Can Hurt You.*

Drinking too much wine with Frenchmen can hurt you, I thought as Kip began his talk on the myths of the golf swing.

But within two minutes I was hooked on what Kip obviously knew all too well, which is that almost everything my father taught me about the golf swing had been wrong.

Handing me that cut-down five-iron that felt like a heavy ax in my hand, my dad summed up the golf swing by saying:

"Keep your head still.

Keep your left arm straight.

Keep your eye on the ball."

Forty-something years later, I learned from Kip Puterbaugh that those three statements have ruined a lot of golfers, not just me.

"What you know can hurt you," Kip told us. "And many of the accepted truisms of the golf swing are just plain wrong."

"Don't move your head." Kip quoted to us. "How many of you have heard that over and over?"

We all raised our hands. I may have raised both hands.

"Well, don't believe it. Talking about keeping your head still produces tension, and tension is never good in any athletic endeavor. To hit the ball with power, you need a free-swinging motion that lets the club acquire centrifugal force. That motion begins with your torso, not with the hands, which is the only way you'll be able to swing the club if you don't move your head."

As he spoke, Kip put on videotapes of some of the best players in the game, and showed us again and again that *good players do move their heads.*

If you doubt Kip's claims—and there's no reason why you should, because he's done pretty well by his number-one pupil, Scott Simpson—you can pretty much follow his points at home. Just videotape the swing of your favorite golfers from tournament coverage, preferably on a shot where the camera is facing the player. Then play the tape, pausing at two or three points in the swing to check your pro's head position.

Hogan, Anneka Sorenstam, David Duvall—Kip put their swings on screen, then marked the spot on the screen where their heads started at address. And did they move their heads? You bet. Moving his head behind the ball was Hogan's *first* move. Without getting behind the ball, how else could he generate any coil and power?

"You've got to get your left shoulder over your right hip," Kip explained. "To do that, you have to move your head."

Okay, so what about keeping your left arm straight?

"Just the idea of trying to keep your arm straight also introduces tension," Kip told us. "More tension in your left arm results in a tighter left grip and . . . once again . . . with starting your swing with your hands and arms instead of with your torso."

"What about keeping your eye on the ball?" I asked.

" 'You looked up!' That's what people tell you. Well, let me tell you, we've never seen anyone at our school with their eyes *off* the ball at impact. But if you concentrate on watching the club hit the ball and keeping your head down, you'll lock your head and the center of your body, which generates your motion. Then you've got a chicken wing with your left arm after impact, which means you'll chunk it."

Even worse, Kip explained, keeping your head down and your eye on the ball puts a huge stress on your back at followthrough.

"Quit trying to *hit* the ball." Kip summarized. "Swing the club toward the target, brush the ground, and let the ball get in the way. Hit it with your swing, not with your eyes."

I didn't have much time to spend with Kip, but it was enough to convince me that my idea of mentally tossing my old swing into the ocean was a good one.

"You all swing the club the same way," Kip told us. "You all have the same swing faults. If you want to correct those faults, you have to say to yourself, 'My old swing is history.' "

"My old swing is history," I said, mentally clicking my ruby shoes together. "My old swing is history."

For far too long, the swing Pip had given me had been a security blanket that I refused to set aside, which is probably why my game pretty much ceased to improve in my teens. Too early, I slammed up against the steepening curve that marks the road to better golf. And because Pip and I shared the same fundamental swing faults, it was impossible for him to boost me further up that steep slope.

Basically, starting again from scratch, it would be up to David Leadbetter to help me along. My new adventure in golf was about to begin.

Fundamentals of Golf

Golf's Biggest Myths

—From *What You Know Can Hurt You*,
by Kip Puterbaugh

Here they are, in five easy lessons, lies, lies, and damned lies,
all guaranteed to screw up your golf game.

1. Keep your head still and your eyes on the ball.
2. Keep your left arm straight.
3. Keep your right elbow in close on the backswing.
4. Keep your left side in control of the swing, and don't use too much right hand.
5. Keep your left heel on the ground to solidify your backswing turn.

Honorable mention:
Your eyes want to watch the clubhead strike the ball.

Remember:
"Don't try to hit the ball; swing the club toward the target, brush the ground, and let the ball get in the way. Hit it with your swing and not with your eyes."

CHAPTER 7

Harvey

"When I ask you to take an aspirin, please don't take the whole bottle."
—Harvey Penick

Though we couldn't afford private lessons from the pro at the San Angelo Country Club, when I was nine or ten I convinced Pip and my mother, Billie, to let me attend a brief municipal golf school. I don't remember anything about the instruction we received, but I have a pretty clear recollection of the nine-hole tournament that followed.

Teeing off on the second hole, I hit my ball into a stand of ferocious Johnson grass that was nearly as tall as I was. Finding the ball—and not having been told the rules governing an unplayable lie—I began to hack away. Thirteen strokes later, the ball finally spurted out of what little was left of the thick grass. I think I made 20 on the hole and posted something close to 70 for the nine. Everyone thought that was so hilarious that I was presented the trophy of a boxer because I'd been "fighting the course." Not the least bit amused, I rode my bicycle down to Santa Fe Golf Course and threw the trophy in the Concho River.

Pip had been right all along, I decided. Lessons will just screw you up.

I was forty years old before I ever received any knowledgeable instruction. I'd been posting scores since I was a teen that were mostly in the eighties, which must have been good enough or I'd have sought help earlier.

While most of my golf pals grew increasingly obsessed with golf tips and tricks like the power move from the top or staying behind the ball, I just stuck to what I'd learned from Hogan's books and from watching good players. Ultimately, my main goal was to simply make a long, smooth swing. The fact that I beat most of the guys I knew who took lessons and thought constantly about the game convinced me that my approach was the better of the two.

"Just hit it," I used to say.

I might have been content to go on like this for the rest of my life if I hadn't screwed up my right forearm by pretending I was an able carpenter. After three straight months of additions and renovations to my decaying house, I learned the hard way that swinging a hammer and swinging a golf club do not go hand in hand.

Having banged in perhaps twenty thousand nails, the tendons of my right forearm were so swollen that I looked like Popeye after a can of spinach. Unable to swing a golf club or to type—a bad combination for a golf writer—the severity of the situation was aggravated by a bum knee. Two different doctors suggested that if I intended to play golf again, I'd need surgery on both my knee and wrist. Barely forty years old at the time, I suddenly felt like an old man.

Wanting to avoid surgery, I visited Dr. John Bandy, now the sports doctor for several University of Texas athletic teams. Through muscle testing, acupressure, and a variety of other things I didn't understand, Bandy worked a miracle on my body, reducing the inflammation and pain in my forearm by 90 percent. The amazing part was, he accomplished most of that miraculous cure in one forty-five-minute visit. I walked into his office in agony and walked out in ecstasy. Nearly a scratch golfer himself, Bandy also suggested that some fault in my swing might be contributing to my physical problems.

And so I found myself at the brand-new Harvey Penick Golf Academy, part of Austin-based Golfsmith International, a company that grew from selling club-making components out of a garage into one of the world's largest retailers of golf equipment. You might think of Golfsmith founders Carl and Frank Paul as the Bill Gates and Stephen Jobs of golf. Over the years, Golfsmith has shipped over $2 billion in clubs and components. Two billion bucks, as they say in Texas, ain't mice nuts.

Having recently enlisted the eighty-nine-year-old patron saint of Texas golf to lend his name and knowledge to a school focusing on his teaching methods, Golfsmith was in need of publicity at the same time I was need of some fundamental swing changes that would help prevent my physical ailments from recurring. So I suppose what separated me from the other students at the Penick Golf Academy was that they all wanted to play better, while I merely wanted to be able to play.

Under the tutelage of the school's director, Bryan Gathright, as well as instructors Larry Gosewehr and Jim Hopkins, I spent three days with a number of other hackers working on all the basics of the game. On day one, Bryan briefly told us how he and other members of his teaching staff met with Harvey to learn how to teach the Penick way, to use Harvey's teaching aids and drills, and to focus on keeping the instruction simple.

"A bad grip," Bryan told us, "is the cause of more bad things happening in the golf swing than all other faults combined."

By the next day, Bryan had switched my thirty-year-old Hogan interlocking grip to an odd-feeling ten-finger grip. I wasn't comfortable with this new arrangement of my big hands until Larry Gosewehr told me that the old grip was putting a lot of stress on my right wrist, the same wrist that was recovering from tendonitis.

Suddenly my resistance to change melted away, and my hands seemed to fit naturally to the club. Guided by Larry, I made a few other minor adjustments in my address position and took a smooth swing with my eight-iron. The ball soared like a bottle rocket and landed on target a hundred and fifty yards away.

Continuing to hit it sweet, by the end of the third day, rather than being half crippled or completely worn down by the hundreds of balls I'd hit, I felt like I was actually gaining strength.

Though he was extremely frail and would live just one more year, Harvey still came by the school on Fridays to spend some time talking to the students, answering questions, and checking player's grips. All of this was quite an accomplishment for a man confined to a wheelchair with impaired hearing and sight.

"Being the center of attention makes Harvey feel like Bob Hope," I'd been told by Bud Shrake. Sure enough, Harvey's entrance was to a standing ovation.

"I'm Harvey," the old pro told us. "My father was Mr. Penick. I can't hear, and I can't see unless I clear my eyes, but I've probably seen more golf shots than anybody who ever lived; too many of them."

We'd all hit so many shots during the last three days, we knew exactly how he felt.

Years later, with Kip Puterbaugh having taken my swing back to square one, I realized that my notes of what was very nearly Harvey's last instruction session on golf might hold the secrets I needed to take ten strokes off my game. Unfortunately, my notes stopped abruptly just as Harvey was getting started. Had I lost the magic key to my quest?

For the next two furious Mad-Hatter days, I rummaged in a panic through thousands of pages of notes, files, stories, and books in my junk-filled office, cursing all the while because, like most men, I can't find anything, while my wife, like most women, can somehow use her uterus as a homing device to zero in on any missing object. Finally, with shelves and cabinets emptied, my glance fell upon something hiding in the back corner of a filing drawer. It was a tiny thing, hardly worth noticing. But I knew immediately that I'd found what I was looking for—a miniature cassette tape just one inch long and a quarter inch thick.

Harvey

Unfortunately, finding my long-abandoned mini-tape recorder still required asking for Christy's help. But when I finally got the recorder hooked up to a large speaker through a variety of adaptors and wires, I pushed the play button and—from beyond the grave—Harvey Penick spoke to me once more.

His voice had been so weak that he was barely audible, even in person. Twice during his talk I moved closer with my recorder until finally I was seated right next to him, trying not to distract him as he told a group of eager students his life's thoughts about the golf swing.

"One thing I've learned," Harvey said, "is that, if you don't have a good grip on a golf club, you can't play good golf. Anything you read about golf or see on TV about golf won't help you unless you have a good grip. If you've got a bad grip, you'll make another mistake to offset that, then you'll make another to offset that.

"You have to choose the grip that's best for you," he continued. "The interlocking grip was made famous by Gene Sarazen, and it's a good grip for people with short fingers: Gene Sarazen, Jack Nicklaus, Tommy Kite. They all have short, stubby hands. The full-fingered grip is good for women, and some other players, too. Whichever grip you use, the important thing is that the V's at the base of your thumbs point to your right shoulder."

Listening to the tape, I could still hear Harvey's passion for the game. Though he spoke modestly of his own game, Harvey told us of a long-ago round at the Austin Country Club when he once shot 30 on the front nine.

"Man, was I hot. Then I got to the thirteenth hole. I hit two bad shots, hit my third shot in the woods, decided I'd go play it, and made a thirteen on the hole. Even with a thirteen, I still ended up shooting seventy."

"Never give up," he told us. "Every shot counts."

Even with his weak voice, Harvey was still a great storyteller from an era that truly valued the art and skill of a good story. We were rapt as he described his friend Joe Kirkwood, a trick-shot artist who used to borrow an expensive watch and tee a ball on top of it.

"Joe could hit the ball every time without harming the watch," Harvey told us, "but on his practice swing he always took a huge divot, which nearly gave the watch's owner a heart attack.

"Titanic Thompson was the biggest gambler that ever was," Harvey continued. "His name was A. C. Thomas. Ben Hogan told me Ti hung around Fort Worth and Dallas, and Hogan told me, 'Harvey, he'll be through Austin sometime, and you can't beat him.'

"So one Sunday afternoon, here comes two fellers, and one of them said, 'I've got my PGA card and my Oklahoma card and can we play?' I said, 'Yeah,' and they asked, 'Would you like to play?' I said, 'No, I guess not.'"

Though millions have read Harvey's books, far fewer were fortunate enough to hear the beautiful, patient melody of his old-style Texas-Southern accent, which caused phrases like "I guess not" to come out as slow as molasses.

"One of my members was a good player and liked to gamble," Harvey continued. "He wanted to play them, so the two of us caught up and said we'd like to play the back nine. And they said, 'All right, we'll play for a dollar, ten, a hundred, a thousand. Doesn't make any difference.'

"So we said we'll just play you for fifty dollars. Some people came to watch, and Ti pulled out a big roll of bills and said, 'You reckon the spectators want any of that?' And I said, 'No, I guess not.'"

"So Ti said, 'Don't you want to give your wife something nice for Christmas?' And I said, 'No, I guess not.'

"We played the nine, and they sunk two putts about eighty feet long, to beat us one up. This was just before Christmas. Ti's partner, Herman Kaiser, won the Masters that spring."

After a while, I asked Harvey to tell us about his book.

"For the last fifty or sixty years," he said. "I've made notes in a little red book. That's the origin of *The Little Red Book*, which some of you know about."

Always modest, Harvey failed to mention that his book had recently become the bestselling sports book of all time.

"The book helps me remember things," he said. "You take Ben Crenshaw, the most natural player that anybody could be. Ben used to putt every afternoon, and I think that's why he is one of the best putters ever. What you should all do is go out there and spend some time with just one ball and really learn to putt.

"And when you're comfortable putting, you ought to work on your chipping game, too. If you don't get down in two from the edge of the green, you might as well have missed that first shot altogether."

When Harvey had answered all our questions, he asked to see my grip. I stood up and took a club in hand, and the grand old man began to study my new ten-finger grip. After a moment, Harvey adjusted my right thumb just a little, and suddenly the grip felt truly solid, as if the club were an extension of my body. I knew then that I'd found what I'd come searching for.

Looking up at me with a smile, Harvey said, "I like that. You keep using that grip, and you won't have any problems."

For seven years, my new ten-finger grip and the words of Harvey Penick kept me playing pain-free and left me generally happy with my scores. Then, in the year before my dad died, it all fell apart. And the more I tried to put things right, the more screwed up I got. And the more screwed up I got, the more I began to consider previously unthinkable ideas like: Why do I care? Why do I even play? And finally, why don't I just quit?

The answer, of course, was Pip. Though my father was far from being a taskmaster—indeed, he'd never shown me anything but love—love for me, for life in general, for the great outdoors, and for the game of golf. In some ways, our greatest bond was our love for the game. I never felt closer to him than I did on the golf course, the two of us walking side by side up the fairway, my bag on my shoulder and Pip towing his pull cart behind him.

So instead of quitting the game, I'd committed myself to a full year of almost nonstop golf that had the makings of being emotionally, physically, and financially trying, one in which success was far from guaranteed. What would Harvey have thought of that, I wondered.

The Old Man and the Tee

Looking through the notes and clippings I'd scattered all over my office in search of Harvey's last tape, I found the obituary I'd written for him. As I read through my words—and Harvey's—I realized I'd been a fool to ever consider giving up a game I truly loved.

A FINAL LESSON FROM HARVEY PENICK

"Take dead aim," Harvey Penick advised in a pearl of wisdom that applies equally well to golf and life. Born October 23, 1904, for most of his ninety years, Penick applied this simple philosophy toward sharing his love and knowledge of the game of golf, and toward being a trusted advisor and a consummate gentleman. In retrospect, the aims of his life were so inseparable from his actual achievements that he seems to have perfected both the teaching of golf and the art of living.

Penick's family was joined last week by hundreds of friends and former students on a rainy morning in Austin to pay their respects to America's most beloved golf instructor. Having journeyed home from Augusta for their final farewells were Penick's two most celebrated protégés, former Masters champion Ben Crenshaw, who began to study with Penick at age six, and Tom Kite, the PGA tour's all-time leading money winner, who started lessons with Penick at age thirteen.

One of the first American-born golf instructors, Penick came to golf as a caddie at the Austin Country Club in 1913. He became the head pro of that club in 1923, a position he held until his son Tinsley took over the job in 1971.

Though his life was devoted to the game of golf, Penick was little known outside of professional golf circles until 1990, when he showed sportswriter and novelist Bud Shrake a little red notebook in which he had for many years written the simple words of wisdom he often used in teaching the game of golf. Would it be possible, Penick wanted to know, to find a publisher for the book?

A short time later, Shrake gave Penick the news that Simon and Schuster was interested in publishing the work and mentioned the figure they had quoted. After a good deal of hesitation, Penick finally said, "Bud, I don't know if I can put together that kind of money." That figure was, of course, the amount to be paid *to* Harvey Penick. Those who knew him could only smile knowingly at how he had underestimated the world's thirst for his knowledge.

In a moving eulogy at Penick's service, Bud Shrake related a touching story that took place one week before Penick passed away, on a day when Harvey was in pain and his words could not be understood. When Ben Crenshaw came in with his wife, Julie, and their two little girls, Harvey's face lit up. Crenshaw and Penick began talking golf, and then Harvey's voice was heard loud and clear as he said, "Go get a putter."

Striving to control his emotions, Shrake described the scene: "Using Harvey's old wooden-shafted Sarazen putter, on the carpet beside what was to be his deathbed, one of the world's outstanding teachers was giving a final lesson to one of the world's outstanding putters. Harvey's eyes were bright, the fog of his age and pain rolled away, and he was back in his own world again, doing what he loved best."

When it was time to say good-bye to the only golf instructor he'd ever had, Crenshaw said, "I love you, Harvey." Harvey Penick replied, "I love you, Ben, and I'll be watching you, always."

At Tom Kite's suggestion, the old Sarazen putter used for that last lesson was buried with Harvey Penick.

"In case they don't have a putter in heaven," said Shrake, "now they do. And now they have the perfect person to teach them how to use it."

Five days after Harvey's funeral service, Ben Crenshaw—who'd missed the cut in three of his last four tournaments—suddenly found his old magic again. Some of that magic, of course, was Harvey.

According to Ben, "It was kind of like I felt this hand on my shoulder, guiding me along."

Tied for the lead in the final round of the Masters, Crenshaw struck a terrible drive on the par-five second. It flew into the woods, struck a tree, and bounced into the fairway. All over the country, golf fans had the same thought. *That was Harvey.*

Crenshaw got another unexplainable bounce from a bunker on eight, and one off a mound on thirteen. In Crenshaw's bag, Harvey was the fifteenth club.

After making a final putt on eighteen for a one-stroke victory, Crenshaw collapsed under the weight of his emotions. "I believe in fate," Crenshaw would say. "I don't know how it happened. I don't."

When all was said and done, one thing was clear. The clubs had been in Ben's hands, and Ben was in Harvey's.

CHAPTER 8

The Big Picture

———

"The gist of the golf swing is not the little bits and pieces. It's the overall—good grip, good posture, arms and body all working in unison."
—David Leadbetter

A full-day private lesson with David Leadbetter will set you back six thousand dollars, a price that prompted Leadbetter student Ray Romano to say, "Yes, but it came with lunch."

Unable to fork over even six *hundred* a day, I worked up the nerve to ask Leadbetter if he'd take me on anyway.

"My idea is to work with five or six of the best instructors in the world," I told him. "I'll absorb everything I can, hit about ten jillion practice balls, and see if I can take ten strokes off my game."

"You go to six different instructors, you may *add* ten strokes to your game," Leadbetter said with a laugh. "But count me in."

To run the new Leadbetter Golf Academy in Austin, David sent one of his key teaching pros, Sean Hogan, a soft-spoken Irishman (if there is such a thing). Having grown up playing tournament golf against the likes of Darren Clark and Padraig Harrington, after frequently coming in second, Sean decided to dedicate himself to teaching. Like all the instructors who work with Leadbetter at Champions Gate in Florida or at other Leadbetter schools around the world, Sean has worked extensively with the boss and is, I soon discovered, well versed in Leadbetter's theories and methods.

Since my whole arrangement with the Leadbetter School was relatively informal, when I arrived at Barton Creek for my first lesson with Sean, I was surprised to find my name printed on a sign marking my spot on the practice tee set up with tripod and camcorder, practice balls, cold water, fresh fruit, and a full array of teaching aids. This was the real deal.

Despite all the equipment, we started low-tech. After I'd hit a few balls, Sean made me hold out my palms like a kid with dirty hands. Inspecting my glove for a moment, he pointed to some severe wear in my glove at the heel of my hand.

"Those wear marks," he told me, "plus the fact that you're swinging the club on too flat a plane around your body, tells me that you've got the club too much in your palms and not enough in your fingers."

Pulling out a Sharpie, he began to draw two parallel black lines diagonally from just above the base of my little finger through the crook of the index finger.

"The club goes around you," he said, "because you're not hinging the club up, and much of that is because of your left hand. If you were trying to hammer a nine-inch nail into several two by fours, imagine how hard it would be if you held the hammer in our palms instead of your fingers. You wouldn't be able to hinge and get leverage. The golf swing is the same way."

Sean's analogy couldn't have been more appropriate, I realized, because ever since I'd hurt myself hammering nails, I'd basically been afraid to put much leverage in my swing.

Not too surprisingly, moving the club more into my fingers felt good, for that's where I'd held it when Harvey gave my grip his blessing. Over the years, I'd simply forgotten how to hold the club.

The Big Picture

Once my grip had been retooled, Sean videotaped a number of swings from behind my line and face-on, then we moved indoors to watch the tape. If you've ever taken a video golf lesson, then you'll be familiar with just how terrible your swing looks when you watch it rather than feel it.

"Feel isn't real," I remembered Leadbetter telling us.

So when I watched the video, I didn't need Sean's opinion to see that what I thought was a smooth seven-iron swing actually had more layoff than Enron.

To explain an overabused golf term like "layoff" —or "laying the club off the line" —let me paint the same picture in words that Sean drew with the use of a computer graphics program on my stop-action swing.

For starters, picture my setup from behind me, looking over the ball toward the target. As I address the ball and am just about to start my swing, Sean freezes the screen and draws a line along the shaft of my club that extends past the grip of my club, through my body, and up into the air behind me. This line indicates my original shaft-plane line, an essential reference point and guide. Ideally, the plane of my swing, relative to the original plane line, goes from a steeper angle on the backswing to a shallower one on the downswing. Add a little timing and I'll have a good chance of hitting the ball relatively straight toward the target every time.

If I roll my wrists as I start the swing, then take the clubhead back well inside of the target line, from that same view, my swing plane going back will be well under that same imaginary line or swing plane. I'll have a flat swing plane which encourages a laid-off position. When I get to the top of my swing, I'll be so out of position that the only way I can get the clubhead back to the ball is to come way over that same line, which means I'll be coming steeply toward the ball. That's generally called an "over the top" swing, and somewhere over the years, my swing had gotten more over the top than Robin Williams after a double latte.

As Leadbetter had already told me, steep is bad. Steep is the fault of most amateur golfers.

Sean had other things to say about my swing, not many of them good.

"Your shoulders are a little too open at address," he told me, echoing John Degen's words about the one fault most common to golfers going through the club fitting at Callaway.

"You also need a more athletic stance," he added. "Your weight should me more on the balls of your feet instead of your heels."

As I'd already noticed, Sean also commented that I was "bringing the club back in a flat and rolled position."

Putting a stop-action video of Ernie El's swing alongside mine, Sean moved Ernie and me through several swing checkpoints to give me a better idea of what I should be trying to do, but wasn't.

"Notice that Els keeps the clubhead in front of his hands a good bit longer than you. Halfway back, his clubhead has hinged up and the heel of his shaft is pointing at an area on the ground between his right foot and his target line."

The heel of my shaft, I could not help but notice, was pointing way out in front of me, almost at the horizon. If I'd had one of Leadbetter's info-commercial laser guides pointing out the heel of my shaft, instead of making an arc on the ground around my body, the laser would have put some poor spectator's eye out.

And Sean wasn't done with me yet.

"Your body is a little overturned at the top of your swing," he added. "Then you have a completely different track back down to the ball."

"So I noticed," I managed to mumble.

Finally we came to the moment of truth, the story of what the clubhead was doing as it reached the ball, the ultimate explanation of why I'd been hitting that deadly mix of pulls to the left and high, weak fades to the right.

"On the downswing," Sean continued, "your hands are lagging way behind your body. If you didn't pull hard to the left, you'd hit the hosel every time. Depending on the timing of that final hand action, you either pull it left or cut it right."

"It may sound like a lot," Sean concluded, "but a few small changes will create very positive results."

To correct my bad posture at address, Sean moved me a little farther from the ball and had me tilt my spine a bit forward and drop my hands and arms more under my shoulders. Doing that naturally gave me more of a right angle between my spine and my swing plane.

"You also need to be more on the balls of your feet," he told me. "Flex your knees and hold that flex all the way to the top of your backswing. That flexed right knee is the anchor that helps keep your lower body stable during the backswing."

For years, various golfers had told me I was locking up my right knee on the backswing. And though I knew that no great players allowed that to happen, somehow I'd convinced myself that the move worked for me. Suddenly a little light switched on in my brain, illuminating a neatly printed sign, which read "You're an idiot." If no good players share your bad habits and faults, chances are they're habits you should give up.

"Okay," I promised. "I'm absolutely going to keep that right knee flexed."

Since I'd been allowing my left knee to turn back with my body, Sean had me take my stance with a seven-iron and stuck a shaft in the ground so that it pressed gently against the inside of my left knee. Keeping that knee in a stable position would prevent my hips from overturning and keep my clubhead coming back on line instead of way inside. A stable lower body would also reduce my overswinging at the top and generate more coil between my hips and my shoulders and arms. Put them together and I'd be coming toward the ball on a good track with more power.

Next he inserted a second shaft in the ground just inside the path of my backswing to help guide my takeaway more on the target line.

This encouraged me to keep my hands in and the clubhead on line during the moveaway.

With the shafts all around me, I suddenly felt like Custer at Little Bighorn. I had zero confidence, and the first couple of swings showed it.

"You need to start getting your wrists into the act," Sean told me. "Remember Ernie on the video? When his arms were halfway back and his left arm parallel to the ground, the club was already fully set with the shaft pointing straight up at the sky."

After a dozen awkward swings, I slowly became more comfortable with the idea of stabilizing my lower body. I was far from hitting the ball perfectly, but I knew where I wanted to go, and that's a lot of the battle.

When we were done, Sean handed me a videotape of my swing alongside of Ernie's, then gave me a recap of what we'd covered.

"This is big-picture stuff," he said. "And you've already been able to make some of these adjustments from the get-go. If we can sharpen up your posture, get you an awareness of what your wrists need to do, get the club swinging, and take care of some of this excess body motion, we'll have sort of a complete swing lobotomy. Any questions?"

"Just one—when's the next lesson?"

Fundamentals of Golf

Grip and Posture

As taught by David Leadbetter

Grip and posture are the two easiest things to get right, and most people have them wrong. If you grip the club badly and stand over the ball poorly, then we know what kind of golfer you are.

A bad grip is the biggest single fault in golf. Most right-handed players grip the club way too much in the palm. If you look at your glove and you have wear marks in the heel, you can be certain you have it too much in the palm. Power is delivered to the ball through your arms, wrists, hands, and then into the clubhead. If you grip the club in the palm instead of in your fingers, it's difficult to create leverage through wrist hinge. That means you won't have much power.

It doesn't look a lot different to grip it in the fingers, but the club is probably an inch farther out. That allows you to swing it back, hold the angle coming down, and then release it. Interlocking, overlap, or ten-finger grip are all okay, as long as the hands work as a unit.

When it comes to posture, if players would just get in front of a mirror, pay attention, and try to understand what they're doing, their golf games would improve tremendously. Just getting yourself in a position where you can balance and get set will make it much easier to make a good swing.

Flex your knees, but don't sit back on the heels like so many amateurs. You want to feel your weight on or around the arches of your feet, to be in a position where you can almost lift your heels off the ground.

The Old Man and the Tee

Keeping your lower back straight, you should stick your rear end out slightly—that enables you to be in a solid, ready position. If you were shooting free throws you'd be in an athletic position—bouncing the ball, knees slightly bent, bending from the hips. Look at Tiger Woods and you can tell what type of athlete he is by the way he sets up to the ball.

CHAPTER 9

A Hundred Balls a Day

—————

"With self-discipline, all things are possible."
—Theodore Roosevelt

I've never been a person of great discipline. Rather than adhering to self-imposed rules, I've accomplished things by a manic commitment to doing what I enjoy. After a year in college at the University of Texas, my parents informed me on my eighteenth birthday that they didn't have a dime to help me continue my education. With a little discipline, I could have found a way around this dilemma, but instead I left UT and enrolled in the school of hard knocks. Somehow it seemed easier.

A year later, just for a lark, I learned to juggle, then became so obsessed with my new skill that I was soon making a living by tossing and catching everything from wicked, curving scythes to torches with searing flames about three feet high. Have you seen the movie *Waiting for Guffman,* Christopher Guest's comic parody of small-town community theater? That's me juggling Ping-Pong balls out of my mouth. BFD.

The Old Man and the Tee

Having learned to juggle by chance, I traveled across America and around the world for the next ten years, tossing and catching all sorts of things with gleeful abandon. I juggled at the world's biggest rock festival in Denmark, on the streets of Pamplona after running with the bulls, and on the pitcher's mound of Dodger Stadium between sets by the Eagles and Elton John. My passing the hat for a living even prompted Pip to start tipping street musicians, a radical change for a guy who'd always considered buying a soda a waste of money.

Moving off the streets, I worked in Vegas showrooms between topless dancers and opened countless shows for Willie Nelson, Count Basie, and even James Brown. After *Caddyshack* took America by storm, I spent months touring with Rodney Dangerfield as his opening act. Somehow I created a career for myself as a juggler, a comedian, an actor—it's hard to say exactly what I was. All I know is that I was completely and totally dedicated to this pursuit. Then one day I woke up and thought, "Done that." And I gave it up.

What can I say? No self-discipline. Besides, I'd learned that life is sometimes more fun if you don't have a clue what's gonna happen next.

Because I was all too familiar with my lack of self-discipline, my ten-strokes mission presented some of the same problems that come with any quest. It's easy to *say* you're going to rescue Helen of Troy from the man she loves, but convincing the most beautiful woman on earth to come home with her stodgy husband may prove a little more complicated than you expected (not to mention the launching of a thousand ships, fighting a ten-year war, and having to hide in a big, smelly horse).

The one undeniable thing I know about golf is that lowering your score is like trying to lose weight. The lower you go, the harder it is to continue your progress. When you first take up the game, it's not hard to cut your scores from 120 to 110 or even to 100. Cutting from 100 down to 90, we soon discover, takes both a bit of work and some real understanding of the game, but it's a goal eventually accomplished by almost half of all golfers.

For most of us, the sweat really starts to flow when you try to take it down another five, with every stroke thereafter becoming more and more difficult. And like taking off the pounds, as soon as you quit working on your game, the strokes fly back on at an alarming rate.

The more you learn about the game, the more you come to realize how good a three- or four-handicapper really is. The players who make it to scratch hear a hundred times a year that they ought to turn pro, but they're actually the very few golfers who truly understand just how good the pros really are. And that's why there are a hundred thousand amateurs for every active PGA Tour pro.

To further complicate matters, almost all really fine players achieve most of their skills when they're relatively young. Thinking through all that, it began to dawn on me that I'd have to work my butt off to have a prayer of taking off ten. That meant changing my lackadaisical attitude and setting minimum amounts of practice and play. Not only would I be forcing myself to put in the time on the range, the putting green and the course, I'd also establish a regimen that could not be distracted by such mundane details as work or money. I didn't want to end up sounding like Pip, who'd told me so many times that he could have been a good player if only he'd had the time.

What Pip didn't talk about was that he'd only played a little with his own father, or that he hadn't taken the game up in earnest until he was thirty years old, at which time he and his friend Don Kennemer had started playing at the Old Santa Fe municipal course in downtown San Angelo.

"Whether it was golf or anything else, Pip and Don loved to *play*," my mother told me recently, giving a definite negative connotation that a lot of people wouldn't associate with the word *play*.

I'd inherited Pip's love of play, but to achieve my ten-stroke goal, I was going to have to work at the game like I'd never worked before. No one has ever become a great golfer without hard work, and without being selfish with their time. My first commitment was to hit a hundred balls a day. A hundred balls every day, rain or shine, in sickness and in health, till death did we part. If a hundred didn't give me the progress I needed, then I'd hit two or three hundred a day—whatever it took. While I was at it, I figured I might as well hole a hundred putts a day as well.

There was no magic number involved; I simply wanted to force myself to find, then ingrain, the new swing that Sean Hogan and David Leadbetter had promised to help me build. At the end of my year, I didn't want to have any excuses. Having played with the old swing for forty years, I had a lot of bad muscle memories to erase.

Luckily, I also had an unlimited number of free range balls to hit at Barton Creek, for when I told their director of golf what I needed, Chip Gist replied, "Canyons has the best facilities; make yourself at home."

Located just fifteen minutes from my home—the Fazio Canyons Course is set in a pristine Texas Hill Country site covered in dense forests of oak, elm, and cedar and bisected by several beautiful creeks and eighteen winding holes. An impressive short-game practice facility has multiple greens for putting, chipping, and sand play. The far end of the double-sided driving range had recently been renamed the David Leadbetter Golf Academy at Barton Creek.

Taking full advantage of my welcome, I started every practice session by pouring a hundred balls out on the ground. When those were gone, I generally did it again. Both Sean and David had told me I didn't need to hit that many balls, that I could accomplish almost as much with the swing drills I was already learning, but I loved banging the pellets and reasoned that I was also building strength and stamina.

When I went back to see Sean for my second lesson, the first thing he did was recheck my grip to make sure I had the club more in my fingers than in the palm. Then he gave my address posture another quick critique to once again get me on the balls of my feet, my knees flexed and butt out.

After just a week, Sean already liked my progress in taking the club back on track. I was no longer hitting any weak fades, but I was hitting it hard left and couldn't seem to do much about it.

"We're seeing a little of the old effect on your downswing," Sean told me several times. "Ultimately, I'd like to shallow out your downswing."

Once again, Sean pulled out his arsenal of putter shafts to help me guide my swing. Behind me—away from the target and outside of my swing, he inserted a long putter shaft in the ground. Then he stuck a second shaft in the ground down the target line, but inside my swing plane.

"The idea," he told me, "is to swing out toward the big shaft on the takeaway, come down underneath it, swinging out toward right field, then finishing over the second shaft."

After four or five swings around the two shafts, I was actually starting the ball a little to the right, then drawing it toward the target, which gave my game a sense of power I'd never felt.

A little pumped, I decided to really go after one and that's when the proverbial shift hit the fan. Or perhaps I should say, the fan hit the shaft. Fanning the club open on the backswing—which I'd repeatedly been told not to do—I took it back inside, then employed, as Sean puts it, "a little of the old effect." Coming over the top as I'd been doing for years, with every bit of strength in my body, I nailed my seven-iron directly onto the blunt top of the putter shaft I was supposed to be swinging inside of.

I mean this was a dead-center, full-on blow, kind of like hitting an anvil instead of a ball. The impact of the club and the screeching halt of my swing felt as if I'd been sledge-hammered in the right wrist. Literally in shock, I looked to the club still in my hand and tried to fathom why my shaft was bent at a thirty-degree angle about eight inches from the head.

Then I felt the pain shooting from my wrist. *"Geee-aaaaiii!"* I shrieked, the opening salvo in a recounting of every foul word I'd ever heard—along with a few new ones to boot. Looking to Sean, I saw that he, too, appeared to be in shock. I could almost read his mind: "Broken wrist."

Thirty years before, I'd broken both bones in the same wrist making a ballsy dive to save a volleyball, only to have another player do the same thing and land full-out on my arm. Why we were both diving for a volleyball on a wooden court in a casual game can only be explained by hormones. We were both trying to impress a girl. Not only did I never see the girl again, that nasty break never healed properly. Now I wondered if I'd screwed it up again.

"I hit the shaft," I finally said to Sean, as dumb a comment as I'd made since high school basketball, when a mountain of a man named Charlie Brown missed a rebound and came down with both fists on my face as I was going up for the ball. Nose flattened into my cheeks and blood everywhere, I staggered over to the sideline and said, "Coach, I broke my nose."

Like any good high school coach, he looked at me and said, "Yeah, I think you did. Now shake it off and get back in there."

Shake it off? If you had rectal cancer, your high school coach would say, shake it off. A severed hand? Shake it off. A vampire reaches into your chest and pulls out your still-beating heart, which you show to the coach. "Coach, my heart." "Yep, shake it off."

With my hand jammed between my legs to cover the pain, the first inkling that I was all right was when a golf joke popped into my head.

Two women are playing golf when one hits a tee shot that duckhooks through the trees toward the next fairway. Hearing a man shriek in pain, the women hurry over and see a guy doubled over in pain, with his hand covering his crotch.

The woman who hit the ball apologizes profusely, then says that she's a nurse and might be able to make it feel better. Then she starts to gently rub the inside of his thigh. "Does that feel better?" she asks. He nods, so she moves higher up his thigh and massages him there for a minute, then she gently pulls his hand away from his crotch and starts to massage him there. After a minute, she says, "Does that feel better?" And he says, "Yeah, but my hand still hurts like hell!"

A Hundred Balls a Day

By the time we finished laughing at the joke, my hand also felt a little better, though I'm sorry to say there were no nurses in sight.

"That's an instructor's worst nightmare," Sean told me a few minutes later, "teacher error, broken equipment, injured pupil . . . who happens to be a golf writer."

"What do you mean, teacher error?" I asked. "You told me to come down well inside the shaft and I whacked it dead-center. That's pilot error."

"If you say so," Sean told me. But then he moved the big shaft about six inches farther out of my swing plane.

Seeing that my seven-iron was going to be out of play until it could be reshafted, I pulled out my eight, made a half swing just to see if I could do it, then I hit the ball, a grimace on my face.

No pain, no gain, I thought. At least I hoped I'd gain. Cause I sure didn't want the alternative of pain, no gain.

At the end of the lesson, Sean wrote out a short list of things for me to work on:

Lower hands at address.
Butt end leads the moveaway.
Swing to right field to start the downswing.

"I think that's enough for this week," he told me.
I had to agree.

CHAPTER 10

Mexico

---

*"They say golf is like life, but don't believe them; golf is more compli-
cated than that."*

—Gardner Dickinson

Early on, I decided I'd play a hundred rounds during the
year. So I wouldn't get tired of playing the same courses over and over,
I figured why not up the ante in my little golf fantasy and travel to some
of the world's finest golf destinations? All that practice would be a heck
of a lot more enjoyable if I was looking out over the Sea of Cortez in
Cabo San Lucas or standing in the covered hitting bays at Turnberry in
Scotland. Besides, playing a few of the world's great oceanside tracks
would tune me up for my return to Pebble and a shot at breaking 80.

Of course, that would mean a lot of solo travel, and I'd be forced
to spend my evenings in pubs and cantinas all over the world. That
was the kind of tough duty my dad would have appreciated, I figured,
and as good as any other approach I could think of in dealing with my
middle-aged vacation from reality.

All I had to do was convince my wife.

A few years ago, several of my buds were planning a guys-only road trip—fishing on the Texas coast, drinking beer, hanging around in seedy bars, that sort of thing. We asked another married friend to join us and suggested he check with his wife for a hall pass.

"My wife!" he said indignantly. "I'll have you know that I am the lord of my manor and have the final decision on all matters, including debauched parties!"

"So you'll go?" we asked.

"Well," he said, "let me just go ask my wife if I *want* to."

So let me just say that when I told my wife I was headed to Mexico to work on my golf game, her reply was "When do we leave?"

Two weeks and a couple of thousand practice balls later, I found myself twenty miles north of Puerto Vallarta, sipping a cup of hot coffee on the veranda of our swank accommodations at the Four Seasons Punta Mita. (And by now I *was* beginning to get addicted to the cushy life.)

I had a round set up for the afternoon on the resort's Jack Nicklaus Signature course, but first had to decide whether to spend my morning snorkeling with my family or banging balls. An hour later, the Four Seasons shuttle dropped me off at the golf course. Instead of my clubs, though, I was carrying a giant bag of snorkeling gear and leading Christy and our two daughters to a spot the concierge assured us is the clearest water along Punta Mita's miles of reef-protected beaches.

Beachcombing our way past piles of sun-bleached coral, we came to a cove guarded by a natural island in the Pacific which just happens to be the green for what may be the most fun hole in all of golf.

Officially named hole 3B and affectionately called the "Tail of the Whale," the tee shot here is a knee-knocking challenge, two hundred yards into the wind, all carry. Assuming you get a ball to the island—and that's a big assumption—when tides and waves permit, you are driven in an amphibious vehicle to putt out on the green. How cool is that?

Swimming instead of driving, we paddled out in fins and masks and were soon snorkeling among schools of brightly colored fish, sea urchins, and rock lobsters. Then my seven-year-old discovered something *really* exciting—a golf ball! Actually, there were quite a lot of them.

Back at the beach a little later, we were drying off when a group of golfers stepped onto the tee that faces the island. Moving closer to watch, I found a group of young men and women playing in the resort's annual employee golf tournament. This was a rare chance for these mostly novice players to knock one toward the distant green, but, alas, the wind and the long carry proved too much for them.

"Mind if I try?" I asked, digging out one of the balls my daughter had found in the ocean.

Barefoot and shirtless, my trunks still dripping wet, I teed up the ball. On a warm-up round the day before, I'd taken three shots at the island without once landing dry. I'd guess one in ten is the overall percentage of shots that make the green. There is no closer shot: the tee is on the mainland; the green is an island; it's two hundred yards into the wind. Good luck.

Swinging a five-wood on loan from a bartender who'd made a fine margarita for me the night before, I was careful this time to do the things Sean had been teaching me—grip in the fingers, stable lower body, swing the handle. Knowing I had to hit a big lick to get there, I came at the ball from the inside and just launched that sucker. I held my breath as the ball sailed over the waves and just caught the green, causing my hosts to let out a cheer.

But how, I wondered, had I been able to strike the ball so sweet without even warming up. The answer, I soon realized, was the green itself: a fantastic target in the ocean, it had called to me. The green had told me I had to have enough club, that I had to swing hard and finish well. Had the green been the same distance but surrounded by grass, I'd have made a less determined swing and hit anything from an average shot to a disaster. Instead, Nicklaus had forced me to think and act like a golfer, to commit to my shot and acquire my target. He had challenged me to focus. What I needed to do, it suddenly seemed obvious, was learn to challenge myself in a similar fashion on each and every shot I played.

While in Vallarta, I received another invaluable lesson from Sam Logan, then the head pro of Robert Von Haage's El Tigre course— the Tiger—so named for its ferocious 7,239-yard length and for its 621-yard par-five closing hole, which might as well be a mile as far as my ability to reach it in three.

On El Tigre's par-four fourteenth, I had one shoe off and one leg knee-deep in the murky lagoon by the green and was about to hit my half-submerged ball when Logan offered the most important golf tip I'd ever heard.

"Keep your eye on the crocodile," he said, referring to a twelve-foot crocodile lurking nearby.

"Crikey!" I hollered, making one of the fastest swings in the history of golf. Both the ball and yours truly flew out of the resulting geyser of water, and I'm still not sure if I was happier about me landing on dry ground or the ball landing on the green. I didn't save par, but I did save my life, so I guess I can't complain.

My seaside golf preparations continued after driving south from Puerto Vallarta to El Tamarindo Resort and Golf Club, my favorite destination in Mexico, which is high praise considering I've been writing about Mexico for two decades.

Surrounded by two thousand acres of tropical rain forest, the fairways of El Tamarindo climb, fall, twist, and turn like some mythical serpent of the gods. Add twenty-eight villas and a great restaurant on a secluded beach and this place really is paradise.

The first time my wife and I stayed here, we were taking an early morning walk when we discovered baby sea turtles emerging from their nest in the sand and struggling toward the water. Returning a year later with our two daughters, we hired a local vaquero to bring his horses for a long ride through the jungle to the deserted Mahajua beach, where we took turns galloping up and down the sand beside the crashing waves. This trip we spent one long morning as the only people on mile-long Dorado Beach, where the powdery white sand is as perfect as my memory of our girls trying to tunnel their way to China.

If your own private beach sounds good, how about your own private seaside golf course? Teeing off at the casual hour of ten A.M., my suspicion that I was the first and only golfer on the course was confirmed by the unmarked dew on the first green. My only company for the round would prove to be Mexican white-tailed deer, javelinas, and literally thousands of crabs, which constantly scurried back to the jungle at the sound of my golf cart.

At three separate coves on the Pacific, the course drops sharply down to the ocean before climbing back into the enchanted forests. The eighth hole is as good as it gets—here or anywhere. From the mountaintop black tees way, way down to the seaside green, it's 328 yards of sheer, unadulterated fun. Take out your driver and swing away, but I bet you can't hit just one, for the desire to drive this green will pound in your heart.

After a steep climb from the eighth green to the par-three ninth tee, it's again almost straight downhill, this time 140 yards to a bunkered green with the rolling waves of the Pacific Ocean crashing in front and a rocky cliff behind. Even better, on the hill above the ninth green is a halfway house with a dramatic view of the ocean, ice-cold beer, and delicious guacamole.

"Cuántos golfistas pasan aquí en el dia?" How many golfers come by in a day? I asked Pedro, the bartender and waiter who didn't seem to mind my Spanish, which reads better than it sounds.

"Sometimes twenty, sometimes ten," he told me, "and sometimes none."

Feeling good with a string of pars under my belt, I asked him to make me one of my favorite drinks, a cold Michelada, a Pacifico Beer on the rocks with lime and salt.

In the hot months, Pip drank his beer on ice whenever it was available, a practice I adopted a few years ago on a fishing trip to

Mexico with both my brothers and my father. The fishing was just okay and the weather unbearably hot, but we did drink a lot of beers on ice, and everyone at the fish camp, as usual, thought Pip was the greatest.

He always introduced himself by saying, "I'm Raymond Pipkin from San Angelo, Texas." He'd ask who they were and where they were from, and the next thing you knew, Pip had made another old friend.

After his funeral and memorial service in San Angelo, Pip's five kids sat around for hours telling stories about him and discussing why everyone loved him so much.

"Pip became the King of Meadowcreek Nursing Home," my brother John told us. "It's not going to be the same there for anyone."

Months after that long and tiring day, my mother ended up in the same nursing home where she'd visited my father daily for over eight years. I made the long drive to San Angelo and as I was walking to her room, I came upon Pip's former roommate, another stroke victim whom I'd never heard speak. Recognizing Pip's son, he lifted his arms to me, the saddest look in his eyes I have ever seen, and he began to cry. Whether these tears were for my loss or for his, I wasn't sure.

What kind of man was my father, I wondered, to inspire so much love? But I already knew the answer—he was a great man—not for the successes of his labors, nor for his accumulation of wealth or power, but for the love he left behind.

"He was kind, loving, and caring," my brother Marvin told us the evening after Pip's funeral. "Plus he was lucky. Pip and I went to Alaska to hunt caribou, which was something he always wanted to do. But he wasn't strong enough or agile enough to catch up with them, and after five or six days he was so exhausted he just gave up and went back to the camp to sleep. After a while he got up to go to the bathroom and said, 'Look! There's a big caribou!'

"Sure enough, this monstrous caribou had walked right into camp. I handed Pip his gun while he still had his pants down around his ankles.

The caribou was running full-out now, a long ways away, and Pip shot it on a dead run. It fell on the landing strip right where the plane came later to pick it up. If that's not the luckiest guy I ever met, I don't know what is.

"All the way back to Texas," Marvin concluded, "Pip kept telling the story to people we met, and he always started it by saying, 'Marvin and I got this caribou.'"

Hearing my brother tell that story, I could not help but think that I'd never heard Pip say anything that started with "Turk and I." I'd had a hard time living up to my brothers' accomplishments in school and in sports when I was a kid, and now I realized that in some ways I'd also failed to measure up as a man. There were so many things we could have done together. We could have played Pebble or St. Andrews, but I was always too busy, and Pip was generally content to just take life as it came. Why fly to Scotland or California to play when he had so many friends in San Angelo?

The love of hunting, fishing, and golf ran deep in his heart, and after moving into the nursing facility he had a difficult time understanding why he couldn't go home and carry on as before.

"What have you been doing?" I asked him one day after making the three-hour drive from Austin.

"Just trying to figure out a way to get out of here," Pip told me, looking around as if he was planning a jailbreak.

Somehow, though, he held his head high and learned to make do with too infrequent visits from his distant children, bingo games for quarters, singing old hymns in chapel service, and a group of coffee drinkers who came every Saturday morning to sit with him and tell outrageous stories. Since most of Pip's lifelong friends had already passed away, the coffee drinkers were more recent acquaintances, and I could never decide whether they were the kindest, most generous men I'd ever met, or whether they were the ones benefiting by all the West Texas bull flying around in the group's stories and laughter. After Pip's service, I realized it was both.

This was Pip's final foursome, and all of them had so perfected the game that they no longer needed clubs and balls. They were more than happy to simply have each other's company.

One of the greatest beauties of golf is that you can play for so much of your life. Is there anything in the game more beautiful than an old man with a pull cart and a sweet swing who knocks it not too far, but right down the middle every time?

Sitting there on the cliff above number twelve at Tamarindo, I sipped my Michelada and realized that golf continues to give to you even after you can no longer pull that cart or swing the club above your shoulder. The patience instilled in you by the game is little different than the patience needed in all of life. It's a long eighteen holes, and if you get to the end of the course with a smile on your face and the same number of balls you started with, then I'd say you learned your lessons well.

"Voy a regresar," I told Pedro at the halfway house. "I'll be back."

Continuing on my private course in paradise, I eventually came to the S-shaped eighteenth, a par five with water right and left and very little possibility of going for the green in two. Knowing the sensible route is a midiron from the tee, I pulled out my driver. If I hit a high hook over the jungle, I thought, I might have a chance at eagle.

I'd already hit a couple of shots into the jungle, so I decided to quit thinking so much about all the things Sean had taught me. This time I was swinging hard for the fences and for my father and for some badly needed confidence. The farther I moved into my twelve months of lessons and work, the more I was beginning to doubt that I'd ever reach my goal.

But I knew that if I got behind this one, generated some coil and really gave it a ride, good things might happen. Off my big swing, the ball flew up and over the first line of trees that separated jungle from fairway, then disappeared. Way past the dogleg, I found the ball sitting on the two-hundred-yard mark in the middle of the fairway.

A five-wood and one putt later, I'd made the first eagle of my quest. Even with the beer break, the eighteen holes had taken well under three hours, which prompted me to head straight to number one for another round in paradise.

Out at the halfway house, I thought, Pedro would have my lunch and another cerveza waiting for me. When I drank that beer on ice, Pip would be with me.

Fundamentals of Golf

The Swing

As taught by David Leadbetter

So many players fail to wind up and coil, which is why I stress the importance of getting behind the ball. Physics tells us that if you want to create power, you have to create some coil. You have to have a firm, stable lower-body position, then you have to get the upper body winding up on top of the lower body. You have to get behind it. You have to get some whip.

To start the swing, the club and the body must work in unison. The chest rotates into the right leg. As you start the backswing, feel a little shift in the middle. Feel your stomach moving slightly to the right. That shift gets you going. You don't just want to turn, or feel like just your arms are moving. You want to feel like the stomach actually moves.

It's important to synchronize the movement of your arms and the movement of your body. Get everything working together—hands, arms, and chest. Feel it all loading up on your right leg. Then you can make your turn.

At the top of the backswing you should be able to lift your left leg (or for lefties, your right leg). If you get to the top of the backswing and can't lift your left leg, I guarantee that you have too much weight on your left side. Get turned and get that chest to the right. At the top of your swing, you can think of the shirt buttons being on top of your right leg.

Remember that the arms, hands, and body arrive at the same time at the top, and as you work through the ball, you feel your arms and body get there at the same time as well, then continue through to the finish.

CHAPTER 11

The Harder They Fall

"The more you understand the game, the better. The more you can understand your swing, the better."

—David Leadbetter

Having hammered my seven-iron squarely on the fat end of a putter shaft, it was obvious I couldn't be trusted to follow instructions. On subsequent lessons, Sean dispensed with the shafts and began spray-painting lines on the grass to show me the proper clubhead path for my backswing and downswing.

Like most middle and high handicappers, I'd been taking the clubhead back way inside of the target line, so the line in the grass to guide my backswing was well outside of where I'd been swinging. A separate line for my downswing moved from inside the target line toward the inside, back quarter of the ball, the kind of line that would have me "swinging for right field," as Sean put it.

These same swing lines, Sean estimated, would be helpful for 80 percent of all amateur golfers.

Following these lines soon had me hitting the ball again with a great sense of power, but there was one problem with this approach.

The only way I could swing the club even remotely along these lines was to have the feel of taking the club way outside the target line going back, then looping the clubhead toward the inside at the top in a fashion that felt like Jim Furyk's famous loop swing.

Though this made my downswing considerably less steep, which was one of my primary goals, it also made me worry about this big "inside" loop causing me problems at some point down the road.

"I know I asked for big changes," I told Sean, "but it feels like we've gone too far in changing my swing track."

Sean's response was to invite me inside, to the air-conditioning, where we watched the videotape of my new "Furyk loop." The only thing was, the video clearly showed that I had no loop. I was taking it back, changing directions, and returning to the ball on a pretty impressive swing plane. If anything, I was still a little steep, but I was definitely not making a loop like Jim Furyk.

"Remember," Sean told me for the twentieth time, "feel isn't real."

What was real is pretty simple. I'd been looping it the opposite direction, coming over the top and steep at the ball for so long that even a good swing now felt false and manufactured. Obviously I had a long way to go.

For the next few weeks, Sean had me working on a variety of drills and exercises for various parts of my game.

With the driver, Sean had to keep reminding me of the setup that Leadbetter had put me in that first day: wider stance, 60 per cent of my weight on the right foot, my shoulders tilted slightly away from the target, which would help me stay behind the ball.

"As it moves away from the ball," Sean told me, "the clubhead ought to move gradually inside the line, but it's just as important that the clubhead stay outside of your hands."

Oddly enough, taking the club back quickly inside the ball-to-target line was what I'd long visualized as the source of my hitting power. Sean was quick to point out to me that what power and accuracy I had were mostly from good timing (when I had it). Still the juggler, I'd relied on hand-to-eye coordination to hit the ball, instead of on the big muscles and the coiling and uncoiling of my body.

With my weight properly behind the ball, I'd be in position to sweep the ball off the tee with a swinging motion, not by trying to smack it at the one moment when the ball might go right. The modern swing of David Leadbetter is more synchronized, more compact, more on line, and more powerful. If you can learn to do it.

I was not a great student. As long as Sean was watching me and helping me make minor corrections, I was really busting the ball. If he stepped away for too long, I'd start to get sloppy and lose what I'd gained. Even worse, once I started getting comfortable with the driver setup, when I switched back to the irons, I was unable to get back in position to hit them. After a while, Sean would once again remind me of my posture with the irons.

"Don't lean to the right side as you do with the driver," he told me more than twice. "With the irons, the right hand being lower on the shaft automatically takes care of the spine and shoulder angle."

I also had a tendency to get all bunched up at contact, and that was bound to throw lots of unpredictable forces into the swing.

"A free, easy swing," Leadbetter had said. But having spent countless hours trying to find it, this mythical swing seemed neither free nor easy.

Through all of our sessions, I was slowly managing to convert my slice to a mere fade, but still found it almost impossible to draw the ball with the kind of power that a 220-pound, six-foot seven-inch guy should be able to generate.

Being tall gives you a unique perspective. My whole life people have been coming up to me and saying painfully obvious things like, "How's the weather up there?" and "Gee, you're tall. You must play basketball!" What's up with that? I don't walk up to midgets and say, "Gee, you're short. You must play miniature golf!"

While most golfers share many of the same swing flaws, tall players in particular find it difficult to hit a right-to-left ball flight.

Bruce Lietzke—a tall guy known on the Champions Tour as "Leaky"—is the prime example of a great player who simply cannot draw the ball. "Bruce's hook," I was told by his brother and caddie, Brian Lietzke, "is a three-yard fade."

I couldn't begin to properly describe all of the drills that Sean and I worked on, though I soon discovered that most of them are detailed in David Leadbetter's various books on golf. Two of these books— *Faults and Fixes* and *100 Percent Golf*—soon replaced my well-worn Hogan volumes and helped clear up the state of full swing confusion that threatened to swamp me about every other day.

Leadbetter had also recently published *The Fundamentals of Hogan,* in which David analyzes Hogan's thoughts about his own swing. In reading this work and studying the book's excellent Hogan photos, I discovered that my laid-off position at the top actually *does* look like Hogan. The difference, however, was that Hogan's hands dropped behind him in the crucial moments as he started down toward the ball, while my hands went there on the way up. If Hogan was a textbook golfer, then I'd become the textbook golfer for over the top. I was Hogan backward.

As Hogan had done, I was practicing at every opportunity, trying to unearth my own secrets of golf by digging them out of the earth with an endless progression of range balls. One exercise I found particularly helpful was similar to an old Harvey Penick drill I'd learned years before at the Penick School. To help with a proper backswing track, Bryan Gathright would have me set up to the ball with my seven-iron, then place a second ball immediately behind my clubhead—making a clubhead sandwich, so to speak. As I moved the clubhead away from the ball I was about to hit, the idea was to roll the second ball straight back, *away* from the target. Then I completed my swing and hit the first ball.

This may sound complicated, but it's amazing how well it works to keep your clubhead on a proper path, moving low and without ducking inside the line. Once you've taken it back on a better path, it's relatively easy to come back to the ball at a shallower angle.

Over the past few years, this drill has been one of my prime methods for rescuing my swing in time of trouble.

Now I had other problems to address. Like so many amateurs, my tendency was to "set" the clubhead late in my swing. Comparing my swing again in side-by-side video with Els, Sean pointed out one of my biggest weaknesses, a fault that is shared by a majority of amateur golfers.

"When Ernie's arms are halfway back and his hands about waist high," Sean pointed out, "the shaft of his club is already pointed straight to the sky."

"When your hands are waist high," he continued, "the clubhead is barely above your hands."

This late setting of the clubhead, I soon learned, leads to the reverse on the downswing, an early release of the clubhead, meaning that before I'd gotten close to even making contact, I'd already lost clubhead speed and wasted most of my power. Els, on the other hand, naturally combined his early setting of the clubhead with a late release, giving him maximum power and clubhead speed at the ball (or just in front of it). That's why my drives went "Bap!" and his went "Boom!"

Giving me a modified version of Harvey's roll-the-ball-back exercise, instead of a second ball behind my clubhead, Sean placed one of those three-foot-long driving range boards that normally protect your space from those wild-swinging doofuses on either side of you.

With the heavy board behind my clubhead, because of its weight and its friction with the ground, the only way I could get it moving was to swing the handle of the club back. If I tried to move it back by rolling my wrists—as I'd started my swings just a couple of months before—all that happened was it hurt my wrists.

But if I initiated a synchronized swing with body and hands and kept the clubhead coming back low, the board would slide quickly back until the point that my clubhead came over the top edge of the board. Suddenly released of the board's resistance, the clubhead would immediately jump up, giving me the early wrist set that I needed. While this was happening, the board would continue to slide back another foot or two, moving it beyond any possibility of being struck on the downswing, and more often than not, I'd hit a good shot.

After I stretched and warmed up at the beginning of my daily practice session, pushing the board back was the single best way for me to get into the feel of my new swing.

One afternoon late in the summer, I was on the range, alternating this drill with a couple of others, and hitting a succession of solid rockets, each with a nice high trajectory. Unfortunately, every one of them was going thirty yards left of the target.

I tried everything to hit those balls to the right, but they just kept streaking left. And even though it was cloudy and probably the coolest day of the summer, I realized after a while that I was sweating all over, and it wasn't because I was working so hard.

It took me quite a while to figure it out, but finally it dawned on me. I was sweating because I was full of doubt. I'd learned more about the golf swing in three months than I had in my whole life, and I still couldn't hit the damn ball any straighter.

Noticing I was in agony, the young assistant pro attending the range strolled over to watch me hit.

"How's it going?" he asked.

Bang—I hit a ball: straight left.

"Terrible."

Bang—straight left, again.

"So what's with the board?" he asked. "I saw you pushing it around or something."

Teeing up a ball, I set the board close behind it, leaving room for my clubhead to slip between the two, then explained what the drill was supposed to accomplish.

"The only problem is," I concluded, "today it's not working."

"Show me anyway," he asked.

With a shrug, I set up to the ball, pushed the board back, let the club set, made a smooth change of direction at the top and hit my first straight shot of the day. Then I hit another, and another. And just like that, whatever was wrong was right again.

I'd even forgotten the guy was watching me, but after a bit he spoke up.

"Those shots look okay to me," he said. The tone of his voice sounded like, "Geez, I wish I could hit it that good."

As he walked away, I could tell that the minute the range closed for the day, he'd be out there pushing those boards back with his seven-iron.

So I hit balls for another half hour, moving through my bag, a few shots per club. After a while I noticed the clouds had burned off and the sun was shining bright. The cool wind had died, and the temperature was pushing past ninety, but I was no longer sweating. Instead, I felt like I could hit balls all day long.

Then I remembered Sean telling me that when I was hitting it good, I didn't have to do it all day. Quit while I'm ahead. Knock off with good thoughts in my head and go practice some short game.

Almost three months into my year-long golf odyssey, I couldn't help thinking that not once in my father's life had he seen me hit a ball as good as every shot I had hit for the past half hour. He would have liked that, liked it as much as I would have like for him to see it.

On the drive home, I wondered if that was what my quest was all about—still trying to impress my father.

"Look at me, Dad! I'm gonna jump off the high board."

"Look at me, Dad! I'm gonna hit it over the water."

"Look at me, Dad! Look at me."

And then I realized, if that was my reason, it was okay with me.

Fundamentals of Golf

The Studio Club Drill

As taught by Sean Hogan

The short-club drill—or "studio club swings" as Sean describes it—is a simple exercise designed to let you use the butt end of the club as an indicator of your swing plane. Since it doesn't require a ball, it's also a great technique to use at home, indoors or outdoors.

Take your seven-iron and grip down on the club, placing your left hand at the bottom of the grip, and your right hand actually on the shaft. Now move into your address position, but with the clubhead well above the ground. Start the clubhead back in conjunction with the abdominal muscles, allowing the left shoulder to work under your chin.

As the shaft reaches halfway back and the left arm parallel to the ground, your wrists should be fully hinged, with the butt end of the club pointing at an area between the ball and the line of your feet. If the butt end is pointing well outside your target line, you know that your swing plane is too flat.

When you finish your turn and start back toward the ball, the butt end of the club should now be pointing to a spot slightly beyond the ball-target line.

Essentially, this drill works the same way as Leadbetter's laser guide attachment, with its red beam tracing where the club's butt end is pointing. With the club shortened up, though, it's easy to do the drill indoors, and it doesn't require any expensive equipment.

CHAPTER 12

Old School

_____

"You learn to putt and you'll really have something!"
—Lee Trevino

Like most golfers, my interest in the game has ebbed and flowed over the years. A missed putt on the last hole in the qualifier for the high school golf team left me tied for the last spot on the team. Exercising his discretion, the coach chose the other kid, a severe blow that took me quite awhile to overcome. Twenty-five years later, while playing one of our last rounds together, Pip mentioned that he was still mad at that coach for "robbing" me of a chance to play high school golf.

I don't know how successful I've been at it, but I've generally tried to avoid the wasted energy of regret. Even so, I couldn't help but think that, had I made that long ago putt, I could have saved my father a lifetime of misspent anger. Having started elementary school just a couple of months after my fifth birthday, I was a late bloomer at almost all sports and only found my legs for basketball and my nerves for the putter *after* I'd finished high school.

The Old Man and the Tee

I played the best golf of my life at age nineteen and twenty, then—unable to take my clubs as I wandered around the world for the next few years—I gave up the game, which created a further rift between my father and me. After our family lost our most treasured possession—my grandmother's ranch on the headwaters of the South Llano River—and after I left both San Angelo and college far behind, almost all the easy connections between Pip and me were broken. I still came home occasionally, but not for long. When I was there, we neither played nor talked about golf, but in many ways, it was golf that saved us and ultimately put us back together as father and son. Though I had given up the game, my old Wilson X-31's had not given up on me. Every time I looked at them, sitting in the closet, they seemed to be waiting for me to wise up and come to my senses.

Approaching the age of thirty, I was recently single and spending wasted days and wasted nights in Texas honky-tonks that never seemed to close. Late one night, seeing that I hadn't slept in about a week, my friend Steve Fromholz invited me to join his weekly golf game at Willie Nelson's Pedernales Golf Club outside of Austin.

I hadn't played a lick in eight years, but golf with Willie sounded too good to pass up. Digging out my sticks, I found myself on the tee one morning with Fromholz, Bud Shrake, and Willie Nelson hisown-self. Nervous about my extended layoff, I inquired as to the location of the driving range. All three pointed to the first fairway.

With a golf ball–sized lump in my throat, I gripped my old Wilson driver and miraculously whacked one down the middle.

"Eight years, my ass!" said Willie, and we were off on a game that's lasted for decades.

Willie's course is pure Texas—pasture pool at its finest, with hard-pan fairways that climb up and down hills with twenty-mile views. Just a nine-hole track, white and blue tees give a different look to the two halves of your eighteen . . . or your thirty-six as Willie has generally played it over the years. On my thirtieth birthday we played either forty-five or fifty-four holes—by the end of the day, none of us could remember exactly how many we'd played, and I was the only one who seemed to think it was worth mentioning.

A day of golf at Willie's in the old days generally meant drive fast, swing hard, move it off the rocks, and don't try to tell a joke if you have to think to remember the punch line. In other words, golf the Willie way.

The rules on the card include such ditties as "No skimpy attire, except on women," "Please leave the course in the condition you'd like to be found," and the one most frequently flouted, "No more than fourteen in your foursome."

If there was such a thing as an average day with Willie at Pedernales in those early years, it involved a constantly rotating group of between five and fifteen golfers scattering shots in all directions, making outrageous bets that would never be paid, and claiming any ball you found as your own.

"I've noticed," Willie once told me, "that the man with the fastest cart usually wins." His cart, by the way, could have won a drag race.

Willie first became known as a golfer when he was quoted as saying, "Par at my course is whatever I say it is. Today I made a fourteen on the first hole and it turned out to be a birdie." Despite the snappy ring, he doesn't remember saying it, and anyone who's played with him knows he'd pick up his ball long before making a 14.

Despite a swing that sometimes looks like he's fly-casting a frozen turkey, Willie really can play. Known among our group as the One-Armed Bandit, he putts one-handed, often holding the pin in his left hand as he knocks in a long putt and says, "You can't lose 'em all!"

Arising from what most golfers would consider unfavorable course conditions—rocks, roots, snakes, or severe hangovers—a local rule known as the Pedernales Stroll states that a golfer in trouble is entitled to "stroll the ball" to a more amenable spot.

"If you play from a bad lie," Willie once counseled as I considered the distance from my ball to the nearest grass, "it's nobody's fault but your own."

The Old Man and the Tee

When I took a stab at a career in Los Angeles, the game at Pedernales was perhaps the thing I most missed about beautiful Austin. The longer I was away from Texas, the more I realized how lucky I'd been to have played with all these sandbagging sharpies, flat-bellied hustlers, and cow-pony golfers.

Once upon a time in West Texas, after an introduction by Pip, I caddied for a cowboy-booted rancher who, on the thirteenth tee at the San Angelo Country Club, pulled a double-barreled shotgun from his bag and blasted a pair of passing doves.

"Hop the fence and go get 'em," he told me as he reloaded. I was back with the birds before he'd even closed the breech, happy just to have kept my pants unsoiled.

Always stand behind your golfer, I learned, especially when he has a gun.

One of the best things about my return to golf was that I also started to play again with Pip, and I think we both had an increased appreciation for our time together on the course. I had left the fold, left San Angelo, left golf, left Texas, and even the States for a year *"at Europe"* as they say in West Texas. I'm not sure my return made me the prodigal son, but it did earn me a much coveted invitation to play with Pip in the San Angelo Country Club partnership, a five-day tourney in which I'd caddied dozens of rounds, but never once played.

My brother John, starting when he was in high school, had played a number of times as Pip's partner, which made sense, for John was the eldest and the best golfer. I've been teeing it up with John off and on for forty years, and I've never beaten him (and you *know* that's a thorn in my side).

When I was in high school, I didn't understand why Pip never invited me to play in the tournament with him. Having won his flight one time with John, he was determined to do it again and perhaps thought his chances better with his pal Marshall Jones as his partner. All I got to do was caddie for Marshall and read putts that I was sure I could make.

But finally, at age thirty, I got the invite. Hitting a lot of balls to prepare myself, I had my game in shape, and we won every match (in the fifth flight) leading up to the final round on Sunday. Only one thing stood between us and victory, that being that I was too much Pip's son. I hadn't been in San Angelo this long since high school, and every day and evening I ran into more and more old friends with whom I stayed out later and later until the last night, when I simply stayed up all night and reported directly to the first tee a little drunk and a little hungover.

Pip was furious with me, despite the fact that I played good enough to keep the match even through fifteen holes without any help on the card from Pip. But on our sixteenth hole—the par-four seventh at the country club—I sliced my tee shot into the woods and made a seven to lose the hole and ultimately the match. Not having bettered my score on even one hole, I didn't see how Pip could put all the blame on me, but no matter, for he never invited me to play in the tournament again.

Partially to make amends—and partially because playing in the tournament reminded me of so many interesting golf episodes from my childhood, I wrote a magazine story for *Texas Monthly* about caddying in my youth. The following year, my story was awarded a golf writer's award in the form of a pair of etched crystal beer mugs, one of which I presented to Pip, for it was as much his as mine.

He was so proud of that mug that I don't think an Oscar would have made him happier. And just like that, we were one again.

The memories of those West Texas characters also launched me into a novel called *Fast Greens*. Searching for the heart of the game at the heart of my book, I used just about everything interesting I'd ever heard or seen about the game, pearls of golf wisdom, backhanded compliments like "good shot for *yew*," and just plain cussedness, which often involved the mention of places where the sun don't shine. I stole lines from golf partners like Willie and Lee Trevino, and even stole names from Fromholz and a hustler named Sandy, who was reincarnated as the eternal blond golfing hero, the kind of player all of us wanted to be when we were young and hitting well-worn balls into the constant winds of West Texas.

My reward for paying some proper attention to the game was the sale of a lot more copies of *Fast Greens* than I'd ever imagined possible (and enough whacky fans of the book that I began to receive nude photos of their girlfriends with quotations from my book scribbled on the back). Inspired either by my success or the photos, I took to golf writing with a vengeance, which provided me some unique opportunities to thank my father for taking me out to the course and handing me that cut-down five-iron.

My game also rebounded, and I shot the lowest round of my life, thinking after, of course, that I'd finally figured out how to master the game. The next day, I returned to the same course and fired a round fifteen strokes higher than the day before. The secret to a low score, I decided, is to get all your lucky breaks on the same day.

As I started receiving invitations to play golf all over the world, I also started to get burned out. Given the choice of running like the wind or writing like the wind, even in grade school I would have chosen the latter. I'd become a writer because I was better at writing than I was at golf.

But as my lessons at the Leadbetter school progressed, I began to realize that for the first time since my childhood, I was trying to be a golfer first and a writer second. I don't care how many lessons you take, writing about them doesn't make you a better golfer. If anything, writing about them gets you even more confused. If feel isn't real, then you can imagine how unreal it is to describe what you can't feel.

I didn't *want* to write about golf while I was on my year-long quest; I just wanted to hit balls, all day, every day. The only problem was that my children suspected I was insane, while my wife seemed sure of it.

The first week of September, I woke up at seven A.M. for a lesson with Sean and saw that rain was pouring down outside. I was about to get dressed and drive over anyway, but then I remembered an old joke.

Rain or shine, every Saturday morning for years and years, a guy gets up at the crack of dawn and heads to the course to play. One morning he's driving to the course, barely awake, when he realizes that it's cold and pouring down rain.

Doing a U-turn, he goes back home where he takes off all his clothes, slips back into bed, and snuggles up next to his sleepy wife.

"It's freezing out there," he tells her.

And she says, "Yeah, can you believe my stupid husband is playing golf?"

Hoping to preserve my spot in the bed a little longer, I rolled over and went back to sleep, dreaming I was playing in the British Open in a driving rain.

When Sean called a little after lunch, I had not won the Open Championship, but it was still raining at my house. Nevertheless, he said it was clearing at the course if I wanted to come over.

Since the progress of lessons is incremental and difficult to isolate, when something big happens, it is definitely memorable. That afternoon, when Sean and I looked at new video of my swing, I was horrified to discover that I was just as laid-off at the top as ever. All the progress I'd been feeling had hardly changed my most basic faults. The clubhead and shaft were still swinging back way inside my target line, and I was still setting the club way too late.

"Your posture and setup look great," Sean told me in his lilting Irish accent, "but your shoulder turn is too flat—you've got to get that left shoulder working down and during the backswing.

"And you still need to get the clubhead set earlier," he told me for the millionth time.

Well, maybe it wasn't quite a million times, but it's like my mother used to say, "If I've told you once, I've told you a million times—don't exaggerate!"

"Try this," Sean told me. "As you start your backswing, let your left hand push the butt end of the club downward. That'll send the clubhead up and help complete your wrist hinge."

I wasn't exactly sure what he meant, so I tried it a couple of times, setting up to the ball and pushing the butt end of the club downward as I swung the club away from the ball. Pushing down with my left hand made my right hand a pivot point and had the clubhead quickly levering upward as I swung back.

"Push the butt end down?" I said. "I've never heard anybody say that."

What I meant was "Why *haven't* I heard that?" Because I knew immediately that it was going to work.

And did it ever.

After hitting just a few shots where I was pushing the butt end down with my left hand during the first part of the backswing, I realized that I could actually *see* and *feel* the clubhead rising up toward the sky. For the first time in my life, I knew what people meant when they talked about "setting the club."

Once again Sean videotaped me, and we headed inside to the computer and screens. Freezing my image at address, Sean extended the line of my shaft with his magic mouse, then stepped through my swing. Lo and behold, hallelujah, for the first time in my life, my downswing was parallel with my backswing. No over the top. No laid-off clubhead. No lower body sway. I looked, and I felt . . . like a golfer.

"Push the butt end down," I repeated. "I should probably try to remember that."

CHAPTER 13

Bogey

"If you want to learn to play better, go back and start at a younger age."
—Anonymous

When everything's going good, that's when you have to watch out."

That's what Bill March Sr. told me once when I was caddying for him in San Angelo. Mr. March was on a long string of pars and, at age thirteen I assumed he was talking about golf. Years later, I began to suspect he might have been referring to life in general.

Maybe it was just too good to be true. Perhaps I should have simply taken Bill March's advice and kept an eye out for trouble just around the corner. Everything was going so well; almost four months into my quest, I could feel my confidence growing every day. And not just on the range.

One afternoon, Sean videotaped a few of my swings to e-mail to Champions Gate so Leadbetter could make comments on my progress. Pushing Send, Sean turned to me and said, "Let's go play."

Despite the ominous clouds building in the south, this was a big moment for me. We were finally taking it to the course.

I've rarely played a Tom Fazio course I didn't like. He's a fine designer with lots of opportunities to work with great sites and big budgets. The result is often a great course like Barton Creek Canyons. Winding its way through a remote Hill Country site, one memorable hole leads to another, with wide fairways compensated for by thick woods, deep canyons, and lots of water.

With no one making the turn, Sean and I stepped up to the 433-yard par-four tenth. If you can hit a straight drive here, avoiding a deep creek on the right, the long, downhill second shot has that same creek in front of and behind the green. With the wind in our face, I played it like a par five and took satisfaction in my bogey. Had I gone for the green in two, I could have made a big number fast.

Not only was I happy to have played smart, but with Sean watching me, I'd found it easy to use the swing keys he'd been giving me. In other words, I was confident.

The clouds were darker and the wind really whipping as we came to the long par-three eleventh. Sensing my discomfort with the shot, Sean gave me a little reminder of what we'd been working on.

"Turn your left shoulder under; push the butt end down with your left hand; slow transition, then swing to right field."

Pulling my five-wood, I smoothed the ball to eight feet from the cup. With Sean around, I felt I could do no wrong.

We played a couple more holes and could have played till dark, but with the storm almost on us, we barely made it back to the parking lot before the skies opened up. We were laughing as we loaded our sticks, and soaked by the time we got in our cars. Since it was raining too hard to see the road, I sat in my truck listening to the thunder booming all around and thought about my progress in the months since my bad round at Pebble.

For the first time in my life, I had a solid visual picture of an effective and repeatable golf swing. I was far from mastering that swing, but I did have a sequence of drills to help me move in that direction. I was hitting the ball farther and straighter than ever before, and my scores were dropping.

In the months before playing Pebble, I'd posted rounds mostly in the upper eighties and low nineties. A couple of times, I'd been up around the century mark, my worst rounds since I was thirteen. Now I was scoring in the low to mideighties and my handicap at Barton Creek had dropped from 16 to 12. Best of all, my confidence was high.

If I'd already made this much progress, eight more months of periodic lessons with Sean—plus a few days with Leadbetter himself—seemed likely to hone me into a golfer of considerable skill. With their help, I was going to keep my handicap coming down and my confidence going up until that final round at Pebble would only be a formality. I was sitting on top of the world.

As I sat there pondering my game and marveling at the power of nature and its thundering roar, a bolt of lightening ripped across the sky just in front of me, a long, jagged streak that seemed to rip the evening sky into two pieces as it raised the hair on my arms and legs with electrical charge.

Catching my breath, I felt the adrenaline surging in me and thought, that's how it feels when you hit it pure, when that ball is sailing up against the sky and drawing in on the flag. That's the part of golf that my father loved; that's what I was striving for.

Unfortunately, I'd forgotten about Bill March's warning.

Two days later, Sean Hogan called, and I knew by the tone of his voice that something was wrong.

"I'm sorry to have to tell you this, Turk," he said, sounding apologetic indeed, "but I have to go back to Florida."

I knew right away that he wasn't talking about returning to Leadbetter's headquarters just for a visit. My teacher was leaving, and he wouldn't be coming back.

"It's a business thing," Sean explained. "David and Club Corp have parted ways amicably and the result is that David will no longer have a school at Barton Creek. We're all pretty sad about it."

It took awhile for the effects of this to sink in. I'd found a great teacher who was a good match for me, and now I was losing him. Sure, I could go down to Florida to see Sean—or David, too, for that matter—but how often could I afford to do that? This whole golf quest thing had already put a serious dent in my family's financial situation. When my credit card bills arrived, I'd taken to snagging them from the mailbox and hiding them in my desk drawer so Christy wouldn't see them. I didn't have a clue how I was going to pay them off, but I did know I wouldn't be flying to Florida every couple of weeks.

As I tried to sort through the situation in search of a good plan, I had the same sick feeling in my stomach I'd gotten when my parents told me that the River Ranch was gone, and again when they said there was no more money for college. The same feeling I had when I learned that Pip had suffered a stroke during his knee surgery. Suddenly, everything had changed.

Fundamentals of Golf

Turk Pipkin-Full Swing Keys
By Sean Hogan

Before leaving Austin, Sean handed me a set of typed notes to help keep me on track.

SETUP

Maintain dish angle in wrists at address.

Stay athletically balanced on the balls of your feet.

BACKSWING

Sense your abs and the butt end of the club starting away first.

Shortly after "takeaway" the left hand pushes the butt end of the club down, thus sending the clubhead up.

Simply follow your thumbs from here to complete your backswing track, i.e., wrists fully loaded with club looking down the target line.

TRANSITION AND DOWNSWING

As your left side starts to work toward the target, you need to feel the butt end of the club working more toward right field!

DRILLS

Left-arm-only swings for a better hand and arm track halfway back. This drill also helps you feel a complete wrist set. Practice your backswing with your back to the wall. Sense the club swinging up the wall to a fully loaded position.

Closed-stance drill: Set up square; draw back your right foot, then swing the club down your foot line for a better in-to-out swing path.

Half-to-half swings with a pitching wedge to encourage a better wrist set and swing plane.

CHAPTER 14

Double Bogey

————

"Things get worse before they get better."

—George H. W. Bush

Have you ever noticed that the first bug that hits your clean windshield always lands directly in front of your face? That coming to a double door, you always push the one that's locked, then pull the one you should have pushed the first time? That the other line moves faster, that children never throw up in the bathroom, that the grocery bag you drop is always the one with the eggs?

I have.

Have you ever noticed that most golf holes play uphill, into the wind, or both? That there's often a raised area just around the cup, but never a lowered one? That 90 percent of your shots headed toward a tree hit something that's supposed to be 90 percent air, that the only shot you hit fat all day is the one over water, that your putt is never a gimme if you're still away, or that, no matter how badly you're hitting it, you can always play worse?

If you haven't, you're not paying attention.

The Old Man and the Tee

Have you noticed that everything tends to go wrong at once, that life finds it easier to kick you when you're down, that you usually forget to take special notice of the good days but take double notice of the bad ones, or that things really do tend to get worse before they get better?

If you haven't, you will.

The day after my one and only golf instructor left Austin, things definitely got worse.

All summer, I'd been having an adverse reaction to the time I was spending in the sun. Summer in Texas is just about what you'd expect—hot—and I'd spent a lot of summers in Texas without any problems.

This year was something different. With or without sunscreen, I was burning up. I started the summer with SPF 15 and had gradually progressed to SPF infinity, which I believe is recycled mayonnaise. With that stuff on, I was just two slices short of a toasted club sandwich because, let me tell you, my skin was on fire.

Within half an hour of arrival at the golf course, whatever skin I left exposed to the sun felt as if it had been subjected to some kind of evil radiation experiments. If I wore pants instead of shorts, and a glove on my left hand, I could reduce the areas in distress to my right hand, both forearms, my neck, and my face. That wasn't much comfort, though, as the skin on my right hand was in danger of peeling down to the bone, and across my nose and cheeks, I'd developed a red butterfly-shaped rash.

To combat this problem, I started going to the range earlier and earlier in the day, but even then, to put in the practice time I'd committed to, the sun still got to me before I left the course. Finally I had to admit that I was worried about my health.

Odysseus nearly failed in his quest because Achilles' mom had failed to submerge his heel when she dipped him in the River Styx. Apparently I missed that whole invincible dip-in-the-river thing, because I didn't have an Achilles' heel; I had an Achilles' body. Or had I become Icarus, daring the golf gods by flying too close to the sun?

With all the time we'd spent playing golf and fishing as kids, my

Double Bogey

brothers and I had already had a lifetime's dose of sun. And we hadn't worn hats when we were kids—we hadn't even *owned* hats. I remember one day when my brother Marvin and I spent about ten hours in the hot sun fishing with minnows. Marvin later told me he'd stared so intently at his red-and-white bobber that the image of that bobber had burned into his retina. Even when he closed his eyes to sleep that night, the bobber was still there. Even in his dreams, he saw it. (And I'm pretty sure it's still there now, because he's as crazy for fishing as I am for golf).

What's also there from all that sun is an accumulation of UVA damage that can never be reversed. Two or three times a year, Marvin goes to his dermatologist to have a few chunks of his skin burned or frozen off. And every time you go in for a procedure like that, you've got to worry that maybe this time it's turned into something that can't be snipped away.

Me, I didn't have bad spots, I was just burning like an old chunk of coal. Skin cancer is such big business in Texas that it took a month for me to get an appointment with a dermatologist. When I did get in to see the doctor, I described my symptoms, and he seemed particularly interested in the butterfly-shaped rash on my face.

"Probably nothing serious," he told me. "Could just be rosacea, but we're going to need some blood work to check out the possibility of lupus."

It was nearly a minute before I remembered to breathe.

Taking home a pamphlet, I began to read, though I already knew more than I wanted to know. Systemic lupus erythematosis, or SLE, is a chronic autoimmune disease in which the body attacks its own cells and tissues, causing inflammation and skin and organ damage. Signs of lupus include swelling, redness, warmth, and pain, all of which sounded a little too familiar. The symptoms of discoid lupus—a variation affecting the skin only that can progress into systemic lupus—include a variety of skin rashes and photosensitivity. Factors contributing to developing the disease are a combination of genetics and exposure to certain triggers, especially the sun.

Twenty years ago, large numbers of people with lupus eventually died from overwhelming infections or kidney failure. Survival rates today are 90 per cent or better, but only with treatment and by minimizing exposure to lupus triggers, especially the sun.

In other words, I translated for my panicked brain, I wouldn't be spending my days at the tanning salon we all call a golf course. To give up golf and all the countless other things I loved about life in the great outdoors was simply unthinkable. I know it sounds trite, but even the possibility of dying didn't seem worse than my love of life beneath the beautiful Texas sun.

On the other hand, until we knew something definite, my worries were all premature. Maybe I was just having a Woody Allen panic attack. "Sleep with the nanny," I hoped the doctor would say, "and call me in the morning."

All I really knew was that the sun was bothering me, so for the first time since I'd started to rebuild my game, I quit going to the range and started doing my drills inside our house. That's probably not the best place to swing a club if you're six-foot seven-inches tall and have a swing arc the size of Cleveland.

Over the years, a number of my golf buddies have had disastrous results from practicing golf indoors. My pal David Wood, with whom I made my first golf pilgrimage to Scotland, became so obsessed with the game that he'd often practice for hours in the bedroom of his apartment in L.A. The resulting holes in his ceiling were just a minor complication compared to the realization years later that most of his golf problems were related to the bunched-up, compact swing he'd created by trying not to do a demolition job on his rental unit.

The crown jewel for indoor golf faux pas goes to my pal Ray Benson—the lead singer of the band Asleep at the Wheel and another tall, ponytailed golf nut like myownself. Ray was at Bud Shrake's house one evening demonstrating some new secret move in the downswing when he took a deep gouge out of Shrake's wall-to-wall carpet. Picking up the dollar-bill-shaped piece of shag, all Shrake could say was "Nice divot." The divot was replaced, though it has yet to grow back in around the edges.

To help with my laying the club off so far behind my body, Sean had recommended that I practice my drills and my swing with my butt against a wall at home, something I'd been unable to do simply because my walls aren't tall enough to accommodate my gangly frame. While I waited for the blood tests to come back, I considered the possibility of remodeling so I could swing inside the house. Perhaps I could leave the front door open and hit seven-irons out into the yard where my golden retriever would locate them and bring them back. I really didn't care how; I just wanted to play golf. Shoot, I'd play at night if I had to.

That's when famed hustler Titanic Thompson practiced and learned the game, both to avoid being seen and to avoid a telltale suntan that would be a clue that he'd been learning golf. Having won bets that he could throw a walnut over a five-story building (secretly switching the chosen nut for one filled with lead) and beaten the best horseshoe players in America (by secretly moving the posts from forty to forty-one feet, the distance at which he practiced), Ti conquered the game of golf alone and at night and won $18,000 dollars in cash off a San Francisco golf pro who apparently couldn't believe such a pale-skinned guy could play the game.

Night golf would have been a good match for me, because I sure wasn't getting any sleep. Going in for the blood test wasn't much comfort, either. Because of the large number of tests they had to run, the lab technician had to take tube after tube of blood. A difficult disease to diagnose, there is no single test or indicator for lupus. Because it develops slowly over time, tests for certain indicators may be negative one time and positive the next. There are eleven criteria for determining whether you have it; positive on four and you've lost the lupus lottery, so to speak.

The best thing I had going for me was the simple fact that rosacea—a common and treatable skin malady—shares one major trait with lupus: the distinct redness around the cheeks and nose. I couldn't find any mention of rosacea and skin sensitivity of the arms and hands and didn't really care. All I knew is I wanted the easy disease, not the fatal one.

A few days later I was sitting back at the doctor's office for the test results, muttering to myself as if I were waiting for a little white ball to fall into a spinning roulette wheel and land in a slot labeled Golf or Life instead of a black ball flying off the wheel and settling into some dark crevice where the sun never shone.

"Give me rosacea," I muttered. "Come on, rosacea!"

The doctor came in studying my lab results.

"What's the word?" I asked after what seemed like an eternity.

He looked up at me with a smile and said, "Rosacea. We'll try a couple of different medicines, and I think one of them will work fine."

I don't much remember what he said after that. I was already looking out the window, checking the clouds and the wind, wondering how long it would take me to get to the course. Sean was gone, but the game was still on.

CHAPTER 15

Mr. Sand Man

"The keenness of golfers varies in direct ratio with the quality of the course they play on. The worse the course, the keener they become, and the more seriously they take their game."

—Henry Longhurst

Unsure what to do about the loss of my teacher, I decided to go in search of the essence of the game I'd known as a boy in West Texas, when the fairways were often brown and the greens were sometimes made of sand.

In the first decades of the twentieth century, as golf swept its way across America, limitations in money, water, and hardy grass varieties often made traditional grass greens an impossibility. The only practical response was to build greens of hard-packed sand that were rolled, dragged, or swept smooth for every putt. Sure, many of these early courses were little more than holes in a hardscrabble field—hence the name pasture pool—but many others were championship designs that we still consider among our finest.

Even Donald Ross's famed Pinehurst No. 2 had sand greens from its turn-of-the-century founding until 1935. And that means that every putt on the course during the 1931 Ryder Cup matches rolled not on grass, but on sand. Pinehurst No. 2 finally got its famous grass greens in 1936, and in the ensuing decades, hundreds of American courses followed suit.

By the early sixties, you only found sand greens in small-town, nine-hole courses. But even at San Angelo Country Club, I sometimes caddied for visiting ranchers who wore cowboy boots with spikes, and who disliked having to walk to the edge of the fine bent grass greens to spit their tobacco juice.

"All this grass," one golfer with a big chew declared, "is a gol-danged nuisance!"

By 1990, the last sand greens in my home state were at the remote Rocksprings Country Club in the Hill Country and at the windswept McClean Country Club in the remote Texas Panhandle. Maintained by the local Lions Club, McClean's fairways were mowed right through the middle of the surrounding wheat fields. As for the greens, they weren't green at all, because they were made of sand.

To avoid having to rake and drag the sand for every putt, Mc-Clean's sand greens featured a long rope attached to the bottom of the pin. Stretch the rope and measure the distance to your ball, then use that same length of rope to move your ball to a single smooth-rolled strip that traversed the green. Raking and rolling one strip of sand instead of the whole putting surface made for a faster round, plus you could read the break by the visible tracks of previous putts.

I'd always found a certain primal satisfaction to putting on sand, so I was dismayed to learn that the sand greens at McClean Lions now have long strips of artificial turf. Use the rope as before to relocate your ball, then putt on Astroturf—an ingenious idea *if* you're not a fan of fading golf traditions.

With pure sand greens in Texas only a memory, I set off on a trip into America's heartland, where I hoped to putt on sand one more time before it was too late. Beneath buttermilk skies—as Willie describes them—I drove hundreds of miles across vast grasslands and eventually came to the town of Big Springs, Nebraska. There, by a dirt road on the edge of town, I found a small, neatly lettered sign that read Cactus Heights Golf Course.

Driving to the top of a hill overlooking a hamlet that seemed to define the image of small-town America, I found a deserted starter's shack and a sloping expanse of grass dotted by occasional patches of brown. I had struck gold . . . or sand, to be more precise. Selecting five clubs that I thought would get me around the track, I stepped to the first tee, which consisted of a wooden frame packed with a mixture of gravel and sand. Sand greens—sand tees: somehow it made sense.

At the green—or "brown," as it should be called—a metal pole was planted in the ground behind the putting surface. Leaning on the pole were two large rakes. The first, a heavy round pipe welded to a long metal handle, was designed for smoothing the sand between the ball and the hole. Having seen a sign on the starter's shack saying "Make all drags toward the cup," I smoothed a ten-foot path from my ball to the hole, then banged my putt twice as hard as I would have on grass. The ball went about three feet, then ground to a halt. I looked at my putter like it was broken.

Three putts later, having finally hit the ball hard enough to hole out, I picked up the second rake, this one with a row of short iron teeth. When I'd arrived, the grooves in the putting surface created by these serrations surrounded the hole in concentric circles. Perfectly raked, the sand looked like a Zen meditation garden. But raking perfectly, I found, was neither easy nor fast. After one hole, a strip of Astroturf was beginning to seem like a pretty good idea.

With all nine holes either up-, down-, or side-hill, Cactus Heights turned out to be a shot-making test. After discovering that the best way to get your approach shots close to the hole was to bomb them in there like lawn darts, I suddenly hit three straight greens in regulation, then hit my putts hard enough to skid over the sand and into the cup. For the first time in my life, I'd made three birdies in a row—a golfer's hat trick—and just like that, I was once again hooked on sand greens.

The Old Man and the Tee

Legendary golf writer Henry Longhurst believed that playing desert layouts and sand greens requires you to "manufacture" shots as you do on the Old Course at St. Andrews.

"To cause a ball to carry an expanse of loose sand," wrote Longhurst, "and pitch on a firm patch with just the right trajectory to run up through the gully and come to rest on a small circle of fast-running asphalt is true golf. Harry Vardon would have done it supremely well; Jack Nicklaus, I think, would not."

The asphalt Longhurst referred to was a coating of oil traditionally sprayed on sand greens to prevent erosion and choke out grass and weeds. With the EPA having banned the use of petroleum products in open applications, many believe that sand greens are no longer viable. Recognizing this, the USGA has granted thousands of dollars to help small-town courses build grass greens and irrigation systems. But a windfall to those communities is another hard blow to an old American tradition. At this point, it seems unlikely that we'll see any more golfers like Steve Jones, who—before winning the 1996 U.S. Open—was a two-time winner of the Colorado Sand Greens Championship. Or like Vijay Singh, who, between his stint teaching golf to lumberjacks in the Borneo rain forest and winning the PGA and the Masters, won the Nigerian Open twice while putting on sand greens.

Moving on to Hemingford, Nebraska, I found more or less the remnants of a sand greens course, still played occasionally, but with both fairways and sand greens dotted with tall weeds. As I gazed out at the course, the first snow of the year began to blow in on a cold north wind. Having driven a thousand miles to putt on sand, not playing this little course because of snow flurries would have been like traveling to St. Andrews and not playing because of rain.

As kids, my pals and I played in weather ranging from 32 degrees in a cold blue norther to 115 in the shade (if there'd been any) with the heat of the land generating giant whirling dustdevils that sometimes grabbed the wedge shots we hit into them and carried our balls away. Perhaps I dreamed that I, too, would be carried away by the towering vortex, to Mexico or British Honduras perhaps, someplace far away, where everything was green and life easy.

Making it all the way to Hemingford, Nebraska, wasn't exactly what I'd had in mind, but in deference to the twenty-degree windchill, I put on an extra layer of clothes and headed out. If you're curious how the course was, I'll tell you: it was cold! My clubs were cold, the flagsticks were cold, and the iron-pipe rake handles were really cold! To comfort myself, I tried to think of a golf joke about playing in the cold, but all that came to mind was an image of blue, dimpled balls.

Taking my search farther west through a land of mile-long trains, I traversed blue highways that are driven seven days a week by Sunday drivers. After hours on the road, I stopped to try the "World's Largest Hamburger" —two fourteen-ounce patties on a six-inch bun with cheese. I ate half, then drove the next hundred miles with all the windows rolled down. (Oddly enough, I also didn't know any golf jokes that involved farting, though I suspect my readers will send me several.)

Finally I arrived at Midwest, Wyoming, where a resident herd of pronghorn antelope looked as if they'd been posed for me behind the sign for the Salt Creek Golf Course. Built as an oil company course in 1922, Salt Creek is the second oldest track in Wyoming, and is considered by many to be the "holey" grail of sand greens golf.

Even on a busy day at Salt Creek, antelope and deer are likely to outnumber golfers. The green fees are two dollars—on the honor system, of course—and the entire track is dotted with large red, white, and blue oil well pump jacks, sucking out the dinosaur wine as they pivot up and down.

My problems on the course were not with the sand or my swing, but with prairie dog holes that swallowed not one, but two of my new Callaway balls. This is a job for Carl Spackler, I thought, *Caddyshack*'s assistant greenskeeper with an obsession for blowing up gophers.

As I walked off the ninth green, strolling down the dirt road toward me was a skinny kid with a beat-up canvas golf bag slung over his shoulder, an almost spitting image of myself as a kid in San Angelo, or of the caddy Billy, whose story is the heart of *Fast Greens*.

"How you like those sand greens?" I asked the kid.

"They're great!" he said without a bit of sarcasm.

I was putting my sticks in the trunk when the kid took a beautiful Tiger-sized cut at the ball, which jumped off his clubface like a rocket and mortared in near the cup on the opening par three.

"Future U.S. Open winner," I thought as I drove off past the antelope posing again at the entrance to the course.

Not forgetting my goal of testing my new swing on a few championship challenges, while I was searching for sand greens, I stopped at Ben Crenshaw's links masterpiece, Sand Hills Golf Club. Built in the vast Sand Hills region of southwestern Nebraska, the course follows an all-natural routing through the seemingly endless grass-covered dunes. And since the sand that comprises the area's soil has the same round shape and noncompacting drain characteristics of the sand required for all USGA greens, the entire course is essentially one gigantic natural putting green in need of mowing.

During construction, both fairways and greens required only shallow tilling, minimal shaping, then an application of seed. As in the original links courses of Scotland, many of the bunkers were already there, natural hollows created by the wind or by sheep burrowing to get out of the elements.

None of this description does justice to Crenshaw's masterful layout or to the simple pleasures of walking this stunning golf course, stopping at Ben's Porch for a fine hamburger lunch, then heading out for another eighteen.

Late one afternoon on the par-four eighth, my drive drifted right and ended up atop a thick yucca plant. Forgoing a drop, I choked down and knocked the ball toward the green, where it nestled into a little shrub under an overhanging bunker lip that formed a small cave *beneath* the green. With my ball just twelve feet from the hole (as the gopher burrows), I was forced to choke down a wedge, play it left-handed and aim *away* from the pin just to get the ball back into sunshine. I almost pulled off a miracle. This time my ball hung off the ground in a clump of weeds on the edge of the bunker. With my ball having perched on a tee, a cactus, a shrub, and a wildflower—but never on the ground—I then chipped it in the hole for the weirdest par of my life.

Even more memorable was the previous hole, where my drive ended up behind what may be the world's biggest bunker. I don't have any stats to back up that claim, but let me say that it looks as wide and deep as the Missouri River. The front lip of the bunker was so high that I couldn't see any part of the green from my angle, much less the hole.

"Good luck," said my playing partner, Clint Svoboda, who, with his wife Barb, manages Sand Hills' excellent clubhouse restaurant and lodgings. "The pin's just over the bunker, and the green slopes away from you."

Sure enough, if I came up even one foot short, my ball would drop fifty feet below the lip of the bunker. Land on the green and I'd probably bounce fifty feet over. There didn't seem to be any alternatives, though, so I pulled my sand wedge and tried to think back to a lesson that Sean Hogan had given me a few weeks before.

"Can you teach me how to make it dance?" I'd asked.

Sean seemed amused by my question. I missed as many greens as I hit, so what good to make it dance? Like most of your run-of-the-mill golfers, every time I see one of the pros put that second-hop *suck* on a low-driving pitch shot, or fly in a high shot that backs up about eight feet to the cup, I am seized with jealousy. Never mind that 90 percent of my iron shots end up short of the pin, I'd still like to be able to back the ball up at will. Why? Because it's fun.

Covering the 1997 PGA Grand Slam on the Hawaiian island of Kauai, I was standing just a few feet from Tiger Woods, whose ball was sitting next to the hundred-yard marker. Checking the wind with the smoke from his cigarette, Fluff Cowan pulled Tiger's sand wedge and handed it to the Man. Gripping down slightly on the club, Tiger lined up the clubhead, moved into his stance, and made just about the most fluid swing I've ever seen. Sailing up smartly, the ball landed twelve feet behind the pin, then zipped back toward the cup with authority. Too much authority, it turned out, for after burning the lip, the ball continued all the way back off the front of the green and trickled into the water.

With a disgusted look on his face, Tiger looked to Fluff, who handed him a second ball.

"Same shot; less spin," Fluff said.

Dropping the ball behind the previous divot, Tiger made what looked to be the exact same swing. The ball flew to almost the same divot on the green as the first ball, then zipped back with a little less force until it fell into the cup for par.

The grins that Fluff and Tiger exchanged were truly something.

Standing behind the bunker from hell on the seventh at Sand Hills, I needed to pull a Tiger shot out of my hat (or from some other spot where the sun don't shine).

So what was it that Sean had told me? A narrowed, open stance, a quiet body as I turn the shoulders back, a smooth change of direction, and accelerate through the ball.

Unable to remember all that, I simply went for smooth.

Flying off my clubface, the ball soared up, headed straight for the pin, then disappeared from my view. A heartbeat later, Clint began to holler from his vantage point at the front of the green.

"Am I close?" I asked in disbelief.

"Close?" he answered. "You landed four feet past and backed it into the cup. I mean it was dancing!"

As I walked to the hole to pull out my ball, through my excitement I was thinking how much easier the game is when you've got Sean, Tiger, Fluff, and Ben helping you out.

CHAPTER 16

Semi-Drunk

"I see myself as a monstrous, manned colossus poised high over the golf ball, a spheroid barely discernible fourteen stories down on its tee.

—George Plimpton,
The Bogey Man

Despite a couple of remarkable holes, the main thing I learned at Sand Hills was that I didn't have the shot-making ability needed for a true links course. The obvious solution was for me to play courses that require the widest variety of shots. That meant I absolutely *had* to go to Scotland—at least that's what I told Christy, who'd begun responding to my ever-increasing travel plans with a rueful shrug.

On the way to Scotland, I stopped in New York to see some pals from my acting stint as Janice's narcoleptic boyfriend on *The Sopranos*. ("Have you heard the good news?") Despite the fact that Tony Soprano tees it up occasionally on screen, James Gandolfini has never played the game. The show's number-one linkster is Steven Van Zandt, who plays club owner Silvio Dante and is also, of course, the lead guitar player in Springsteen's E Street Band. Over dinner at the set one evening, Steven told me about taking up the game a few years

earlier in order to spend more time with his father. With his dad having since passed away from Alzheimer's, the father-and-son rounds
they shared are no doubt more special to Steven than ever.

Yet another great thing about the game of golf is that, even though
Steven and I hardly know each other, we share an important bond,
and it has nothing to do with *The Sopranos.* What we share is the good
fortune to love the same game our fathers loved. Whether it be golf,
baseball, or ice fishing, everyone should be so lucky.

Wishing more than ever that I could tell Pip about my lessons and
travels, I began at this point to write in earnest about my golf
odyssey, and had the opportunity in New York to seek advice from a
master of the game—the writing game, that is.

In a small bar on the Upper East Side, I joined my onetime tournament partner, author and actor George Plimpton, who had turned
much of his life into art in his books about playing quarterback for the
Detroit Lions, flying on a trapeze for the Clyde Beatty Circus, and
playing percussion with the New York Philharmonic, where he inad-
vertently banged the bells so loudly that Leonard Bernstein stopped
the concert to applaud him. Another of Plimpton's books, *The Bogey
Man,* chronicled his woeful attempt to compete in the PGA.

Trying to find some method in the madness of my ten-stroke
quest, and hoping to write a book that might cover some of my mount-
ing debts, I asked Plimpton if he had any advice for me on the subject
of participatory journalism.

"Don't be afraid to come across like a dumb ass," he told me in his
genteel Harvard accent. "I lost thirty yards in five plays for the Lions
and was certain I'd ruined my book. It wasn't till much later that I discovered my ineptness made the pros seem all that more powerful and
skilled. My failure turned out to be a success."

"But I'm essentially competing against myself," I told him.

"Well," he said thoughtfully, "in that case, you could be in trouble."

I'd met Plimpton a couple of years earlier when Bud Shrake suggested that the two of us play as a team in the Dan Jenkins Goat Hills

Partnership tourney in Fort Worth, a raucous outing affectionately referred to as the Meatloaf Sandwich Open.

At the opening-day practice round, my partner mentioned that it'd been a while since he played a full round.

"How long?" I asked.

"Years."

Seeing the look of panic on my face, George reassured me that he'd recently undergone a custom club-fitting at Callaway Golf where he'd also taken a couple of lessons and even played nine holes.

"Nine holes," I repeated.

"I didn't play very well, though," he added. "I was picturing a midget standing just in front of my tee, then trying to hit the midget in the ass with my driver."

"A midget?" I asked.

"A little guy who's pissed me off."

"So you hit him in the ass with your club?"

"Don't knock it till you try it," George advised. Then he teed up a ball and smacked it down the middle of the first fairway.

"Did you get him?" I asked.

"Right in the ass," George said, flashing me a smile.

We were halfway around the course when Plimpton related what he thought might be more of a problem than an extended absence from the game.

"Am I going to need any money?" he asked. "I've only got fifteen dollars and I didn't bring a credit card."

I looked at him dumbfounded for a few moments and then realized that, hell no, he didn't need any money. He was George Plimpton. As if to prove that point, after a fine Mexican food dinner and many margaritas at Joe T. Garcia's restaurant that evening, George asked me to take him to Billy Bob's, the world's largest honky-tonk.

There was a line at the door and a cover charge, but George just walked by everyone and we sailed inside. After a tour of the indoor bull-riding arena and other outsized oddities, we sat in front of a large bartender who looked at George and said, "Hey! You're that guy from *Good Will Hunting!* Wait! Wait! Don't tell me your name!"

"Buy us each a drink and I'll give you a free guess," George told the bartender without missing a beat.

"Okay," the bartender said. "You're Buck Henry, right?"

George shook his head, we drank our whiskeys, then the bartender poured and guessed wrong again. It was true; George really didn't need any money.

You don't meet many Harvard men who've teed it up on tour with Arnie or lined up in a scrimmage opposite Alex Karras, so for the next hour, I listened to one incredible story after another while the mammoth bartender returned every few minutes for another wrong guess and another round of drinks.

Though Plimpton seemed to think the world of Arnold Palmer, he was most passionate when speaking of Ernest Hemingway, who had slugged George to the ground in an impromptu bare-fisted boxing match in Hemingway's writing room.

"Looking up at Papa," George told me, "I realized we were going to continue to spar and he was going to pound me senseless. So I jumped to my feet, ran behind him, and said, 'That was incredible. Show me how you did it.' So instead of getting killed, I got a boxing lesson."

Still in Cuba, a couple of days later, George arranged a meeting between two of the greatest men of American letters, Ernest Hemingway and Tennessee Williams.

"Papa and I sat at the bar at La Floridita waiting for Tennessee," Plimpton told me as the man-mountain bartender guessed wrong again. "An hour late, Tennessee came in wearing an all-white sailor's outfit, complete with the hat and gold piping. I introduced the two, then Papa turned around, looked Tennessee over from head to toe, and said just three words: 'Not even close.'"

With that, Hemingway turned back to the bar and Tennessee melted away in embarrassment.

When we finally stood up to stagger back to the hotel room, the bartender stopped George and said, "Wait! You have to tell me your name." In his most graceful, dulcet tone, the Bogey Man leaned forward and said, "George Plimpton."

A blank came over the bartender's face as he tried to process this information. We were almost to the door and picking up speed when we heard the bartender call out loudly, "Who the hell is George Plimpton?"

Over seventy years old at the time—and with twin two-year-olds at home—all the margaritas and whiskeys might have been a bit much even for George. The next morning, he showed up at the golf course with one eye about three inches lower on his face than the other, though that may have been the result of my vision, for I wasn't in much better shape.

Played on Z Boaz golf course—named one of "America's Worst Twenty Courses" —the Jenkins tournament is a celebration of Jenkins's 1965 *Sports Illustrated* story, "The Glory Game at Goat Hills," which told the hilarious tale of Dan's well-wasted youth on a hardscrabble course in South Fort Worth. Populating his story with characters like Cecil the Parachute (who swung so hard he fell down), Weldon the Oath (a swearing postman), Grease Repellent (a mechanic), and Foot the Free ("short for Big Foot the Freeloader"), Jenkins was only proving the old adage that truth is funnier than fiction. May the writer with the best memories win.

Through the decades, it's amazing how little Fort Worth has changed. Many of these characters still play golf with Jenkins and the golf course at Z Boaz is no less colorful than the long-since bulldozed Goat Hills track. The fourth at Z Boaz plays past a topless bar (in case you've forgotten what breasts look like) and the seventeenth overlooks a check-cashing liquor store (in case you've lost your own shirt). When I played in the tournament the previous year, a guy in the group in front of us found an elderly man's body floating facedown in a ditch on the course.

The only bodies Plimpton and I were in danger of stumbling over were each other's. After having a sleeve of new Titleists stolen out of our cart while we were warming up on the putting green, George and I played like old men who'd been drinking as if they were young men, and that was good enough for us.

Reminiscing about all this in the bar in New York, George told me he hadn't teed it up again since our outing in Fort Worth, and I asked him if he wanted to return to Texas the following fall and reteam for another shot at Goat Hills glory.

"I'd love that," George told me, though I think we both suspected that his golf days were behind him. Seventy-five years old, with the *Paris Review* to edit and his memoirs still to write, the last hole of golf he'd ever play would turn out to be number eighteen that day at Z Boaz.

In the usual assortment of crazy Dan Jenkins rules, on the final hole teams were allowed to *buy* a four-hundred-yard drive. Digging into his wallet for the first time all weekend, George pulled out ten of the fifteen dollars he'd arrived with and purchased the best golf shot of his life. Dropping a ball on the designated spot four hundred yards down the closing par five, George knocked a ball onto the green, then made the putt for an eagle.

And so, thirty years after *The Bogey Man*, Plimpton finally beat the game.

Without a clue that George would not live another year, in a bar in New York, I raised my glass to him.

"To the Eagle Man," I toasted.

It's wasn't easy to trump Plimpton in the word game, but I could see he liked that one.

"Any advice?" I asked him as we stood to go.

"Play golf," he told me, "then write about it."

There was no bill from the bartender. I was with George Plimpton, and life was good.

CHAPTER 17

A Wee Dram

———

"I do not believe anyone should fundamentally alter what comes natu-rally to a golfer."

—Colin Montgomerie

Seven of us climbed off the red-eye from New York, sleep-less and bleary-eyed, and headed straight to Turnberry Resort and Golf Club—host to three British Opens—where our caddies were waiting on the first tee. With temperatures in the low forties, we looked out over the course to Ailsa Craig, a granite island eleven miles off the coast of this historic Scottish resort.

"If you can't see Ailsa Craig, it's raining," the locals like to say. "If you can, it's about to rain."

With the rock in view, we had a glorious front nine as we danced through the gorse-covered dunes of Turnberry. On the par-three sixth, perhaps the hardest tee shot in Scotland, with the wind coming hard off the ocean, I aimed a five-wood thirty yards onto the beach and hoped the wind would bring it back. I made my best swing of the year, and the ball streaked off the clubhead and flew in a gentle arc al-most directly at a video crew to the left of the green. Before I could yell fore, the ball had sailed over their camera, hit a few feet short of the hole, and curled just over the lip for what was nearly an unforgettable hole-in-one.

"Did you get that on film?" I asked the cameraman when I got to the green.

"No," he said excitedly, "but I saw it!"

When I asked my caddie to take a photo of me with the flag blowing sideways and Ailsa Craig in the background, Robert happily obliged while the other caddies snickered.

I had to ask what was so funny, and the others explained that Robert was infamous for taking bad photos. Driven nearly mad by Japanese golfers who ask the caddies to take their pictures at every possible moment, Robert had perfected the subtle trick of pointing the camera just a bit low on every picture. When the tourists develop their film back home in Japan, they discover they have forty or fifty photos of their feet, a prospect the Scottish caddies think is simply hilarious.

Though everyone assured me that *my* picture had been framed perfectly, when I got back home, I had one particularly good photo of Ailsa Craig and my feet.

Before boarding that red-eye flight in New York, I'd spent several days walking miles and miles of cold concrete canyons and come away with painful shin splints and a rheumy chest. Arriving at Turnberry's famed lighthouse hole at the same time as the driving rain, golfers and caddies alike were shivering like an eightsome of epileptics.

Ducking out of the cold rain in the halfway house, we all felt the need for a wee dram of scotch. I drank a single shot of twelve-year-old Turnberry single malt, and suddenly felt a fire in my belly that quickly spread to every inch of my body.

"You call this rain!?" I asked my group after a second dram. "You call this wind? This is nothing! Nothing!"

Buying two more of the little bottles of scotch, I dropped one into my bag for an emergency, gave one to my caddie, and the game was on again. By the end of our round, I'd soaked all seven gloves I'd brought for the trip, including two right-handed gloves, which are indispensable in the cold. In this kind of weather, the great pleasures of the day come from simple things, like a string of two or three pars, by pulling off a particularly tough shot, or simply by sharing the joy and misery with your partners and caddies.

Reviewing my round of 89 that evening, my conclusion was that I'd played well, but thrown away nearly ten strokes by my inability to navigate Turnberry's pot bunkers or hit the bump-and-run approach shots required in the kind of wind we'd experienced.

To prepare myself for more deep bunkers to come, the next day I headed straight to the Colin Montgomerie Links Golf Academy. Sandwiched between the two championship courses at Turnberry, the academy offers instruction ranging from a basic forty-five-minute links lesson to the Full Monty, a daylong course of private instruction coupled with a playing lesson on Monty's nine-hole Academy Golf Course.

Whatever lesson you choose, your day of links learning starts with Montgomerie's Twenty-six Ball Warm-up, a great way to get loose for a lesson or a round of golf.

"Why twenty-six balls?" I asked Monty later that day as he gave me a rundown on his operation.

"That's two shots with every club but your putter. Starting with your sand wedge, the idea is to hit one ball with every club, gradually moving up to the driver, then reversing the process back to the sand wedge. If you warm up with any more balls than that, you're practicing, not warming up."

Of course, Monty wasn't telling me anything new. I was always practicing.

Once you're warmed up, your links lesson will take you through a circuit of the links golf shots you'll need in Scotland. Throwing myself on the mercy of Academy Director Chris Brown, I asked for a deep bunker lesson, Colin Montgomerie style. What that lesson entailed was both simple and effective: ball forward in my stance, feet, hips, and shoulders open to the line, clubface square to the target line, weight on the left foot, and accelerate through impact.

After just a few swings—and a few reminders on each of these points from Chris—I was lofting shot after shot toward the pin, shaking my head at how easy it suddenly seemed. After going through the setup in order, I'd conclude each swing by accelerating through impact, which lofted every single shot onto the elevated green. With each shot, I could feel a weight being lifted from my shoulders. I had ten rounds left in Scotland, and I didn't have to fear the sand.

Free at last! I thought. Thank God, almighty, I am free at last!

"Chris saved me a lot of shots today with a bunker lesson," I later told Monty.

"That's the whole idea," Monty told me. "I feel like I've saved as many shots as possible in my career, so I want to stop people from walking off the course saying, *if only . . .*"

Montgomerie has had a long love affair with Turnberry. Having grown up twenty miles north in Troon, he first played the Ailsa course at age thirteen when his mother became a member of Turnberry. Three decades later, he partnered with golf architect Donald Steele to create one of the rarest things in golf—a good academy course. Using parts of the former Arran course as well as a piece of Turnberry's World War II Royal Air Force runway, Montgomerie and Steele created a mix of par threes and fours that may be the most challenging nine-hole course you'll ever play. Like Ailsa and Turnberry's new Kintyre links, the academy course has deep rough, gorse-lined fairways, and plenty of wind.

Playing in a hard-fought grudge match, on the tee of the par-three seventh, I watched the other golf-writers hit high seven-irons into a thirty miles an hour wind and saw each of their shots blow so far off line we weren't sure which course they came down on. Pulling my five-iron, I placed the ball back in my stance and took the club back low and slow as Chris Brown had shown me. Hitting through the shot with a low follow-through, I watched in amazement as the ball leapt off my clubface, bored straight into the wind, and hit soft on the green, leaving me an easy putt for the win and the skins.

When we finished the nine and headed to the hotel to warm our toes in Turnberry's pub overlooking all this magnificence, two of the other guys were recounting their failures. I couldn't hear the whole conversation, but one phrase was loud and clear. "If only . . ."

Fundamentals of Golf

The Bump and Run

As taught at the Colin Montgomerie Links Golf Academy

There is no more useful shot on a true links course than the bump and run. When around the green, the goal is to land the ball on the putting surface and let it roll out to the hole. Distance is the most important aspect of the shot, so club selection is essential.

If the roll is three times the length of the flight, a seven-iron is the proper choice. Half-carry, half-roll calls for a nine-iron or wedge. More carry than roll requires a sand iron. (If the shot is uphill, you probably need to decrease your loft by one club. If downhill, you increase your loft.)

Once you've envisioned the shot and chosen your club, set up with a narrowed stance, ball in the middle of your stance, and your weight 70 percent on your left foot. Grip down slightly on the shaft and place your hands opposite your left thigh, then make a rhythmic, pendulum-style swing.

Keeping your weight on your left side, make a smooth stroke with your hands and arms, keeping your wrists "soft" so that the clubhead never passes your hands.

CHAPTER 18

A Boy Named Clyde

———

"In the galleries, there were lots of dogs, which never barked, and lots of
children, who didn't howl or fuss, which is the way it is in Scotland."
—Herbert Warren Wind

There are a number of ways to undertake a Scottish golf pilgrimage, and as far as I'm concerned, all of them are good. My first trip almost fifteen years ago was on the absolute cheap—budget airfare to London, train to Edinburgh, and bargain bed and breakfasts.

Though the trip was intended to be a vacation with Christy and our seven-month-old daughter, I took the liberty of inviting my number-one golf buddy, David Wood, a.k.a. the Woodman. For the Woodman and me, the trip was a grand success; for Christy, that would probably be an overstatement. Unbeknownst to us at the time, children are not allowed in Scottish pubs, so every time David and I raised a pint after a glorious round in the old country, Christy and baby Kate were unable to come inside.

Somehow my marriage survived.

This time I managed to class up my act by joining Haversham & Baker Golf Tours for nearly two weeks of nonstop golf and off-course celebration. H&B really knows how to do Scotland right. For starters, travel is aboard a Mercedes motor coach with twenty captain's chairs and a bar. Other than being sober enough to play golf, the only requirement is that your bags be outside your hotel room on the travel days and that you show up before the appointed departure time for the bus.

"The bus waits for no man," we were told solemnly by Sam Baker, one of our hosts and the "B" of Haversham and Baker. There is no "H" of H&B, which I suppose is a good thing for the "B."

In addition to Sam—pronounced "Sahm" by the Scots—our group consisted mainly of disgruntled misfits who, had it not been for the intervention of the game of golf, might otherwise have been involved in some ugly incident at the post office involving supervisors and unrequited love. No doubt, our obsession for the sport has saved us from many felonious actions.

Sporting new nicknames within hours of arrival, we consisted of the Hit Man (an Italian-American who dislikes Italian stereotypes), Ball Game, the Sniper, Five-minute Tom, Sparky, and a boy named Clyde. Never mind that Clyde is my first name, and one that hadn't been used in normal conversation since I tried to deck a kid in the third grade for making fun of it. I was in Scotland, and there is no more Scottish name than Clyde.

The name Clyde Turk was passed down to me from my grandmother (also named Clyde Turk Pipkin), whose grandfather Turk came to Texas from Kentucky after the Civil War. While the Turk family came to the New World from Ireland over 250 years ago, my Clyde ancestors trace back to Scotland's famed Clyde Valley surrounding the banks of the Clyde River in the region of Strathclyde. Like my grandmother, I was christened Clyde, though it took me nearly half a century to realize how proud I was of the name.

As a kid, I'd never heard of Strathclyde or its proud golf heritage. Today the region is home to 160 golf courses, including Turnberry, Troon, and Western Gailes Golf Club, considered by many to be the finest of the three, despite the fact that it has never hosted an Open Championship. The fact that the course is unsuitable to large galleries is clearly one of its charms. A private club originally built in 1897, Western Gailes is rarely played by Americans, which only served to increase the excitement of our group of golf nuts as the H&B bus pulled into the parking lot.

With snow visible on the Arran islands across the Firth, and the wind howling at us at forty mph, the logical course of action would have been to sit in the bar and drink. But if we were willing, so were our caddies. On a day when the United Kingdom was enduring what the newspapers would label the "storm of the century," with significant tree blow-downs, structural damage to buildings, and seven deaths, our group was happily playing golf.

A ribbon course laid out on a narrow strip of links land between railroad tracks and the Firth of Clyde, Western Gailes normally plays downwind on the first and last four holes, with a long stretch in between playing down the coast against the wind. We saw it exactly the opposite, with the caddies grinning on the first tee, certain we couldn't keep the ball in play hitting into this vicious zephyr.

Luckily I had a couple of secret weapons at my disposal—first, that I'd grown up playing in windy West Texas, and second, that many of my swing faults arise from my loosey-goosey swing. When I play in the wind, I tend to minimize all that extra motion to help me make solid contact. Oddly enough, that makes me one of the few golfers I've ever met who actually plays better in the wind.

I'd also just received an excellent lesson in hitting the knockdown shot, which was just the shot I needed to bore my ball under and into a four-club wind.

By the time we turned back with the wind, the others in my group had pretty much given up on keeping score. Having hit all four greens in regulation, I'd made two birdies and was looking at a string of downwind holes that boded well for a miraculous round.

"What's your handicap?" my dumbfounded caddie asked me after I hit a long drive down the coast.

"I was at sixteen five months ago," I told him, "but I've got it down to eleven now."

"Eleven?" he said. "I'd like to have you and eleven in the Open."

Perhaps this compliment was intended to increase the size of his tip at the end of the round. If so, it certainly worked.

Despite my worsening shin splints, I strode proudly down the fairway, looking out past the whitecaps and windblown waves of the Firth of Clyde to where a majestic rainbow arced across the sky. Never had I felt closer to my father and his Scottish family. I'd returned to my homeland and even had a Scottish caddie complimenting my game. It was a miracle.

The rainbow, unfortunately, was soon replaced by ominous clouds heavy with black rain and then with rock-hard bits of hail that drove into our rain suits like thousands of tiny nails. Despite all this, our group played on.

About the time of our third rainbow, fourth hard rain, and second hailstorm, we had to admit that there was no beating Western Gailes this day. Teeing off into the wind on sixteen, I hit it low and left, and the last time I saw my ball it was soaring high and right, flying over the railroad tracks and looking as if it were never going to come down. Reteeing for my third shot, I staggered in for an 82, which I considered to be about five under par in a hurricane. In many ways, this was the proudest round of my life. As the bus pulled away from the clubhouse and bade farewell to the Firth of Clyde, I didn't see how our trip could get any better. Luckily, I was about to find out.

The next morning our group loaded up for what Sam calls the "greatest day in all of golf"—thirty-six holes at the home of the Honorable Company of Edinburgh Golfers, known to us mere mortals as Muirfield.

"I have to warn you clowns," Sam told us on the bus, "some people come to Muirfield, and they don't understand what it's all about. They don't *get* it!"

When David Wood and I drove to North Berwick fifteen years earlier, we'd stopped at the gates of Muirfield to simply gaze out upon its historic fairways. While we oohed and aahed, a gentleman in a navy blazer and tie asked what we were doing.

"We're playing all over the country and just wanted to *see* it," we explained.

"And what would you be doing tomorrow?" he asked.

Suddenly a wave of nausea swept over me. "Flying home with my wife and baby," I told him.

"And you, sir?" the gentleman said to the Woodman.

"Playing Muirfield?" David asked brightly.

"Be here at eight."

And so I missed the greatest day in all of golf. Now I was getting a mulligan to play the club where the original rules of golf were written, a course that has played host to fifteen Open Championships, or what we Yanks call the British Open.

In many ways, Muirfield is a personal experience, different for each person who plays it, but a glorious combination of Old World grace and brutally tough golf. "Four balls and two balls," they call the day.

After playing eighteen on our own balls in the morning—and a tough eighteen it was—we moved to the beautiful old locker room and changed out of our sopping wet clothes and hung them in the drying room. Even with a Gore-Tex rain suit, the water crawls out of Muirfield's thick, wet grass and climbs up into your clothes. The drying room, at a temperature of about 140 degrees, makes those clothes playable for the afternoon.

Looking natty in our coat and ties— "No golf shirts with ties," Sam had warned us, "or it's back to the bus" —we headed for the dining room for an incredible buffet of roast everything. I'd describe the various offerings, but if I did, we'd both have to put down the book and go get something to eat.

A great clubhouse is one of those secret joys of golf. You may watch the Open Championship on television and thrill to the course, but the cameras will not take you to the inner sanctum. When Pip and I played together in my early years, though minors were not permitted in the men's locker room, he sometimes allowed me to go in with him to change clothes or have a bowl of soup in the nineteenth-hole bar, which was generally populated by old men drinking cocktails and clicking dominoes as they shuffled them in sweeping motions on the table.

Eventually I earned the right to sign for a hamburger, fries, and iced tea in the nearby grill room. My pals and I would play or caddie eighteen in the morning, drink a gallon of tea with our lunch, and head back out to play till dark.

Though we quaffed a pint of bitters with our meal at Muirfield, the next stop was the coffee and smoking room, where a port and a cup of coffee or tea prepared us for more golf.

The two ball afternoon match pits you and a partner in an alternate shot competition against two others. As my partner, I'd drawn the group's A-player, Teddy "Ball Game," and had high hopes for our chances. If you've never played alternate shot, the format pushes the game along at an astounding pace. As one player hits his tee shot, the other is already walking two hundred yards down the rough. While the second player hits to the green, the first has hopefully passed him. It's quite an ingenious system and ought to be played more in the States.

For us, though, it was a different story. Ball Game hit a couple of cold toppers on the first, but promised to get back on form. I was already down the fairway on the second when he swung from the tee. My caddie and I watched for the ball to come down, but saw nothing. On the tee, my partner was waving for me to walk back toward him. We kept walking back, and Ball Game kept waving us closer, until finally I was standing at his side.

"Where is it?" I asked.

"Right there," he said, pointing into the gorse twenty feet to the right of the tee. Apparently Ball Game had taken full advantage of the free-flowing pints and ports at lunch. I wanted to throttle him, but knew immediately that would prompt Sam to send me back to the bus, so I sucked it up and hit the ball. After only a couple more disasters, the cold wind revived my partner and we were back in the hunt. Walking my second round of the day on a course I thought I'd never play, I had a smile on my face at every shot, good and bad.

So how tough is Muirfield? Well, the rough is so thick that finding an errant shot requires one miracle, while hitting it back into play demands another. With the light failing us, the Hit Man found his ball deep in the left rough of the eighteenth. As he made a mighty swing, not one, but *two* balls flew out of the cabbage, both of them reaching the fairway. When you can't see a ball directly under your ball, that's thick rough.

Back on the bus, we cracked an expensive bottle of Irish whiskey that Sam had just been given by the Captain of the Irish National Golf Team. This was a glorious present, but we were gloriously happy and opened that sucker for a toast.

"You were right," we all told Sam. "It *is* the best day in all of golf." Sam just smiled. "I'm glad you got it," he said.

Between my gimpy legs, the flu, and walking thirty-six a day, I was beginning to wonder if I'd even survive the trip. Over the first seven rounds of our pilgrimage, I seemed to have literally transformed into an old man. Every step for the past five days had been painful, so I almost wept for joy when I saw the $22 million spa at the Sheraton Edinburgh, where a waterproof plastic watch with your very own electronic password admits you to wonders of steam, hot and cold aroma therapies, and scalding water that holds the glorious promise of boiling your frozen carcass to the bone.

Slipping into a vast steaming pool, I swam out through a covered portal into the cold night air, where giant spouts of hot water pounded down on my neck and shoulders. Four floors up, I was eye-level and just across the street from historic Edinburgh castle, with snow flurries flying all around.

"Pip never saw nothing like this!" I said in my West Texas drawl.

.   .   .

Much improved, I rejoined my gang the next morning and on we played, teeing it up at the unique seaside North Berwick links and at the new Kingsbarns course, which, though it lacks the history of its older neighbors, is otherwise the equal of any track in Scotland.

Abandoned by my driver, my long irons, and occasionally by my caddie, I began to rely more and more on my Callaway five-wood. Every evening on the bus after our round, the Hit Man would tell a new tale about my ball being completely out of sight in the rough, me standing knee-deep in the thick grass and smashing the ball back into play with that trusty five-wood. I wouldn't have sold the club for a thousand hundred dollars.

Growing more and more confused about how to do all the things that Sean and Leadbetter had taught me, I was having to make do with small victories, not low scores. And in some ways, that's the secret of Scottish golf.

Having agreed in advance that we'd move on if we didn't each draw a tee time in the Old Course daily lottery at St. Andrews, we drove north through the Scottish highlands and back down to the sea at Nairn Golf Club, host course for the 1999 Walker Cup matches. Another fine old links track, Nairn starts and ends along the Firth of Moray with an unusual midround swing through a stand of inland pines. Jack Fosyth, my seventy-year-old caddie for the afternoon round, had played eighteen that morning, but thought nothing of toting my bag on a pull cart, or trolley as the Scots call them. More than once, I had to hurry to keep up with Jack, for golf had kept him young.

And then we came to Royal Dornoch, that mystic links course which—located at the same latitude as Juneau, Alaska—is the northernmost of the world's top twenty courses. Or is it in the top ten? For me, it is perhaps number one.

We stayed at the Royal Golf Hotel, and the next morning walked the fifty yards from the hotel to the Dornoch clubhouse, where I met my caddie, Steve Reeves, an English lad in his fifties who could pass for both younger and Scottish. First visiting Dornoch after reading a 1983

Tom Watson magazine story about this magical course, Steve decided almost immediately to move here from London. A nine handicapper, he's a member of the club, owns a house just a short stroll away, and splits his work between caddying and working as a software consultant. If I didn't have such a wonderful family back home in Texas, I'd probably join him.

The previous summer, Steve had caddied for Joe Keller, a young man from Chicago who became the first American ever to win the Dornoch Shield, a historic and grueling tournament that involves two days of medal qualification play, two days of thirty-six-holes-a-day matches, and a Sunday final with a gallery that would eclipse most Champions Tour events.

To give you an idea of how tough the course can play under this kind of pressure, let me tell you of another American competitor— a sixteen-handicapper who showed up fresh off the plane from the States hoping to put in a few honorable rounds. Despite the fact that the man's caddie was six-time club champion Stewart Ruddy (a two-time Shield winner himself), the 16-handicapper shot a staggering 141, arguing all the way with his caddie about club selection, strategy, and the breaks of the green.

"He went out in 81, but it was downwind coming home, so I brought him in with a 60," Ruddy told me over a pint in the clubhouse's second-floor bar overlooking the first tee and Dornoch's famous five flagpoles.

"What were you arguing about?" I asked.

"Well," Ruddy responded, "people's opinions about their golf games seem to operate in inverse proportion to their talent."

"So, the better you become, the more you realize how much you still have to learn," I offered in translation.

"And the more you moan about your bad breaks," said another gentlemen, "the less chance you'll ever have of learning anything."

The night before, we'd broken bread with Dornoch's general manager, John Duncan, a retired British army officer who was wearing the

Duncan clan's traditional tartan kilt along with a modern red shirt and tie. Fascinated by the differences in maintenance between American parkland courses and the links of Scotland with their mottled shades of tan and green, I asked if the club supplemented the area's mere twenty inches of annual rainfall.

"We do have a watering system," Duncan told me. "The water comes from the spring-fed Witch's Pool, where the last witch in Scotland was burned in the 1700s."

Witch-brewed water, I thought. That couldn't hurt.

"How often do you irrigate?" I asked.

"As little as possible," he told me.

However much he watered, it was the right amount, for Dornoch was simply a gem. I have never been more captivated by a golf course, and even though I trashed my chances for a low score with a couple of horrendous drives, the round was as memorable as if I'd broken seventy.

Playing in gorgeous weather with Sam Baker, the two of us came to the eighteenth, both knowing this was the last round of a golf trip as good as we would ever know. Our group had given our all, been triumphant at times and totally destroyed at others, talked endless hours about golf over endless rounds of drinks, told and heard a thousand jokes both good and bad, and become the best kind of friends there are—golf buddies.

All my lessons had put me into a state of confusion that I could not conquer, but somehow, those same lessons always came through when I most needed to hit one good.

Hitting our drives to almost the same spot in the eighteenth fairway, both Sam and I made triumphant shots up the last big hill and onto the green below the Dornoch clubhouse. Having worked on putting less than any aspect of my game so far, I left my putt hanging on the lip and stood back as Sam stroked his firmly into the cup, a beautiful birdie at the end of a perfect day.

That night at dinner, we all rehashed our favorite memories of the trip, many of them about our sardonic Scottish caddies.

On a tight par four at Kingsbarns, my caddie handed me my driver.

"But the fairway looks like a ribbon!" I exclaimed. "Why should I hit driver instead of three-wood?"

"Because I've seen you hit your three-wood," he replied.

Taking his advice, I hit the driver and split the narrow fairway.

The Hit Man told us he asked a caddie, who was hustling from one player's ball to the other's, what was the record for the two drives farthest apart by two players for whom he was carrying double.

"Two hundred seventy-three yards apart," the caddie replied without blinking an eye. "I stepped it off."

As usual, Sam Baker won the day, not with his swing, but with his stories of twenty years on the Scottish links.

"I'm out playing one day with Sandy Pipey," Sam says in reference to the legendary Dornoch caddie, "and we're trying to figure out what shot to hit from one spot and another, trying to calculate the wind, the bounce and mounds. And Sandy says in his beautiful brogue, 'Sahm, Dornoch is like a beautiful woman—you have to learn what *pleases* her.' "

Toasting her with one last pint, I went back to my room feeling as if I'd made as many proper approaches to the lovely lady as I'd ever be able to muster, having perhaps not quite soft enough a touch, but satisfied in a way I've almost never felt after a round of golf.

Sure, I'd like to have not blasted a ball seventy-five yards into the gorse off the eighth tee, but I took my knocks and got back in the game. Without a doubt, if my father had been walking that course with me, he'd have come back to the clubhouse bar filled with pride at simply having watched my round.

He'd have swapped stories with caddies and bought a round when it came his turn, and in all probability I'd have had to help him up to his room after he had a few too many. I would have liked doing that, but instead, the best I could do was drink a pint in his honor, then say that's enough.

Someday I'd be back to Royal Dornoch, wind-kissed lass of the north, wooing her with sweet swings and a soft touch. When I return, Dornoch will show her advantage over any woman I'll ever meet, because even if I'm walking one of the last rounds of a long and happy life in golf, there's a good chance this beautiful woman won't have changed at all since my first round, or Sam's, or Sandy Pipey's. For she is timeless, like the game we all love.

CHAPTER 19

The King of Golf

"When you hear someone shout, 'You da man!' if he ain't shouting at Arnold Palmer, then it ain't da man."

—Ron Green

After an eighteen-hour journey from Dornoch to Austin, I had about five hours sleep before I was due to introduce Arnold Palmer at the opening of his new Austin course, Lakecliff Golf Club. Unfortunately, I brought the weather from Scotland with me, as the temperature was barely in the forties, with a light but steady rain. That did not deter Arnie's army of fans, many of whom would stand naked in a tornado at a thumbtack factory to get this close to the King of Golf.

Helping owner and course developer Bobby Day with the event, I took advantage of my limited privilege to peek into Arnie's Callaway bag, and boy, did I get an eyeful.

"My God, Arnie's got a seven-wood!" I mumbled. "What in the wide, wide world of sports is going on?"

Not only did Arnie carry a seven-wood, he was proud of it. When someone in the crowd asked him what was in his bag, the seven-wood was the club he seemed most excited about.

The Old Man and the Tee

"There are a lot of new players in the game, plus some of us are getting older, "Arnie told us. "If you don't hit a long iron good enough, you hit a lofted fairway wood."

And though Arnie carries what some players would say is an old man's club, he still has a young man's perspective.

"A pretty lady asked me if I'd teach her to play golf," Arnie continued, "and I said, 'Okay, I'll teach you. We're gonna start with the irons . . . and then we're gonna go into the woods.' "

Between jokes, the King of Golf also told us you can learn a lot about the game in a half-hour clinic.

"When I was learning as a youngster, my father never spent more than ten or fifteen minutes with me. He'd place my hands on the club and say, 'Keep them there.' Well, they've been there a long time."

With it still raining, still cold, and Arnie still seventy-three years old, he headed to the first tee and proceeded to make five straight pars before saying, "Let's have a press conference."

Beneath the cover of a small tent, I introduced Arnie as, "My father's favorite golfer, my favorite golfer, and probably your favorite golfer, too."

Lakeside is the second course Arnie and Ed Seay have built outside Austin for Arnie's friend Bobby Day, and it's obvious that they dedicated a lot of work and care to the course. The $15 million Bobby spent on construction didn't hurt either. In addition to miles of flowing creeks, waterfalls, and sixty-eight sculpted white-sand bunkers, all eighteen bent grass greens are built atop sub-air ventilation systems, which allows the injection or vacuuming of heated or cooled air and moisture from pipes beneath the green.

"This place is a real gem," Arnie told us. "I'm looking forward to coming back and playing it again next spring if I live long enough. At my age, I don't even buy green bananas any more."

When the writers had quit fawning over Arnie and asking questions he'd been asked a thousand times before, I managed to steal a private moment to tell him about my ten-stroke mission that I was dedicating to the memory of my father. Though Arnie is ten years younger than my father, he reminds me of Pip in his patience, his love of life, and especially his kind, but wrinkled eyes.

One of the current owners of Pebble Beach, Arnie suffered an agonizing stretch of near victories on the course, so there was hardly anyone alive who could give me a more informed opinion on Pebble's difficulties and my chances.

"So," I concluded, "do you think it's possible I can take ten strokes off my game and break 80 at Pebble?"

Having listened intently to my every word, Arnie thought about my story and question for a moment, then he looked to my hands.

Shades of Harvey Penick, I thought.

"Ten strokes?" he repeated.

"Yes, sir," I told him.

Raising his gaze to mine, Arnie said, "You can do it!" Then he put his hand in mine, gave my hand a firm squeeze of encouragement, and added, "I know you can."

And then he was gone, swept up in a clutch of other fans with other questions, signing balls, hats, shirts, and programs, generous to all, but especially to the kids who'd waited in the cold to say a word to the greatest King of Golf who will ever be.

At the opposite end of Lakecliff's practice range is the new facility of Chuck Cook, 1996 PGA Teacher of the Year and the coach of Payne Stewart, Tom Kite, and Corey Pavin when each of them won their U.S. Open Championships during the nineties. Though Chuck admits to strong preferences for certain swing styles, he also acknowledges that everyone has a unique way of swinging the club and may not have the ability or desire to change the fundamentals.

"Chuck doesn't overteach, he simplifies," says Tom Kite. "He doesn't demand change, he suggests it. And he gets results."

Having stalled in my progress, I was in desperate need of results. Even though my five-wood and the links golf lesson saved me in Scotland, I knew all too well how many fairways I'd missed, how many drives I smothered into the left rough, and how many midirons I sprayed almost everywhere but the green.

In Chuck's new state-of-the-art studio, I began hitting shots for the video cameras and telling him the particulars of what I'd been working on.

"Waiting for me to hit a good one?" I asked after a number of swings and no comments.

"Nope. You can't fool me," Chuck said. "That was good, but you still can't fool me."

After a dozen shots, we moved to the analysis screen and I once again began to watch stop-motion video of my various swings.

"All the stuff you talked about that you're working on, we're going to see," Chuck told me. "But I'm going to give you a little different way to look at it.

"Part of the reason you're over the top or a little bit flat is that you stand a little close to the ball," he explained as he began drawing lines on the screen. "The plane of your back and the plane of the club should form a right angle. The reason that's important is because if you stand too tall, as you rotate your shoulders, they'll rotate through too high and the club goes behind you. If you bend over a bit, the shoulders will automatically rotate under.

"So you just want to move back a couple of inches and widen your feet a little, too. In effect, I'm trying to make you shorter. I want you to feel that it's easier to swing more around and not so much up and over the top."

Essentially, these were changes that Leadbetter and Sean Hogan had made in my address position. Had I reverted to where I started, I wondered, or had I not changed enough?

But that was just the beginning. Chuck also wanted me to cock my right hand more upward, and turn my shoulders more going back so that my left shoulder was more over my right foot at the top, instead of above the center of my body.

Putting me in a side-by-side comparison with Tiger—footage that

Chuck had shot at the previous Masters—Chuck compared my swing to Tiger's at the moment of impact.

"By the time Tiger makes contact," Chuck pointed out, "the club is right back where he started, but his shoulder has worked under considerably, and his hips are rotated open into a position of power."

My hips, on the other hand, were square, as were my shoulders, a position from which I'd never hit with authority.

"To recap, I want you to widen out, get farther from the ball, and have less hands and more turn in your swing."

Moving back to the tee, I hit a long succession of irons, with Chuck speaking up whenever he felt it was necessary. It didn't take long for us both to realize that I wasn't getting it, so Chuck decided to try something else. Stepping close, he held my hands as I took the club back, keeping the clubface pointing at the ball.

"What's that feel like?" he asked.

"Like I'm rotating the club shut as I take it back," I replied.

"Then that's what I want you to do! Take it back, rotating the club in a counterclockwise motion, then hit a punch shot to right field."

I had my doubts about the whole approach, but doing as Chuck said, I made a little punch swing and absolutely hammered the ball with almost no effort.

"Good!" Chuck told me. "Really good!"

Continuing to rotate the clubface shut as I took it back, I hit a succession of solid punch shots, all of them flying farther and with a higher launch angle than any of my full swings when we started.

Back at the monitor, Chuck used the stop motion to show me how my body was now turned open at impact, that I also had considerably more extension through my hands and arms at contact.

As far as I was concerned, the lesson was already a success, but Chuck wanted more. Standing opposite me, he held out a golf shaft horizontally so that it gently touched the outside of my right shoulder.

"As you swing, I want your right shoulder to go back along the shaft until the left shoulder touches the shaft."

Doing as he said, I felt as if I were about five miles behind the ball.

"Good!" Chuck said. "You're turning back over the right heel more, and your hands are behind the ball."

Moving from the irons to my driver, I then lost the feel of everything I'd been trying to do. Perhaps I was getting tired, but, either way, Chuck decided to take another tack.

"This is the way Harvey would have done it," Chuck explained as he rotated my hands a little farther to the right on the club. "He wouldn't even fool with trying to get you in a conventional grip to do that. He'd say, 'Give me another knuckle, and don't let it hook. To do that, move your hands to the right on the grip, then swing to the right.'"

So that's what I did, and I hit it absolutely sweet! Then another, and another. Other than the fact that I couldn't quit hitting these great drives, it was obvious that the lesson was over.

Handing me a videotape of everything we'd said and done, Chuck gave me one last summary.

"On your short irons, work on shutting the face and hitting low punch shots. On your long clubs, take a strong grip, then a big turn back and through. You don't have to make it any more complicated than that."

Unwilling to leave when I was hitting it so fine, I moved out to the range and continued to just murder the ball!

The next day, I went back to Lakecliff and shot 76 from the tips, the greatest round of my life. Blessed by Arnie and guided by Chuck, I felt as if I could do no wrong.

Three days later it was gone.

Fundamentals of Golf

Torque and Distance

As taught by Chuck Cook

One way to hit longer shots is to create more clubhead speed through the use of torque. Torque is created by your upper body making a full turn during your backswing, while your lower body really resists turning.

This creates tightness in your body. The release of this tightness is similar to releasing one end of a stretched rubber band.

To develop a feel for this, straddle an upside-down milk crate or driving range basket. Now practice hitting shots with a full turn of your upper body without letting your legs hit the box. Restricting your lower-body turn will create tightness that helps you unwind faster, gaining clubhead speed that results in longer shots.

If you can't create this torque because of a lack of flexibility, you need to start a regular series of stretching and flexibility exercises.

CHAPTER 20

Don't Think No Negative Thoughts

"Man is not made for defeat," he said. "A man can be destroyed but not defeated."

—Ernest Hemingway,
The Old Man and the Sea

You hear people say that fifty is just middle-aged. I'd feel more comfortable with that idea if I knew a few more folks who were a hundred. My father made it to eighty-two. At ninety-nine, ball-stealing Bob Hope was getting close, but the only person I'd known who'd actually reached the century mark was Gregorio Fuentes, Ernest Hemingway's boat captain, great friend, and the inspiration for *The Old Man and the Sea*.

In Cuba a couple of years ago, I hired a man with a '57 Cadillac convertible to drive me to the fishing village of Cojimar, where I found the old man having lunch overlooking the harbor at La Terraza restaurant.

Despite our language difficulties and the fact that Fuentes was born in 1897 and I in 1953, we shared a love of the sea, of Hemingway's stories, and of good cigars. Fuentes told me his preferred smoke was a Monte Christo number two; luckily, I had two of them in my pocket.

For the length of one fine cigar, we talked of fishing, friendships, and baseball, about the joys of being young and the pains of growing old. Our waiter helped me translate when the old man told me about the lions he and Papa had seen on the beach in Africa. Finally, Fuentes told me how, following the Cuban revolution, Hemingway had given his beautiful yacht, the *Pilar,* to Fuentes as a gift of friendship and thanks. In *Pilar,* the two had cruised between islands in the stream searching for billfish and—during World War II—for German U-boats. Unable to own a yacht in a communist country, Fuentes had donated his treasure to the Cuban government. In return, Castro gave Fuentes the gift of free meals at La Terraza for as long as he lived. At the time, Fuentes thought he'd gotten screwed on the deal, but after three meals a day for forty years, he was beginning to look wise indeed.

When our cigars were short and our ashes long, the old man asked me to come see him again sometime, and I promised that I would try. Before I could fulfill my promise, just a few days before my father died, Gregorio Fuentes passed away in Cojimar at the age of 102.

Having lost *the* Old Man and my old man, it's no wonder that I suddenly felt like I'd hopscotched right over middle age. Maybe that's the way it's meant to be. When I was very young, I thought my dad was very old. Looking back now, I realize that, when I was five and feeling my first urges to learn about golf, Pip was still in his thirties, hardly an old man.

Maybe it's just that we start to *sound* old. Barely in his forties when I began to caddie for him, Pip was already telling me how far he *used* to hit the ball. I'd heard myself say the same thing a few times, then bit my lip. I wasn't ready for that, not yet. The idea of the new equipment is to get longer, not shorter. The idea is to beat those scores down.

Around the time of my round in Pebble at the start of my year-long quest, I'd been constantly fighting to break 90. On my trip to

Scotland in October, my scores had averaged mideighties in tough conditions. By Thanksgiving, I was notching scores in the upper seventies and low eighties. That was no guarantee I'd break eighty at Pebble, but it felt pretty darn good. Most encouraging was the fact that, despite six months of hard work on the full swing, I had yet to begin serious work on my short game and putting. When I started, I'd never dreamed I could take a full ten strokes off my handicap, for handicap is not an average of your strokes over par (though it should be), but an indicator of your potential, a percentage of your best rounds. Ten off your handicap is huge, and I was halfway there.

Perhaps I could post a double-double—ten off my handicap *and* ten off my marker round at Pebble. Aside from the personal satisfaction, that would show beyond a doubt that good clubs properly fit, solid instruction from knowledgeable teachers, plus a little blood, sweat, and tears, really can change your golf life.

That was the upside.

On the downside, after a smooth 76 at Lakecliff, my scores began to rise like the coming of summer: 78, 80, 84, 85. Unfortunately, summer was a long ways away. What was I doing wrong?

Well, for starters I wasn't returning to any of my instructors to retune what we'd worked on. Sean was back in Florida with Leadbetter, and Chuck Cook was on the road working with several pros. In the meantime, my credit cards were a moneylender's wet dream, and I was still looking at six more months of this nonsense, as Christy could not help pointing out.

Christy and I have been married—at least the way we describe it—for thirty-eight years. That's nineteen for her and nineteen for me. Our most persistent problem for most of those two decades has clearly been money, for I'm like a dumb squirrel who never sees winter coming and plays with his nuts all summer long.

As the bills mounted higher, Christy began to hint that I should ease up on the golf and write something commercial, like that screenplay I'd set aside. Not only had I forgotten about the screenplay, I couldn't even remember what it was about.

My solution to paying the bills, on the other hand, was to take even more golf trips and write a variety of magazine stories on Dallas, San Antonio, South Padre Island, Cabo San Lucas, and Lajitas, a new West Texas track with an incredible green across the Rio Grande River in Mexico. Add it up and that's thirty more days on the road and twenty more rounds. Unfortunately, the more I played, the harder it was to concentrate on my swing. The more I tried to concentrate, the more I became confused.

Confusion is the death of golf. At ninety miles an hour, it's impossible to choose between two alternatives. Better to have a wrong idea and commit to it than two opposed ideas, both of which seem right.

Should I turn my left shoulder under going back, as Sean had told me? Or should I turn my right shoulder back along that imaginary horizontal shaft, which had worked so well with Chuck Cook?

Should I set the clubhead by pushing down with my left hand, or by cocking my right hand up instead of in?

With my seven-iron, should I rotate the clubface to keep it square going back, or simply follow my thumbs up into the slot?

Even when I hit it good, I didn't know if I'd done the right thing. My biggest problems were still with the midirons and long irons. From sand wedge down to eight-iron, I felt pretty comfortable, but put even a seven-iron in my hand and doubt would creep in.

Doubt is the other death of golf.

Leadbetter had jokingly warned that if I went to six different teachers, I might *add* ten strokes to my game, and now I was beginning to wonder if he was right.

As I was hitting balls at Barton Creek one day, the director of instruction, Tom Bennett, walked over and asked how I was doing.

"Up and down," I told him. "Mostly down with the irons."

Perhaps sensing that I didn't need any more swing thoughts at the time, Tom watched silently for a while, then offered a commentary on my game in general.

"You don't approach your iron shots with the same care as you do on the greens. When you putt and chip, you know exactly what you're trying to do, then you do it. But with your irons, you look like you're hitting before you're set."

I thought about what he said for a while and finally decided that I was simply too eager to hit a good shot to consistently pull it off. Maybe I wanted it too much. Maybe the way to get my scores back on track was to quit keeping score.

The place where you don't keep score, of course, is Willie's. Having agreed to do a magazine interview about his impending seventieth birthday, I figured we might as well talk on the golf course.

Early one morning, I found Willie at his hilltop cabin already playing guitar with Ray Benson as the two ripped through the complex chord progression of Fats Waller's "Ain't Misbehavin'." Coming to an improvised finish that sounded like the musical equivalent of sliding into home, Willie looked up to Ray with a big grin.

"Close enough for jazz," Willie quipped. "What else you peddling?"

Just two days before Christmas, Ray picked out " 'Tis the season to be jolly," though Willie sang, "Check the balls out on that collie!"

Ray and I were still laughing when Willie said, "Let's play some golf."

"Hundred thousand a hole," Ray declared.

"Pay up after every shot," added Willie.

Like Willie Nelson's life, the golf game at Pedernales has matured from a hopping party to a measured beat, which makes a pretty solid background for a conversation about golf, life, and women, in no particular order.

"How's that ten-stroke thing going?" Willie asks as I take a practice swing to warm up on number one.

"Okay. But I'm confused."

"Then you're thinking too much," he says. I'm about to agree when he adds, "Or you're not thinking enough."

"Thanks for clearing that up."

"Let's pretend like we're working," I say as we drive down the first fairway. "Your grandmother taught you to play music. Who taught you to play golf?"

"It's mostly Trader's fault," Willie says of his longtime golf pro, Larry Trader. "People want to know everything about the golf swing, but Trader always told me to 'just hit the ball.' It's not anything special. Little kids usually hit it great the first swing. Lots of people do. But when they start getting instruction, they go all to hell. Maybe that's why golf is the great humbler."

"Some guys think women are the great humblers."

"Okay, golf *and* women," Willie allows. "That's why a woman golf pro can be deadly."

Distracted by the burden of entertaining me, Willie hits a terrible shot, and I ask if he wants a mulligan.

"I've hit so many bad shots, I don't care anymore," Willie tells me. "I like to think of it as cowboy-Zen golf."

Cowboy-Zen golf. That fits Willie to a tee.

"So why do you think we keep playing when we're not all that good?"

"The best thing about golf is, you can play it a long time. The way I see it, it'll keep you from weaving baskets."

"You don't seem worried about basket weaving."

"I'm just worried about this shot."

Swinging hard, he hits one over the water on number three and flies it up close to the pin.

"Hey, I may turn pro!" he says in triumph. "And right after that, I'm gonna take up brain surgery!"

"When do you have to start acting like an old man?" I ask.

"That's up to you," Willie says with a smile. And he's right. I am the one talking like an old man.

"So what have you learned in the last decade?" I press.

"Nothing," Willie tells me. "I don't think I've learned anything since I turned thirty."

"What'd you learn then?"

"I can't remember. But I'm sticking by it anyway. My motto is to keep doing it wrong until I like it that way."

"So what's the secret of life?" I ask.

"Clean living and dirty thoughts," Willie quips as he leaves a putt on the front lip.

"Never up, never in," I say.

"Makes for a boring marriage," he adds. This is one of those days when Willie has an answer for everything.

With the weather turning cold, after six holes we head across the road to Willie's old western movie town, Luck, Texas. "When you're not here," Willie says, "you're out of Luck."

After beating him at a game of pool, I pour two cups of coffee and he draws a couple of shots of a clear liquid from a wooden cask behind his saloon-style bar.

"A little moonshine will help your chess game," he tells me.

"I doubt it."

With the coffee and the shine, we sit down to two games Willie's really good at—chess and conversation. By the time we get the pieces set up, our contest is already like watching a war of words on CNN.

"We were talking about things we have and haven't learned," I remind him as I move a pawn out.

"Golf is better than no golf," Willie replies with a pawn move I've never even seen.

"Good golfers don't listen to bad caddies," I reply.

"Bad caddies don't listen to anyone."

"Okay," I tell him, taking a sip of the shine, which burns rather like, well, moonshine. "Good bartenders don't listen to bad drunks."

"The last drink," says Willie as he takes my knight, "is always a mistake."

"Safe sex is better than Lite beer," I say as I take a pawn in return. Already I'm losing.

"The devil doesn't drink Lite beer," he adds.

"God doesn't drink decaf," I add, switching from the moonshine to the coffee.

"Horseshit," Willie says flatly.

"What?" I ask, realizing a moment too late that I've moved my bishop into a trap.

"Horseshit," he says again. "All the whipped cream in the world won't improve it."

Between the chess and the conversation, I don't know where to move or what to say. Into my silence, Willie tosses the following little ditty.

"Breast-feeding," he says.

"What about it?"

"Nothing. Just breast-feeding."

We think about that a while, then Willie asks what I've learned.

"Listening is more mysterious than talking," I tell him.

And he says, "What?"

Almost out of material, I decide to go for the whole enchilada. "Work for yourself," I say. "The best bets in Vegas are casino stocks. And beautiful women are trouble."

He thinks about it, then adds, "All women are beautiful."

Moving his queen forward, he says, "Check."

I move my king, but can see I that I'm toast.

"No one story is true," I say. "They all are."

"Did you write that?" Willie asks.

"No," I confess. "Hemingway. And Shakespeare wrote the Bible."

"That's what *he* says."

About three moves ahead, I think I see a way to get out of Willie's trap and put him in mine.

"What's the best golf advice?" I ask, making my first move toward the win.

"Don't think no negative thoughts."

"So what's the best age?" I've almost got him now.

"This one," he says. Then he slides his rook down opposite my king. "Checkmate."

"Dang," I say.

"Breakfast of astronauts," Willie trumps.

Don't Think No Negative Thoughts

"Still confused?" he asks as I stand to go.

"Always."

"But you hit the ball good out there today," he tells me.

I think about it and realize he's right. I did hit it good.

"What kind of golf stuff were you thinking about?" Willie asks.

"I don't remember."

"There you go," Willie says in conclusion. "There you go."

CHAPTER 21

Champions Gate

"It's not an odd little tip that's going to help you; it's not necessarily buying a new driver. It's understanding fundamentals and then sticking to them that will help you become a better golfer."

—David Leadbetter

Welcome to Champions Gate!" Sean Hogan told me as I stepped onto the practice tee at David Leadbetter's worldwide headquarters in Orlando, Florida. And what a facility it is. Surrounding a large office and instruction building is an array of practice areas—a gigantic driving range with covered hitting tees, a separate hitting area where David works privately with pros and duffers like me, and numerous pitching areas with multiple targets for practicing approach shots with distance accuracy. Add an eight-acre short-game practice area with lots of greenside bunkers and giant putting greens, and you get a good idea of why Nick Price flies his helicopter here for his lessons with David.

Indoors, the facility has two separate rooms with V1 computerized video systems, four other video monitor rooms for lesson analysis, and a network that hooks up all the instructors' computers.

If a Leadbetter-taught pro is having problems on the road, all the pro has to do is videotape his swing, save it on his laptop, then e-mail it to David at Champions Gate or wherever else he happens to be. That same technique—which Leadbetter's team calls the Distance Learning Program—will soon be available to the general public.

In a lower tech but still efficient mode, a couple of the rooms have wall-to-wall mirrors, which show infinite, ever-diminishing reflections of your swing, which I call the "Barbershop Learning Program."

The school also has a physical therapy room, and a pro shop with clubs, books, videos, clothes, and swing aids on sale. As the most successful instructor in the history of the game, Leadbetter is an industry all to himself.

Sean and I hadn't seen each other in the four months since he'd left Austin, and we were both eager to get to work on my swing. I was scheduled for two solid days of instruction with him, plus as much time with David as he could squeeze in.

Once again, Sean and I started with my hitting a number of seven-irons and drivers for the video camera. When we moved back inside to look at the video, Leadbetter stopped in to get an update on my progress. Despite my recent troubles, after David watched just a couple of my swings on tape, he was confident they could get me started back in the right direction.

"Sean's going to work with you on some specific drills," David told me. "And I think you'll make big strides in the next six weeks doing these drills without a golf ball and giving your muscle memory a real run-through."

Then Sean and I got down to work. After a thorough refresher of the things we'd worked on in Austin, Sean reduced my focus to four simple stop-and-go positions that I'd be able to rehearse with or without him present. Repeat the positions enough times, and eventually I'd be able to groove a proper swing path.

First, starting from a solid setup, I'd turn my body and take the club halfway back in a fully set position, the shaft pointing to the sky. And then I stop to give myself the feel of this position. At this point, both thumbs are also pointing up along my swing path.

Second, I simply follow my thumbs up, completing my shoulder turn until the club is set at the top, with my right arm feeling high above my shoulder. And then I stop again.

Third, the move from the top is just a slight transition, a shift of my weight from my right side onto my left toe. This is the downswing starting from the ground, not from the top. Having moved only slightly, again I stop.

Fourth, I give myself a tiny bump up to regain some momentum, then swing under to the inside quarter of the ball.

"Set; thumbs to the top; transition to the left toe; pump and swing," Sean coaches me, "then the club releases in front of you to a high finish."

When I'm more or less comfortable with this sequence of positions, Sean instructs me to do the same thing without the stop-and-go.

"I want you to hit all those positions at regular speed," he says, "but with your eyes closed."

It's strange at first, but with my eyes closed, I really can feel the positions.

"Now do it all at regular speed with eyes open; and finally I want you to do it at regular speed and hit a ball. That's four times through the positions for every ball you strike."

I do as he says, but I'm still not coming at the inside of the ball. The "old effect" is still in place.

Searching for the problem as I continue the drill, I find that thinking of moving my weight to the left toe seems to make me come over the top.

"It's almost as if my right shoulder wants to go to my left toe," I tell Sean. "If I think of the transition going to the ball of my left foot, it seems to work better."

Making this slight modification, I hit a long, high draw, and Sean nods his head in approval.

"You're doing a little drill here," he tells me, "and even in these stop-and-go positions, you're hitting pretty great shots. With the improved positions, a little rhythm and a little perseverance, you're ball striking is likely to go through the roof."

The Old Man and the Tee

Though we work on other things as well, for much of the next
two days, I continue to repeat this sequence: stop-and-go through the
four positions, then regular speed but with eyes closed, then with
eyes open, and then concentrating on the same positions as I hit a ball.
And the more I repeat this drill, the better I hit the ball.

After a much-needed lunch break, I'm again doing my drills when I
notice that Charles Howell III is hitting drivers on the tee next to me.
Wearing a short-sleeve shirt that reveals him to be as big around as a
beanpole, Charles is almost six feet tall, weighs maybe 150 pounds,
and is absolutely ripping his drives.

In the last four tourneys of his rookie season, Charles won $1.4
million with a four-tournament total of 67 strokes under par. In 2002,
he won the Michelob Championship, earned $2.7 million, and was
ranked number one in total driving.

Even knowing that, I still can't believe how far and how accurately
he's hitting those drives. They're all traveling what I figure to be well
over three hundred yards, and they all seem to be stopping in an area
about the size of a small green.

I'd met Charles at Pebble Beach when he received his 2001 PGA
Rookie of the Year Award, the night before the fateful phone call about
my father. When he takes a break at Champions Gate, I can't resist asking him about working with Leadbetter for half of Charles's twenty-
two years on earth.

"From twelve on, I spent a lot of time with David and his assis-
tants. Even when I wasn't here, I always knew what to work on. Price
and Faldo were great role models—they'd spend hours on the range
hitting balls."

"And you're still here hitting balls."

"David's like a second father to me," Charles says with pride. "I
live in Orlando for the sole reason of David Leadbetter. I've even got
him playing again. We're having a lot of fun."

"So what's the best thing you ever learned from David?" I ask.

"Work ethic," Charles tells me. "Without a doubt, it's work ethic."

With that, of course, we wish each other luck, and both go back to work.

By midafternoon, I'm getting seriously tired. My legs are starting to cramp, and my hands feel like boiled potatoes. Still, it is a rare privilege to be here, and I didn't want to miss any opportunity to pick up something I might need.

After an hour on my own, my shots are starting to pepper the entire range when Sean drags over a cube-shaped cushion about twenty inches across.

"Straddle this," he tells me.

Astride the hard cushion with both knees resting lightly against its sides, I address a ball in front of me.

"That'll keep your lower body stable," Sean tells me. "And don't forget to slow down a little. Take your time between swings and during your swing."

With the cushion stabilizing my legs—and hitting at a less obsessive pace—within a dozen shots, I can feel my trajectory and accuracy returning. Months later, whenever I feel my legs getting loose, I can still imagine that cushion between my knees and regain that stable base. And the first thing I try to remember when I put a club in my hand is "Slow down."

At the end of the day, Leadbetter strolls over to watch me hit a few while Sean videotapes my swing. We all move inside to watch the tapes, but David has already seen all that he needs. The videotape is not for his understanding, but for mine.

"Fantastic progress!" Leadbetter tells me. "But you can still do better."

Putting a seven-iron in my hands, he swings my arms back to the top of my backswing.

"You're getting the club higher, pointing pretty much at the target, which is good. But having it laid off so much for so long, the more you can feel that the club at the top is pointed slightly *across* the target line, it'll be easier to get the club coming down inside the line."

"Pointed a little right of the target at the top," I repeat.

Lifting my hands gently, David pulls my arms higher, though my lack of flexibility at age forty-nine makes it difficult for me to get my arms and the club where he wants them to be.

All year, the big hole in my game-improvement plan had been physical training. I'd meant to get into a serious program of stretching and weight training, but just couldn't make myself do it. As far as I know, my dad hadn't exercised or been in a gym since he was on the swim team at Texas A&M in 1939, and I was a nut that hadn't fallen far from the tree. The fact is, I hate the gym. I had been swimming a half a mile or more several times a week and stretching on my own, but that was it. Push comes to shove, elbow bends are more fun than squats, and feeding a beer belly is more fun than starving your abs.

If my arms wouldn't get as high as David wanted them, then I was prepared to pay the price. The funny thing is, David seems to see it the same way.

"If you can't reach that high, it's okay," he tells me. "You don't want to twist your torso, which will then make the club swing around your body the way you used to do it. Wherever you get it to, when the club is lined up at the top, it should be above your right shoulder. From here you can hit the ball. Can you feel that?"

Putting the club up there, I make a move at the ball.

"That's it," David tells me. "Keep your knee-flex, less activity with your legs, then close your eyes and feel that."

"Remember," he adds, "everyone's swing is different, so everyone has different points to check. For you: check your posture, make sure your knees aren't dancing all over the place. Check to make sure your right arm is in a supporting position instead of this trapped look with the club behind you like you had before. You've got to get that right elbow into a position where the club is up above it. If you do all that, you can continue to make progress."

By this time, I'm so tired I can barely hold the seven-iron and my right arm at the top. Somewhere in my slow-ticking brain, I can almost grasp the positions Sean has given me, plus the higher position at the top that Leadbetter wants. They're there, but at the same time, I can't quite get my mind wrapped around them.

All those years ago when I was given one first impromptu juggling lesson, I couldn't quite understand the rhythm involved in the exchange of balls from hand to hand. For hours that afternoon, I'd tried to keep those balls in the air, but just couldn't do it.

Lying in bed that night, I was almost asleep—my conscious mind letting go of its rigid control on my body—when it all suddenly became clear. Even with my eyes closed, I could *see* myself juggling.

Hopping out of bed, I switched on the light, grabbed three chess pieces, and began to juggle as if I'd been doing it for years. All I had to do was let go of my conscious mind and let myself juggle.

Drained after a day of hitting balls at Leadbetter, I fell into a much larger and cushier bed at the Villas of Grand Cypress than the bunk I'd been in all those years ago when I learned to juggle in the middle of the night, but as I began to slip into dreamland, I had the same awakening in my mind. Suddenly I could *feel* the things that Sean and David had been teaching me. Even with my eyes closed, I could see myself in those swing positions. All I had to do was let go. Deep down inside, I knew how to play golf. I just had to let myself.

Springing out of bed with the excitement of a five-year-old at Christmas, I was rehearsing my positions when I glanced over at the clock.

It was three A.M.

Man, I have lost my mind! I thought. Apparently that's what I needed though, because my new swing suddenly felt very natural.

Fundamentals of Golf

The Price of Steep Golf

In the words of David Leadbetter

Of all the geometric angles in the swing, the most important is the plane of the downswing. Every poor player for the most part gets too steep on the ball, with the club coming down on too vertical an angle.

We call this an outside-to-inside swing, but that's just the appearance. Very few people, if you take the target line, actually swing outside the target line. The big problem is that their swing path or plane is way too steep.

If you do certain things correctly, the club almost swings itself. In order for that to happen, you've got to get the club up on a steeper plane on the backswing. If it gets too flat and moves around your body going back, then the club will have a tendency to get out and steep on the downswing.

When people are too steep, we get them to practice hitting balls on a side-hill lie, with the ball higher than their feet. That's probably the best way to feel what it's like to swing on a more correct plane.

CHAPTER 22

Gentle Ben

————

"We're only here for a short time. Never hurry. Never worry. And always take time to smell the flowers."

—Walter Hagen

Ｈow ironic that thirty years ago, just as I befriended a guy who would soon be one of the most famous golfers of our time, I was on the verge of leaving the game. But there I was, a freshman at the University of Texas and a fraternity brother of co-NCAA golf champion Ben Crenshaw. Every time I saw Ben back then, I wanted to ask him for a putting lesson; I wanted to know what he knew, but I didn't want to impose.

Flash forward thirty years and two green jackets for Ben. Not long before my dad died, I hosted a golf-book panel at the Texas Book Festival. Before a packed house in the beautiful Senate chamber of the Texas capitol, my panelists were three of the greatest names in Texas golf—Dan Jenkins, Bud Shrake, and Ben Crenshaw.

That afternoon was one perfect round of golf. We were a great foursome on a course with mile-wide fairways and cups the size of basketball hoops. If we went even slightly astray, the crowd just kicked the ball back into play.

I'd ask Dan to talk about Hogan, Bud to talk about Penick, and Ben to talk about his recent Ryder Cup captaincy and victory. It was funny, touching, and inspiring. We all left feeling privileged to have been a part of it.

And that's how, thirty years after Ben and I were fraternity brothers, I finally worked up the nerve to ask him for that putting lesson. Crenshaw had met Pip when we were at UT, so despite the fact that Ben is busy with golf, work, and family, he agreed to help me out. Ben had lost Harvey and his wonderful father, Charlie, so I think he knew what I was up against.

There is a brotherhood of loss, I was learning, in simply growing old.

We met at Ben's home course, the Austin Golf Club, another natural Crenshaw design, this one located in the Hill Country west of Austin.

I could not have looked more out of place, or less like a golfer. Having been cast in the upcoming Disney movie *The Alamo,* I'd let my beard grow long and my hair even longer. Six-foot-seven, my weight up to 240 for the movie, and shaggy all over, I looked like Bigfoot in *Harry and the Hendersons.*

At age fourteen Ben Crenshaw pulled out a Wilson 8802 blade putter he'd found in a barrel of putters in Harvey Penick's pro shop. He then made a few passes with it. Turning to his father, young Ben said, "Dad, I'd like to have it."

Making one of the best decisions of his life, Charlie Crenshaw Sr. bought the putter that helped Ben win two Masters and over $7 million on tour. The cost of the putter? Twenty dollars.

Ben's description of his favorite tool is a bit more modest.

"I'm still putting with the same putter," he told me.

Stolen twice, broken at least once, Little Ben fits in Gentle Ben's hand as if it had grown there.

"I heard something incredible about putters last night," Ben said excitedly. "I drove to Houston for Jackie Burke's eightieth birthday, and he said, 'Ben, it makes no difference what a putter looks like; you're still gonna end up with flat steel down there.'"

Hands, eyes, flat steel—all that Crenshaw needs.

Dropping a ball on the expansive practice green, Crenshaw assumes the role of teacher.

"When I go out and putt," Ben tells me, "I mostly think about how hard to hit it. Unless you're very close, the pace on a putt to me is so much more important than the line. Almost anything outside of six feet is a pace putt. And every day I just work on how hard I'm going to hit it."

Looking to a hole about ten feet away, Crenshaw strokes the ball, which breaks left and falls in the cup.

"There are two things I never heard any teacher other than Harvey say: Just get comfortable to the ball; and don't try to look like anybody else. What that meant to me when I was a young kid is you had to develop your own style. You do what's comfortable for you. Some people stand more left-sided. That's what I do. If I feel a little more weight on my left side, it feels more natural and a little more like a chip."

Dropping another ball, Ben makes another ten-footer.

"When I was a kid," Ben continues, "Harvey was such a stickler for little shots around and on the green. One day he said, 'I don't understand why people don't putt a little bit more like they chip.'

"What Harvey meant was to putt like a plain little running seven-iron shot—play the ball a little on your left side and keep your hands running in front. I guess that's a microcosm of what I try to do in putting. I try to have my hands just in front and my weight on my left, then keep my hands nice and low through that putt. I'm trying to let that putter swing out on that line."

Another ball aimed at a different hole, and Ben makes a twelve-footer to demonstrate his hands leading the putter head. Though I'm trying hard to listen to his every word, I'm also distracted by wondering if he's ever going to miss.

"So let me carry this one step further," Ben explains. "The idea is that I start with the shaft a little bit forward. To me, in any good golf shot, your hands just barely lead the clubhead when you hit the ball. And that's what I feel when I putt well; I feel like my hands get there just slightly before my clubhead."

Stepping up to one of the balls, Ben shows me his setup and grip.

"I like to grip it lightly and let the weight of the putter do the work. I'm trying to just take the putter and let it swing on its own, so a starting position with hands forward is fairly critical to me. That way, I can let the weight of the putter settle at the back, then move it through the ball."

Choosing a fifteen-foot downhill putt, Ben makes number four in a row, with the ball just reaching the hole before it drops. Then he begins to talk about speed.

"I never saw any good putters go racing by the hole. Jack Nicklaus was one of the best. He never put a lot of pressure on his putting, because his distance control was unbelievable. When he wasn't hitting the ball well and left himself longer putts, he could almost always put it up there close and assure himself of a two-putt."

Aiming at a still farther hole, Ben strokes yet another ball into the cup. By now, his inability to miss is almost all I can think about. Ben, on the other hand, seems perfectly capable of putting and talking about putting at the same time.

"Bobby Jones made more sense to me than anybody when he wrote that 'any little shot in golf is still a swing.' A two-foot putt you miss sometimes because you forget it's a swing. A bunker shot, a chip shot, or a two-footer—it's still a swing. Basically, Bobby Jones said putting is three things: how to gauge the slope accurately, how hard to hit it, and the basic putting stroke is a sweep.

Searching for the correct words, Ben tells me he knows another good Bobby Jones line: "Anybody who hopes to reduce putting to mechanics and some wild theory can expect disappointment."

"So what do you think about Pelz, who places mechanics above all else?" I ask.

"Dave's very good," Ben tells me. "When you practice, you practice mechanics. But when you play, you rely on what you've worked on *and* you need a little mechanism for what's going on in your imagination and what you see. Putting is very much in your eyes, your brain, *and* your hands."

Over the years, I've noticed that whenever Ben thinks of Harvey, a smile comes to his face and eyes. Now he showed me that smile again.

"When we grew up, we practiced putting by having a putting match against somebody. Harvey always thought that was the best practice, because you were putting at different holes. You were working on your touch and your imagination and your timing, plus you were placing some pressure on yourself at the same time.

"Harvey would say, 'You should never practice the same putt over and over. That practice is good for that particular putt right there, but you'll never have that putt again anywhere for the rest of your life.' "

The thing I was most interested in was the shape of Ben's stroke.

"What about the debate about keeping the putter square to the line," I ask, "versus the way you do it—opening the blade on the backstroke and closing it as you come to the ball?"

"It's good to be cognizant of those things," Ben tells me, "but still the things that count are knowing how hard to hit that putt, how solidly you hit that ball, and letting that clubhead swing out to what you see. There has been every conceivable kind of stroke that worked. Billy Casper putted with the ball very close to his feet and he'd just pop the ball—he'd pop it!

"In 1972, I played Merion the first time with a friend who said, 'Ben we're gonna play with a guy today, and you're not gonna believe the way he putts!' His name was Bud Humphrey, and he was a very good player—about seventy-five years old at the time. I'll never forget it as long as I live—he'd take the club straight up behind the ball, and he'd come straight down on it and cut it! He'd just drop the putter on the ball and he'd put the ball in the hole."

Ben shows me the guy's impossible stroke, and, sure enough, Ben makes the putt.

"What about reading putts?" I ask. "Seems like very few middle-handicappers realize a lot of their short-game problems are rooted in poor green-reading."

Pointing thirty-five feet up a hill, I indicate a cup just over a small mound.

"How about that one up on top of the hill there?"

"That's a fun putt," Ben says. "It doesn't break much, but you can tell that the speed is extremely important."

Ben drops a ball in front of me, and I putt it up the hill. Despite his advice, I'm thinking break, not distance, and I leave the ball ten feet short. Setting up to a second ball, I stroke this one ten feet past.

Ben drops his ball, stands over it, his stance open to the line, and strokes the ball up the hill, leaving it about eight inches short. This is the first putt he's missed. A second ball he rolls two feet past, and a third one he makes.

"You have a pretty long, slow backswing on that long putt," I tell him.

"I've got to," Ben tells me. "I'm trying not to *hit* it. I'm letting the weight gather back there. If I take a nice long syrupy type of back-stroke, I can get the putter back to where it doesn't take so much effort in hitting it."

Trying the same thing, I let the weight gather behind me, and twice in a row I put a ball close to the distant hole.

We walk to the balls, and Ben picks a long, downhill, left-to-right putt. I ask if he's looking at a line on my golf cart past the hole, but he walks down and shows me the place he's looking at, a dark spot about halfway to the hole. He's picking his line by looking along the line of the putt, while I'm staring off in the distance like a sightseer.

"On a putt like this," Ben tells me, "I think the worst thing you can do is let the ball get away below the hole. On a breaking putt, I'm always looking for the highest line I can possibly put it on, high and soft, always on a putt like this. On a downhill breaking putt, your margin of error is a lot wider above the hole than below it."

Putting the ball, Ben rolls it over the dark spot he indicated earlier and slides the ball down the hill near the cup.

. . .

For over an hour, we wander around his spacious practice green, picking out holes and talking about line and speed and the joy of putting just for fun. And putt after putt, it seems that Ben can't miss.

Moving to the clubhouse for lunch, the talk switches to architecture and green design, with Ben telling me about his affection for Dr. Mackenzie's contoured greens and the memorable putting surfaces of Cypress Point, Shinnecock, Augusta, and Pine Valley.

"All of them are challenging to your approach shot *and* your putting," he says. "I like that."

We talk about the fine walking course he's built at Austin Golf Club, and the majesty of Sand Hills, and about other projects he has under way. But still the conversation keeps coming back to putting.

One thing I'm curious about is where Ben looks when he sets up to the ball to putt.

"That's a good question," Ben tells me. "Bobby Jones said he didn't want to stare a hole in the ball. I'm conscious of the area—the ball *and* the putter—and I try to swing the putter through that area.

"Like any golf shot," Ben adds, "when you putt there's no substitute for hitting a ball in the middle of the clubface. Harvey was such a stickler with all his students. He'd say, 'I always want you to hit that ball on the sweet spot.'

"They use contact tape now to see where the ball hits, but Harvey used talcum powder. He'd put it on the ball, and it would leave a mark on the putter."

"Despite all that," Ben says in conclusion, "I'd rather see people make a free-flowing stroke than worry about absolute precision. Most of the time when I putt poorly, I'm not swinging the putter well. Maybe my grip is too tight. The important thing is, you want to get that pace, then let the putter head do all the work—just hang on lightly and let it swing."

And then we ate—good food, old friends, and a fine view. Inspired by the putting lesson, neither of us missed a single bite.

Fundamentals of Golf

Five Steps to Basic Putting

As taught by Ben Crenshaw

1. *Setting up to the ball, it's essential that you be comfortable and relaxed.*
2. *Make a natural sweeping stroke, letting the putterhead do the work. Remember the words of Bobby Jones, "Any stroke in golf must be a swing."*
3. *Your main thought is distance more than line. Any putt over six feet is a pace putt.*
4. *On keener greens, you need to be more pace oriented because your errors are going to be magnified.*
5. *Let the ball die in the hole. This what Harvey meant when he said, "Give luck a chance."*

CHAPTER 23

I Survived the Alamo

"Give 'em what-fer, Davy!"

—Buddy Ebsen to Fess Parker,
in *Davy Crockett, King of the Wild Frontier*

Just as in Willie and Waylon's song, my mama didn't want her babies to grow up to be cowboys. She didn't let 'em pick guitars and drive them old trucks. Let 'em be doctors and lawyers and such, she declared. And so it came to be.

Growing up on a West Texas ranch during the Great Depression taught my mother that there wasn't much future in riding and roping. Running another ranch with my father during World War II did not improve her opinion of the cowboy life.

During his time in the nursing home, though Pip was unable to recall my name, he could remember every detail of those years on the River Ranch. He'd never been on a horse, Pip told me, and had one day to learn the ranch's entire layout and operation from his brother-in-law, Marvin, who was leaving for pilot training in the Army Air Corps (from which Uncle Marvin would never return). The two of them spent twelve hours in the saddle that day, the first brutal, butt-blistering day of three long years of solo cowboying for my dad.

No wonder my parents didn't want their kids to grow up in the saddle. About the closest I came to being a cowboy was wearing a Davy Crockett coonskin cap I got for Christmas and pretending I was one of the heroes of the Alamo.

It's funny how life happens. When I started my ten-stroke quest, my commitment to my game was to take precedence over all matters— work, writing, even women, as my wife and daughters had promised to help me free as much time as possible. But the one thing I hadn't taken into consideration was that coonskin cap.

I met screenwriter John Lee Hancock almost ten years ago at the Austin Film Festival soon after he was asked by Warner Brothers Studio to adapt *Fast Greens* for the screen. John had all the work he could handle at the time, but we remained friends. Several years later, he asked me to play a small part in a baseball movie he was about to shoot in Austin called *The Rookie*. The only trick was, I'd have to cut my hair short. To my everlasting regret, I told him I was waiting to hear if *The Sopranos* was going to bring me back for their fourth season on HBO, in which case I'd be expected to show up with the same long hair I'd had when I played that narcoleptic guy the previous season.

I'd been cast in *The Sopranos* after meeting the show's creator, David Chase, at the Austin Film Festival. So, if you want to work in movies, I'd recommend you attend the Austin Film Festival. And if you're wondering what any of this has to do with golf, after *The Rookie* was a critical and commercial hit, Disney made John Lee Hancock an offer no Texas boy could refuse. Did he want to direct the most expensive Western in history, a $100-million retelling of our epic tale, the Alamo?

Having missed *The Rookie,* I practically jumped over the proverbial Texas Lone Star when John Lee gave me a second chance. Did I want to be in *The Alamo?*

"Does the pope wear a funny hat?" I replied. "Is wrestling fake? Is a six-pound robin fat? Yes, yes, and yes. And yes to *The Alamo,* too." If you grew up in Texas, you can't say no to a coonskin cap.

Though the movie was scheduled to film for the final five months of my yearlong golf quest, I wasn't too worried about its effects on my game. My role was small, and the nature of movies is that actors spend most of their time waiting. I figured I'd just build myself a little driving range and practice out back behind the Alamo.

Like all the actors in the film, my work started with Alamo boot camp, which served as my first warning that my golf skills were about to get trampled under a stampede of hoofbeats. For two long weeks, we worked hard trying to make ourselves look like we were born in a saddle, drilling with and firing flintlock rifles and loading gigantic cannons that had to be rolled by hand back into the blocks before we fired them. It was literally a blast.

Needless to say, I wasn't hitting any golf balls, but my worries melted away when I put on my Alamo costume—thick cotton pants, shirt, and vest, topped by a long buckskin coat that looked as if it'd been slashed and left to die in a dumpster. Instead of a kitsch coonskin cap, I had a beat-up buckskin hat, which was even better. With my beard cut back to giant muttonchops that made me look like a homeless Neil Young, I was literally the Big Man at the Alamo.

Striving for historical accuracy, the final Alamo battle had been scheduled for a month of night shoots. Called to the set in late afternoon, we'd eat breakfast—which is what a movie crew calls the first meal, no matter the time of day—and be in makeup and wardrobe by dark.

Not only would it have been impossible to hit balls in the darkness, there wasn't a moment to spare. Put on your wardrobe, go to set, then work till lunch—which is what a movie crew calls the second meal, even it's at one in the morning—then we'd go back to the set and work till dawn. Dragging my butt home with a smile on my face because I was living out my childhood fantasy, I was happy, but far too tired for golf.

The Old Man and the Tee

I played Isaac Millsap, leader of a group from Gonzales known as the Immortal Thirty-two. The only reinforcements who came to the aid of the Alamo defenders, the thirty-two died like Crockett, Travis, and the rest at the hands and under the bayonets of the Mexican army.

One of my scenes was a midnight ride at the head of my men as we snuck into the Alamo under cover of darkness. It wasn't until I was mounted on my horse—and at this point I hadn't been on a horse since training six weeks before—that I learned the scene had been changed into a fast ride across open ground as we tried to gain the safety of the compound before the Mexican army cut us down.

Complicating my ride was a heavy tangle of gear and straps— a long muzzle-loading rifle, a wooden canteen, all kinds of satchels and powder horns, plus a pigsticker that would have made Jim Bowie's famous knife look like a letter opener. Riding beside me was my friend Blue Deckert, and close behind us were thirty stuntmen, professional riders every one. Inside the compound were one hundred and sixty actors and extras in full costume and a crew too numerous to count. Casting a beautiful blue pall in the winter fog that enveloped us were gigantic trucks and towers holding the world's largest lights— the same units used to illuminate the demolition of the World Trade Center. Surveying the scene, I saw the weak link in all this effort, and it was me.

With all that gear and my on and off riding experience, I found myself once again suffering from a lack of confidence. On the other hand, I was living out my greatest childhood fantasy, which happens to be at the heart of so many things Texan. Knowing they'll be given no quarter, two hundred odd defenders hold out for eleven days against a force of four thousand, all in the name of freedom. *That* is why people remember the Alamo. You want to know why everything in Texas seems bigger than life? Because the Alamo really was bigger than life. And now it was up to me to not screw it up.

On the first rehearsal, as we rode tight through the main gates, my horse bolted at a whirring high-speed camera, which sounded very much like a rattlesnake. Hanging on, I loped in as fast as I could, jumped off on my mark, and approached Billy Bob Thornton, who looked every bit of his part of Davy Crockett.

"That was great!" I heard from the darkness when we finished the scene. "Now let's try the ride full speed."

Full speed? I thought. That *was* full speed.

Climbing back on our horses, we rode back out, turned around, and did it again, faster. After that, we did it faster still. About fifteen takes later, I was so tired from climbing on and off that horse with all that gear that I wasn't sure I could get up there one more time. At that moment, the assistant director said, "Great! Moving on to the next shot!"

By the time I filmed my favorite scene—in which my character writes a letter of farewell to his blind wife and six children—my saddle soreness was gone, but, unfortunately, so were my golf lessons. Having focused on horses and guns, I didn't have a *clue* how to hit a golf ball. I knew that the way I *used* to hit the ball was no good for me any more, but I simply couldn't find the new swing that I'd worked so hard to create and groove.

With just three months remaining till my rerun at Pebble Beach, there was little doubt that I'd remember the Alamo.

I did, however, finally get in a little Alamo golf. A month after my work on the movie ended, the cast and crew of *The Alamo,* along with various ringers and sandbaggers, reconvened at Austin's Forest Creek Golf Club for the Alamo Golf Tournament. Playing in a four-man scramble format, the teams represented various departments on the film—wardrobe, camera crew, wranglers, and so on.

Dennis Quaid and I were going to be the center poles of an actors' team, but Dennis had a family commitment. My partners weren't as famous (and weren't four-handicaps like Dennis), but they had names like Kondo and Slab, and I thought we looked like winners.

Coming up the eighteenth fairway, we were informed we needed one more birdie for victory. Playing my pal Reed Clemmons's perfect drive seventy-five yards from the green, I got a big cheer from the gallery when I stuck a sand wedge ten feet from the hole. Then we all missed the putt and lost the Alamo again, this time by a single thrust of the blade.

And the victors, you may wonder? Who else? The Mexican army. I guess history really does repeat itself.

CHAPTER 24

Three Days in the Valley

———————

"It's not how you putt, it's where you putt from. You want to be a better putter? Chip the ball closer to the hole."

—Dave Pelz

About the time I finished my work on *The Alamo* and was trying to find out how to get my game going again, I received an e-mail from my friend Curt Sampson, who is a rare combination of fine writer and skilled golfer.

"I have an idea of how you can achieve your goal of ten shots," Curt wrote, "First, stop taking lessons, except for the short game. Second, third, and fourth, practice your short game. And when you do hit balls, try hitting every club in the bag 120 yards. This will get some feel in your shots and some play in your play."

Reminded that I'd almost waited too long in my year to dedicate myself to the short game, a week later I set off to see if the Dave Pelz Scoring School could get me back on track.

"Three days that will change your game forever." That's Dave Pelz's motto for his short-game academies, and you have to admit, it's got a pretty good ring.

The Old Man and the Tee

There's probably not a player in the world—Tiger included—whose game wouldn't be improved by three days of intensive short-game instruction. If you think you don't need what Pelz has to offer, keep in mind that sixty-six tour pros have *paid* to attend the Pelz schools. Among those pros are Vijay Singh, Lee Janzen, and Phil Mickelson, the undisputed king of the short game.

A former NASA physicist decided to take a scientific approach to the question of how to score better at golf. For the past twenty-five years Dave Pelz has studied every conceivable aspect of golf around and on the green, written several bestselling instruction books, and created all kinds of teaching aids to help you get the ball in the hole.

Though the headquarters of the Dave Pelz Institute is located not far from my house, there is no Pelz school in Austin, which is why I found myself in La Quinta, California, for three days of short-game and putting instruction.

Being a Palm Springs rookie, I arrived expecting Pelz's Ranch at La Quinta to be part of the classic La Quinta Resort and Spa where I'd booked a room for the weekend. Silly me, the whole *town* is called La Quinta. Ten minutes from the resort, the Dave Pelz Scoring Game School is located at the former Ahmanson ranch, whose original owner built his own short-game course surrounding his Palm Springs retreat.

Our instructors are PGA pro Stefan Carlsmith, former head pro at Mauna Kea on the Big Island, and Dennis Close, who's been a golf pro for nearly four decades since growing up in the Midwest, where he was once the sand greens champion of the State of Kansas.

From eight to five for three days, seven of us will be learning the Pelz approach to the short game, and practicing what we've learned with nearly constant feedback. After stating our goals for the weekend—which can pretty much be summed up as lower scores and less humiliation around the green—we're each assigned a series of putting and chipping tests to assess our current lack of skills.

I complete all of these with a fair degree of success, making a higher than average number of putts from various distances, bouncing some sand shots into circles surrounding a hole, and twice beaning Pelz's painted face on a target net forty yards away. Though I still have things to learn at the school, I figure this confirms my short game is already pretty solid.

It won't take long for me to realize how wrong I am.

The first step in learning new skills, says Pelz, involves understanding what you'll be trying to do, so before we start any serious work on the practice facility, our group sits down for some basic schooling in the Pelz approach to lower scores.

According to Pelz, the short game accounts for over 60 percent of all golf shots, and almost 80 percent of shots lost to par. One mis-played chip or one weak putt and you've made bogey. You can either get used to it, or you can fix it by getting the ball closer to the hole.

One of the first things Pelz discovered in his studies, Stefan tells us, is that golfers' errors in the power game are more direction than distance. The opposite applies on shorter shots, where golfers' errors are more distance than direction, with your misses more likely to be short or long.

Listening as Stefan explains these concepts, I suddenly realize that—like most golfers—I've spent most of my life working on the wrong things. On the power game, where accuracy of direction is the key, I've primarily tried to hit the ball longer. On the short game, where distance is key, I've spent most of my time thinking about line.

Never again, I vow. From now on, it's accuracy from the tee and distance control around the greens.

"The key to efficient learning is feedback—immediate, accurate, and reliable," Stefan continues. "You can't learn without it."

The type of feedback we'll receive at the school will vary from video review and the use of Pelz inventions like his simple alignment guide made of PVC to direct feedback from measuring our results or simply holding our followthrough after a shot to see how our result compares to our intent.

Add in feedback from the instructors, and it suddenly becomes easy to feel what you're trying to do.

"Practice doesn't make perfect," says Pelz. "Practice makes permanent. Smart practice is what golfers need to do to improve."

Most amateurs, says Pelz, think of a short swing as a miniature version of their full swing, but different aspects of the golf game require different skills.

To maximize distance, the power game requires a hitting stroke with active body and hands.

For maximum accuracy, the putting game requires a pendulum stroke, where there is no body rotation and dead hands (which eliminate mistakes created by the strong muscles in our hands, muscles that tend to get us in particular trouble when the adrenaline is pumping).

The short game, on the other hand, requires what Pelz calls "the finesse swing," which combines hitting and the pendulum stroke, giving up unneeded power to achieve consistency and precision, but preserving the dead hands for maximum repeatability.

"Think of the short-game stroke as an effortless swing," Stefan tells us, "a synchronized turn of the upper and lower body, with dead hands through impact."

To demonstrate that your hands should pull the clubhead through impact, not push it, Stefan pulls a golf trolley across the room. The cart follows his hands effortlessly. But when he pushes the cart, it swerves right and left, and he must constantly steer it to keep it on line.

The same principle applies to your golf swing. Pulling the clubhead through your shot will result in a more stable, repeatable swing path through contact. If nothing else, pulling your wedges through the shot will often result in playable mishits instead of total disasters. Pulling through the shot also means you're accelerating through impact, with the maximum velocity of your clubhead in front of the ball, not behind it. Rather than teaching the idea of acceleration, which Pelz has found prompts his students to reactivate those "dead" hands, Pelz teaches his students to follow through higher than their backswing.

"If you swing too far back on a forty-yard shot," Stefan explains, "the mind says *too hard!* and you decelerate through the shot, which makes all kinds of bad things happen."

The key is a shorter backswing and a longer followthrough, a nifty piece of information that forever alters my understanding of the short game for the better.

I can't possibly reduce what we learned in three days to a few pages of description, but it's important to understand the Dave Pelz system of distance control, which involves dividing the backswing into four positions: 1. Getting started. 2. Hands back to belt buckle high, with a full wrist cock. 3. Lead arm parallel to ground and the club vertical. And 4. All the way back.

The corresponding positions in the followthrough are also numbered, with the addition of number five, which Pelz calls "a world-class finish." In the world-class finish, your hands are high on the followthrough, with your belt buckle and sternum facing the target and the butt of the club pointing at the target as well.

Because the followthrough is always longer than the backswing, a short chip would have a 1 backswing and a 2 finish, while a sixty-yard sand wedge might have a 4 backswing and a world-class finish, meaning you'd committed fully to the shot.

Having learned an overview of the short game, we divide into two groups, which turn out to be guys and chicks—either because the guys have been playing longer or because the chicks don't like us—and we move to the practice tees and putting greens to put theory into practice.

"To leave here chipping well is your main goal," Stefan tells us on day one.

On little chips around the green, most of us have been taught to minimize body movement and simply chip with a putting stroke. But Pelz found that when people try to use only their putting stroke to chip the ball, they tend to get flippy with their hands.

To prevent using the hands too much, a little synchronized turn of your body back and through helps you maintain the hand and club angle. Maintaining the angle you started with is the definition of "dead," or soft, hands. But don't start thinking that turn means you're generating coil or power with your lower body; the essence of the chip swing is a triangle formed by your arms and shoulders that swings back and through without the triangle changing shape.

Remembering the backswing and followthrough positions, Stefan reminds us, the chip swing is basically a 1 back, 2 finish.

To keep from hitting the ground first, the ball position is way back in the stance, off the back ankle, and the weight is a little forward.

"That'll help avoid the old the *groundus interruptus*," says Stefan. "Otherwise known as the chili dip, the power chunk, or simply hitting it fat."

Once I understand the shot, I don't need the first video review to show me that my wrists had been breaking down on contact and I've been flipping the clubhead at the ball. Now I have a good understanding of what I need to do.

On the second day, I'm still having trouble when Dennis comes over to tell me that my hands are still too active. I'm still trying to be a juggler.

"Imagine that the shaft is the barrel of a gun. You don't want to point that barrel at yourself or anyone else. The hands are forward at setup, so the barrel is pointed into the air in front of you. As you start back, it's still pointed up in front of your body. Same thing as you go back through. You have to pull through the shot."

Coming through the next one, I still let my wrists break down at contact.

"Bang! You just shot yourself," he says. "Every time you practice this shot, I want you to watch where it goes, then hold your position and say, 'Did I shoot myself?' "

The distance wedge swing—trying to fly a high soft shot to a target thirty to fifty yards away—is everyone's favorite shot at the school.

Like the other short-game shots, the distance wedge swing is a synchronized, effortless turn of the body. A shorter backswing to a longer followthrough lets the clubhead do the work. The ball is in the middle of your stance, your left foot turned halfway to the target and your weight 55 percent on your left side.

Despite the fact that I'd beaned Pelz's picture in the nose, a video review showed that I had no concept of what I was doing. Though I felt I was accelerating through the shot, I was instead swinging long to short, trying to impart spin on the ball with my hands instead of simply using the loft of the club. My lower body was also swaying like a hoochie-koochie dancer, which does not make a pretty picture.

"We'd like you to have on Chicago overshoes," Dennis told me. "Cement up to your waist and nothing moves except your arms and shoulders."

Hitting into a net thirty yards away, we were making a 2 backswing to a 3 finish. Another target at fifty yards required a 3 backswing pulling through to a 5, or world-class, finish.

"You want the ball to land like a butterfly with sore feet," Dennis said, quoting my fellow Texan Lee Trevino.

Ever since a long-ago one-hour lesson from Austin instructor Bill Moretti, I've been able to hit a great flop shot, but never really knew why. "Circus shot," my pals used to call it. On day two, Stefan said something that explained why I could hit that high, soft cut and which just illuminated my understanding of the short game.

"The trajectory of the shot mimics the finish of your swing. If you punch the ball and finish low, the ball-flight is low; if you make a high world-class finish, the ball flight is high."

All these years, I'd been trying to adjust the height of my short shots by the position of the ball in my stance, moving the ball forward to hit it high. But moving it forward often meant I'd strike the ground before the ball.

Every swing has a natural bottom to it, says Pelz. And that's where the ball needs to be in your stance. The loft of the shot is controlled by a combination of the loft of the club and the shape of the swing.

To get the shape I wanted, I just needed to choose the right finish to my swing.

Distance control on the shot is a combination of the right club and the right backswing. You can read the details in *The Dave Pelz Short Game Bible,* but as an example, I discover that I hit a sand wedge with a 3 backswing about fifty yards. Keeping the same backswing and followthrough, but switching to my lob wedge, I hit the ball about forty yards.

Combine three backswings with three wedges, you've got nine different distances. It takes me a little practice to learn the right combinations to hit from particular distances, but by the end of the second day, I am practically a deadeye with these distance wedge shots, using the length of my backswing and club selection to control the distance, and making certain to pull through to a full finish.

Through countless rounds of golf, I've worked to protect a terrible secret: *I ain't worth a damn out of the sand!*

I've drawn railroad tracks in the sand, aimed feet left and my clubhead at the hole, lifted the clubhead, turned my shoulders, and tried to pick it clean, not necessarily in that order. I've invoked assistance from the gods of golf and even considered voodoo. The reward for my efforts has been a sand save percentage that's far less than the interest I pay on my credit cards.

The lesson at Monty's school had kept me from leaving shots in the bunkers of Scotland, but, even so, I'd rarely gotten up and down. A Pelz video review of my sand technique showed a lot of errors: ball not far enough forward in my stance, my swing decelerating before contact, my body not finishing the swing.

Back in the bunker, Stefan gives me a recap of what he'd talked about inside.

"Everything points a little left—body, stance, shoulders, and swing line. Open the clubface. Make the same swing as the distance wedge shot—a 3 backswing with a 5 finish. The difference is that you're going to hit the ground first, so the ball position is farther forward in your stance, just off your left or lead instep. Do all that and you'll hit a high, soft shot."

"Aim left, ball forward, face open," I say to myself.

"A little more weight on your left side," he corrects me. "Then open the clubface, until the grooves point just in front of your left toes."

I do all of this, take a swing, and skank one into the lip of the bunker.

"Don't lay it off. Take it back on the target line with less wrist break."

I gave it a try and hit a low rocket straight right.

With summer coming on, it's hot in Palm Springs, well over a hundred degrees on all three days of our school, and I am now fighting a return of my sun problems from the summer before. Every time we move down into the practice bunkers to work on our sand shots, it's like stepping into a solar pizza oven.

"Pull, don't push," Stefan tells me. "You have to pull through the shot with the left hand. Finish high."

By this time, the other students don't even want to get in the same bunker with me. I'm as dangerous as a disgruntled postal worker on unpaid overtime. I'm trying to do what the boss tells me, but somehow it never works out.

So once again, it's back to video review, where—finally—another little light goes on in my head.

"What you should be trying to do," Stefan tells me, "is pass the ball with your clubhead."

Picking out one of my few good swings, he shows me the clubhead accelerating past the rising ball and leading the sand to the green, with the ball following just behind on a higher track.

"Use your body back and through, and swing through the ball to a full finish."

"Anything else?" I asked.

"Relax. It's just golf."

So that's what I do, and it works fairly well.

But did I conquer my fear of the sand? Did I take the weakest part of my game and make it one of my strong points, as Pelz recommends?

Well, the truth is, the sand shot is still hard for me. I do have a better understanding of how to do it, but to execute it well, I have to practice the shot before I play. I have to rebuild both my technique and my confidence.

On the other hand, how is that different from my driver or my long irons? With all the changes I've made in my swing, I can't play for beans if I don't hit a few warm-up shots, so why should it be any different from the sand?

At the very least, when I step into a bunker now, I have one final swing thought to carry me through.

Relax. It's just golf.

CHAPTER 25

Do You Have That in Red?

"You have to learn to take the bitter with the sour."

—Billy Wilder

Hoping to convince my wife that the trip to the Pelz School was about generating some income, and not just another part of my growing golf obsession, I followed the school with a swing through Southern California, where I watched for hitchhikers who might turn out to be big-time film producers in need of a screenwriter.

I know that doesn't sound like the best way to get hired, but for the last year it had turned up exactly the same number of assignments that my big-time Hollywood agent was able to produce—exactly zero.

The long and the short of unemployment, I guess, is that I once again had a lot of time to play golf. When I lived for almost ten years in Los Angeles—playing comedy clubs and writing television—finding a place to tee it up was not easy. To book a time at the old L.A. munis like Griffith Park or Rancho, you first had to consult an astrologer and

a Gregorian calendar, then get up hours before dawn and perform an-
cient mystic speed-dial rituals over your phone in hopes of getting an
answer from the Parks and Rec reservation line. If, by some miracle,
your incantations worked and an operator answered your call, the only
available times would be something like five in the morning or seven at
night.

That made it all the sweeter when I did get an invitation to play in
a celebrity pro-am in exchange for doing a little comic shtick. Of
course, the downside was when I showed up on the first tee, the other
guys in my foursome generally asked, "Which celebrity do you think
we'll get?"

Telling them that *I* was their celebrity, not Michael Jordan or Bill
Murray, was not the best way to start off a round of golf.

One of my favorite events was the Maury Luxford Tournament at
Lakeside Golf Club. Maury had been the original host of Crosby's
Clambake, and his memorial tournament was hosted by Bob Hope
himself.

"Golf's a hard game to figure," Hope told the audience one year at
our after-dinner show. "One day you slice it, shank it, hit into all the
traps, and miss every green. The next day, you go out and for no reason at all you really stink!"

Each year, we watched Mr. Hope grow more and more frail, but
when my pal Roger Reitzel or I introduced him at the evening show,
Hope would transform almost instantly from decrepit old man to the
comic pro who never met an audience he didn't like.

"I was so bad today, the gallery hung my bag in effigy!" he'd say.
"Last week Arnold Palmer told me how I could cut eight strokes off
my score . . . skip one of the par-threes!"

I was no longer sure he could even hear the laughter, but Hope always knew exactly how long to wait before the next joke.

"My opponent said he'd give me a stroke on fourteen if I gave him
a free throw. That sounded pretty good until he picked up my ball and
threw it in the pond!"

There wasn't a pond on fourteen, but the audience didn't care.

My God, it was Bob Hope! That was *better* than God! Hope had been playing so long his handicap was in roman numerals!

When he got too old to play in the tournament, Hope still wandered around the course. One year, David Wood had just hit his drive when Hope drove up in a cart, picked up David's ball, and drove away.

"He stole my ball!" David squealed in astonishment. "Bob Hope stole my ball!"

Maybe Hope had a garage full of balls he'd picked up on the course, I don't know, but the next year, I was about to tee off on a par five when a cart crossed into our fairway and stopped about three hundred yards from our tee.

"Is that Bob Hope?" I asked.

Sure enough, it was. We couldn't tell what hole he was playing—he still lived in a house adjacent to the course he'd founded with W. C. Fields and Bing Crosby, so as far as we were concerned, he owned the whole course. Finally, after five minutes of his just standing there and everyone in my group saying, "He's *way* out of range," I decided to hit.

When someone's in the driver danger zone, there are generally just two possible outcomes. Either you wait till they leave, then skull one about forty yards. Or you decide they're out of range and nearly skull them.

Guess which one I did.

The ball was barely off my clubhead when my entire group screamed "Fore!" in one deafening voice. We could have waked the dead across the way in Forest Lawn Cemetery before Hope heard us, of course, for he was deaf.

And while the longest drive of my life soared straight at America's most beloved comedian, I realized that I would forever be known as "The Man Who Killed Bob Hope." I was still yelling when the ball missed Hope's bobbing head by a matter of inches.

Appearing to have felt the wind of its passing, Hope looked up and saw my new Titleist about fifteen yards ahead of him. Picking up his own ball, Hope hobbled to my career (and near career-ending) drive, then whacked my ball back to the adjoining hole where he'd come from.

That night when I told him I was about to introduce him to the audience, Mr. Hope asked me where his drink was. He had mistaken me for the waiter (and the drink was in his hand). I didn't see how he could possibly remember his jokes. But once he was on stage, the magic was still there.

"An old man came up to me this morning," Hope began, "and he asked if I wanted a caddie. I said okay, so he picks up my bag and my partner's bag and runs to the tee.

" 'How *old* are you?' I asked. And the guys says, 'Ninety-four. But this is nothing. I'm getting married tomorrow.'

" 'Why would you want to get married at ninety-four?' I asked.

"And the old guy answers, 'Who says I *want* to?' "

The laughter sounded like a bomb going off. Mr. Hope waved and started off the stage. And all I could think was, Boy, I'm glad I didn't kill him.

Failing to find a screenwriting gig in L.A., I drove down the Pacific Coast Highway in my rented red convertible and checked into the palatial St. Regis Monarch Beach. The next morning I teed off at the St. Regis's seaside Robert Trent Jones Jr. course, playing with Henry Cho, yet another fine comic. Of Korean descent, but raised in Nashville, Henry opens his act with a loud, "How ya'll doing?"

"I *know* . . . what you're *thankin'*," he says in reference to his Korean face and redneck accent. "What's *wrong* with this picture?"

There is nothing wrong with Henry's act or his golf game as he continues to beat me handily. Four of us played a round robin, each partnering with one of the others for six holes as we danced in and out of the receding and advancing Pacific fog and sweet ocean air.

The Pelz school had me doing great things until we made the turn. There I checked my cell phone and found a string of urgent messages from my brothers.

This time it was my mother who'd suffered a stroke.

Do You Have That in Red?

Flashing back to the almost exact call at Pebble Beach about my father, my mind raced through the scenario: How long to get off the course and pack my bags? How long to drive to LAX and catch a plane? Is it even possible to get there before the end of the day?

But when I called my brother Marvin for an update, he said, "Don't do anything until we get some more information."

Continuing around the course, I plugged away totally distracted, hitting one bad shot after another. On the short par-three thirteenth, I hit three balls in a row into the pond in front of the green. I was miserable.

The lesson, other than the fact that you can't play golf while worrying about a loved one, is that you also can't play golf without a plan for each shot and the confidence and concentration to execute it.

We were on the last hole when my brother called back with a medical update. "She might not be as bad as they thought. Finish your round and your business, then we'll see where we are."

With a couple of X's on my card, I wasn't able to post the score, but my best estimate was 41–52 for 93. Nine months of lessons and I was worse than when I started.

Packing away my sticks, I climbed back into my convertible and headed north for LAX. I didn't bother to put the top down.

That my mother has lived to the age of eighty-four is a miracle, not just because she has overcome incredible assaults on her own health, but because my misadventures would have killed a woman whose heart was less strong. As a child, I was what they called "accident-prone." That's the term my mom used, but it was just a kind way of saying I was an inattentive spaz.

Among my misadventures, I fell off a dam, was scalded from head to toe in a cousin's science fair project gone awry, and was hit by a schoolbus, which sent me flying a hundred feet and left me unconscious for hours. I even managed to flip a golf cart at the San Angelo Country Club. When this accident didn't kill me, I was sure Pip would, though he seemed to take it in stride and, most important, didn't curtail my golf privileges.

Even at age twelve, I was already working in Pip's clothing store, a job I would continue to hold until he sold the store around the time I left San Angelo for college. Starting as a janitor at fifty cents an hour, then working my way up to a salesman at minimum wage, I spent thousands of hours in the store, few of them with Pip, however, who often came in just long enough to grab a twenty from the beautiful old cash register.

Pip had always liked nice clothes, but had known nothing about selling them when he bought the store in the fifties and renamed it Pipkin's Men's Wear. Looking back on it, I can see now that the store probably made no more profit than the spending cash it put in Pip's pocket. Luckily, both of my parents had inherited a little money from their parents, and somehow they managed to make it last, at least until my first year of college.

Twenty-five years later, after Pip finally came to accept the fact that he was never going home again, he had to make some decisions about what to do with all the things he'd accumulated over the years. His most prized possession was a gold Rolex watch that he'd worn as long as I could remember.

Probably the most emotional moment I ever shared with my father took place, not on the golf course, but on the front porch of the nursing home when Pip pulled out that Rolex watch and its original case and began to search for words that would not come. The aphasia from his stroke, which made it impossible for him to remember my name, would come upon him in the most frustrating ways. At the dinner table he'd point at something and say, "Pass the hammer . . . the briefcase . . . the radio . . .," shaking his head after every wrong word until finally someone guessed what he wanted— "The salt?" — and he'd shake his head in relief.

Now he had something important to tell me, and the words would not come. At last, Billie intervened and explained for him—for the two of them, really—that Pip wanted me to have his watch. That his prized watch should come to me and not to one of my older brothers was incredibly moving, but almost before I could react, I learned that a story came with it.

I didn't have any idea when or how Pip acquired the gold watch I now held—with Raymond G. Pipkin engraved in golf on the back of the case—but Billie explained to me that they had bought the watch earlier in the same year they'd been forced to tell me there was no money for me to continue college. For thirty years, they'd worried that, compared to my brothers and sisters, all of whom they'd somehow financed through advanced degrees, I'd been shortchanged out of an education.

Talk about confusion. In the same moment that I learned my father was giving me his watch, I also learned they'd spent several thousand dollars to buy it, money that could easily have kept me in school another year. To tell you the truth—and it's not easy to do so—I didn't know what to think. There were tears in my eyes—and in my father's, too, but they were not tears I could have easily explained, so I thanked my father, gave him a hug and a kiss, then took the watch home and put it away in a drawer. I never wore the watch until Pip's funeral, and then I put it away again.

Though the doctors insisted that my mother had suffered a stroke, she was more insistent that they were wrong. "Take me back to the nursing home," she ordered the doctor at the hospital. So they did.

Look up the word "tough" in the dictionary and you may find a picture of my mom. She raised five kids, kept our family afloat, beat cancer twice, survived two heart attacks, and was told by the doctor who diagnosed her with severe rheumatoid arthritis that the disease would kill her within seven years. That was twenty years ago.

My mother visited my father daily for over seven years at Meadowcreek Nursing Home, but just months after he passed away, Billie was unable to live alone, and moved into a room at Meadowcreek just down the hall from my father's old room. Visiting her after her stroke that wasn't a stroke, I could see that she'd slipped back down another big step on the precarious ladder she's been fighting her whole life to climb.

Despite my parents' devotion to each other through fifty-five years of marriage, there had long been a rift between them that neither spoke about. Sneaking up on my fiftieth birthday, I decided it was time to find out what all the fuss had been about.

"Why were you mad at Pip all those years?" I finally asked her.

And just like that, she told me what I considered to be the great secret of their lives.

"After World War II and the hard times we had on the ranch in the middle of nowhere, Mama set us up to move to San Angelo to start our lives over. We had a young baby to take care of, so Mama sold all the stock on the ranch—cattle, horses, sheep, and goats—and she gave us the money to help us get by."

"And?" I asked.

"Pip drove up to see his family for the weekend and called me the next day to say he'd done something really wonderful."

I held my breath. This didn't sound good.

"He'd taken all our money and bought a red convertible! It didn't even have a backseat!"

Well, I could see that this had been a very bad decision on my father's part. When a decade of national depression is followed by a world war, you don't really want to spend the milk money on a flashy car. At the same time, I could barely contain the smile that was growing deep inside me, not because my father had blown it big-time, but because his rash action was so much a part of who he was and why people loved him. And because we were so much alike. The coincidences were actually kind of eerie.

When I was sixteen, after working for years picking up pecans, mowing yards, caddying, and working in the store, I went to Pip and told him I'd found a car I wanted to buy. The car needed work, but it was gorgeous, and I wanted it more than life itself.

"What is it?" Pip asked.

Do You Have That in Red?

"A 1953 Jaguar convertible!" I told him. "And it's red."

Shoot, I'd never even seen a Jag before, but I knew a thing of beauty when I saw it, especially for the Cracker Jacks' price of $300, one of the greatest steals in the history of classic automobiles.

"I don't think that's such a good idea," Pip told me. "Billie may not like it."

I insisted he was wrong, but he was in fact correct. No matter how much I begged and wheedled, my parents would not approve. And it was *my* money.

But the story gets better, because when Pip's mother died, she left me a small quantity of stock in the Piggly Wiggly grocery company. Cautioned by my parents that I should hang on to this stock as my one and only investment, I waited till I was twenty-five, sold it, and bought a red MG-B convertible. With the top up, my head threatened to pop through the top like Dino the Dinosaur driving this thing, so I simply put the top down and left it that way for six years, rain or shine. The trick during the rain, I found, was to drive really fast so that the rain flew over the open car.

Still without knowing about my father's disastrous red convertible escapade, when Christy and I moved to L.A., I bought a '67 Le Mans convertible, red of course, and drove it until we moved back to Texas.

Though my parents saw my red convertibles on several occasions, they never mentioned the critical lapse of judgment that my mother held against my father for more than half a century.

With five kids and life a lot tougher then than now, Pip could never have done something as inane and insane as wasting a year of his life to work on his golf game, so all the better that I was doing it for him. When I finally got back home, I again called Hertz to reserve a convertible for my birthday round at Pebble.

"Red, please," I told the agent. "It's important."

CHAPTER 26

In My Own Backyard

"Drive for show; putt for dough!"

—Everyone

Despite an incredible lesson from Ben Crenshaw and many hours of putting instruction at the Pelz School, I hadn't been practicing enough on the putting green. Though my intentions were good when I went to the range, I invariably spent longer than I intended trying to solve my long-game problems, which left little time to putt before I had to get back to those little responsibilities like children and work, which I could no longer ignore.

Statistics show that the player in 125th place on the PGA tour money list could add over a million dollars a year to his earnings by simply making just one more putt per round. And even if your putting won't ever make you rich, you'd probably *feel* like a million bucks if you could knock in few long ones now and then.

"Putting accounts for forty-three percent of the average amateur's total strokes," says Dave Pelz. "But that same golfer spends less than fifteen percent of his practice time on the putting green."

For ten years I'd been saying I was going to build a putting green at home. I'd even buried a cup and flag in my yard and mowed as short as I could around it. That looked kind of cool, and was okay for practicing pitch shots now and then, but I didn't have the time or the money to build a real green, and I knew it.

But while I was in Florida working with Leadbetter, I'd stayed long enough to play a round on the Grand Cypress New Course, a Nicklaus design inspired by the Old Course at St. Andrews. Though central Florida looks nothing like Scotland, the New Course does have some fairly gigantic greens, and the guy I played with made just about every putt in sight.

The secret to this guy's skills with the flat blade, I learned, was that he had an artificial putting green in his backyard and could practice anytime he liked, day or night. That hardly seemed fair, until I took into consideration that my playing partner was also the president of a company called Putting Greens Direct which installs artificial putting greens all over the world.

"We've built greens for a number of PGA pros," Gary Poole said as he pitched me on the idea of my own artificial green. "Davis Love III, Paul Stankowski, and Joe Durant all have our greens at their homes."

By the end of the round, I was already rehearsing the pitch to Christy on why a backyard putting green was worth ten grand.

"We'd have less yard to maintain; it'll add value to our house; someday our daughters will make a fortune on the LPGA."

Perhaps she was just glad I'm not the kind of husband who spends ten grand on a mistress, but to my amazement she went for it. Life is good when you're married to a girl like Christy.

It wasn't till later that I realized my pool table might have something to do with it. Hoping to convert the largest room in our house into a yoga studio, Christy asked if I wanted to sell my pool table, a suggestion I declined. A few weeks later she asked again. This time I wavered, but I still thought our daughters should continue their billiards education. A few days later, when she asked a third time, I replied that maybe it was a good idea, and Christy said, "Great! The movers will be here tomorrow!"

Following her example, I soon had two installers from Putting Greens Direct spray-painting outlines in my grass. Jason Meersman and Michael Zumpone had already converted backyards all over the country into golf fantasies, so I figured they'd have no problem working their magic on the barest, most sunburned part of my own yard. "If grass won't grow here," I told them, "then it's the perfect place for the artificial stuff."

When we were happy with the outline of the new green, Michael used a sod cutter to remove the existing turf, then a giant dump truck dropped eighteen tons of crushed aggregate stone, which was spread and shaped into a firm foundation.

Though I'd intended to make only occasional checks on the construction process, my excitement soon had me working alongside the crew. Crenshaw had told me that his design philosophy called for a course to have greens that were challenging, so I was determined that my green have character and shape. As Jason contoured the surface with a large, flat rake, I directed him to add a little here and take off a little over there.

After a while, I said, "Screw it! Lemme give it a try."

"It's *your* green," Jason told me. "You should get it the way you want it. Paul Stankowski did all the final shaping on his big multitier green."

Of course, the difference was that Paul Stankowski has won over $4 million simoleons on the PGA tour and knows exactly what he's doing. I, on the other hand, once won a dozen golf balls, all of which I lost.

Luckily, Jason is a low handicapper who once held the course record at the Fazio Treetops course in his home state of Michigan. "The green is going to be faster than you realize," he explained when my contouring got a little extreme. "You want it to be good, not goofy."

After one last compacting, we were ready to roll out the putting surface, a giant piece of rubber-backed nylon turf that immediately transformed the site from glaring white rock to a lush green putting surface. Using a commercial carpet cutter, Jason created some graceful sweeping curves on the edges, then made matching cuts in a large piece of artificial fringe turf, which would provide areas from which I could practice my chipping. When all the turf was seamed together, the cups were cut into the putting surface and dug into place.

The final steps were the spreading of a layer of fine-grained sand on the putting surface and brushing it down into the turf to give the whole green a uniform roll.

One thing I was curious about was just how fast this artificial green rolled. If it was too slow, it might hurt more than help when I got to Pebble. I didn't know anyone with a Stimpmeter, but I did have access to something better, the new Pelzmeter, which Dave Pelz designed as a more accurate way to determine the speed of a green.

Dave was out on tour, so his son and partner, Eddie Pelz, brought over the new gizmo, which has multiple tracks for rolling three balls at a time, a mechanical switch to release the balls cleanly, and even a built-in tape measure to check distances. After both an uphill and downhill test of my green, Eddie punched the results into an onboard computer and pushed one last button.

"You're green is a nine," Eddie told me. "That's the same speed as a Stimpmeter nine; it's just more accurate. And nine is a great speed for practice."

Having the Pelz seal of approval, I set about taking full advantage of the putting lessons I'd received at the Pelz Scoring School.

The single most important thing I took away from my time at the Pelz school was my new setup with the putter. One of the first skills tests I'd taken involved a small mirror that was adhered to the face of my putter. After I aimed my putter at a small laser against the base of a nearby wall, the laser was switched on, sending a beam from the device to the putter and back toward the wall.

If the blade of your putter is square to the line, then the laser reflects straight back to the source. If not, then you know you're screwed up. Trying this exercise from three different lengths, each student discovered just how poor their aim and setups really were. My results from the short and medium distances were actually pretty good, but on the longest putt, the reflection was hitting the wall about two feet *above* the floor. By trying to get my eye line behind the ball, I'd also moved my hands back and added loft to my putterface. That would explain why I'd been hitting so many long putts that hopped and bounced their way across the green. Crenshaw had already told me to keep my hands in front of the putter face and ball, but it took Pelz's feedback to convince me that the advice actually applied to me.

More feedback came on the face of my putter in the form of impact tape, which showed that most of my contact was outside of the sweet spot, generally toward the toe. As they say in West Texas, I had a bad case of *tolio*.

Pelz, of course, has also done a study to reveal the effects of mishit putts, or "impact error" as he calls it. Not too surprisingly, heel hits go left, and toe hits go right. I'd been missing a lot of putts on the right lip, and now I had feedback to tell me why.

Paying closer attention to my setup also helped, but it occurred to me that a more foolproof solution might be to use one of Odyssey's two-ball putters. Invented by Dave Pelz, the two-ball quickly became the bestselling putter in history. Unfortunately for Dave, he had already sold the putter's design to Callaway Golf for a flat fee, no doubt costing himself a small fortune in the process.

Pelz research has shown that—despite the *feel* putting style of Crenshaw and other master putters—the most reliable and repeatable putting stroke is a pendulum stroke with a slight acceleration, which means the backswing is a bit shorter than the followthrough. The arms should be fully extended and hanging under your shoulders. To eliminate aiming angles, your eyes are over the ball, and pretty much everything else is square to the target line.

Guess what? I wasn't doing any of this. Crouched over like a hunchback, I had my arms all tangled up in my chest, my stance open, and my putter aimed left of the target.

Changing into a better setup was surprisingly easy. Standing taller and bending less at the waist allowed my arms to hang and swing like a pendulum. To square up my stance and get my eyes over the ball, I stood above a Pelz putting mirror, which has a red line down the middle to indicate the ball position, and a second white line parallel to it that serves as a guide to square your shoulder position.

Eyes over the ball, shoulders lined up to the white line—and suddenly you're square to the line.

Though I'd started my new taller and square setup at the Pelz school, it was on my new putting green where it really started to feel comfortable. For years I'd been uncomfortable over any two-footer. Now I found myself feeling like those really were gimmes.

On longer putts, just as Crenshaw had taught me, I worked on distance.

"On a good putt," says Pelz, "the length the ball travels is not determined by how hard you hit, but by the length of your stroke."

Most of us hackers, unfortunately, don't see it that way. When you leave a putt short, we generally tell ourselves something like, "Hit it harder, you idiot!" But you don't need more "hit"; what you need is a longer stroke.

Late one night I was watching some bad TV at home and found myself thinking about the kind of stroke I needed on a long putt. Crenshaw had taught me to let the weight of the putter gather at the back of the stroke; Pelz had taught me to use the proper length stroke to get the ball just past the hole. Combining those two images, I suddenly had the perfect concept of what I needed to do. It was dark outside, but I'd put up some little Christmas lights by my putting green and the moon was out, so there I was at midnight, stroking a ball from hole to hole around my new green.

If someone had seen me out there, they might have thought I was nuts. And you know what? They'd probably have been right.

Maybe I need to join Golfer's Anonymous, I thought. That's a group that, every time you feel compelled to play golf, sends a foursome of strangers over to drink with you.

Fundamentals of Golf

Seventeen Inches Past the Cup

As taught by Dave Pelz

One of the biggest questions facing a golfer on the green is how far he should try to roll a particular putt. Should it die at the hole, or should it roll boldly by in the fearless fashion of Tiger Woods?

After rolling thousands of putts with his mechanical True Roller, Dave Pelz came to the conclusion that seventeen inches is the optimum length an average putt should roll past the hole.

There are a number of explanations for this, the chief one being what Pelz calls "the lumpy donut"—a badly trampled area around the hole (from which most golfers playing ahead of you on this day, have stroked their second putts) which causes softly struck putts to veer away from the cup. The lumpy donut is caused by golfer's spike marks and their overall weight compacting the green close to, but not touching the hole. Only an area just around the hole is left elevated, the shape of the trampled area being . . . a lumpy donut.

That is one of many reasons why good putts sometimes miss and bad putts sometimes go in.

Remember: A bad read combined with a bad stroke may be perfect, but does that mean you have no control over your own destiny? Far from it. Putt with enough speed to get seventeen inches past the hole, and give yourself the best chance to save a stroke.

"The race may not always go to the swiftest," as the gamblers say, "but that's the way to bet."

CHAPTER 27

Fromholz

"Golf has never failed me."

—Donald Ross

No matter how you slice it, when you steal a guy's name, you're bound to owe him something. Nearly twenty-five years ago, when Steve Fromholz invited me to join the greatest, longest-lived foursome of my life, he was already known as the writer of "Texas Trilogy," which many consider the best song ever written about Texas. Willie Nelson and others had scored hits with Steven's tunes, so Fromholz was well on his way to becoming a thousandaire, and may not have needed anyone to steal his name.

On the other hand, it's a pretty great name.

When I first wrote *Fast Greens* as a screenplay that could be shot on a low budget in Austin, the idea was for Willie to star as the lead golfer turned reluctant granddad. I also wanted Fromholz to play the one-eyed Vegas hit man who also hits a great four-wood. Did I mention that Fromholz hits a great four-wood?

Instead of making the movie, I turned the screenplay into a novel, but by then Fromholz's character and name were far too memorable to change. When the novel came out and Warner Brothers bought the movie rights, all the Hollywood producers on the project had a different idea about who best to play Fromholz. Joe Pesci, Samuel Jackson, and Dennis Hopper were a few of their suggestions.

"What about Fromholz?" I'd ask, which would prompt the mention of more actors who were just right for the part—say Steve Buscemi or Randy Quaid.

"No, *Steve* Fromholz," I'd say. "He's been in half a dozen movies, he's got a squinchy eye, and he hits a great four-wood."

So all the Hollywood guys would look at me like I was crazy, then we'd once again postpone the question until it was finally resolved—like most Hollywood questions—by the movie not getting made.

I guess that meant Fromholz got his name back, not that he ever seemed to give a damn, cause he was still writing songs, leading white-water boat trips, and wrangling horses into the mountains of Mexico, singing for his supper (and for everyone else's) along the way.

When most of our original foursome was in Austin, we'd play a little golf at Willie's, and Fromholz could still hit that danged four wood like a dream. It didn't matter how much he was down, sooner or later, he'd end up 210 yards from the hole, straddling a patch of cactus, his butt up against a 'bob-wire' fence, and we all knew before he swung that somebody ought to run down there and pull the pin.

In the year since my father died, I hadn't seen Fromholz much, even though I really wanted to reconvene the old foursome so I could steal their new jokes.

"Did you know," Fromholz sometimes asks his audience, "if you drink a shot of tequila and hold the empty glass up to your ear, you can hear a whole bunch of Mexicans laughing at you?"

If you doubt his claim, feel free to give it a try. It sometimes takes several shots.

I was still waiting for the right time to call everyone when Fromholz's sister called *me,* and I knew I'd waited too long.

They say bad things happen in threes, and I was starting to agree, for, like my father and my mother, Steven had suffered a stroke.

This was not good. When a hard-living guy in his fifties gets stroked down, the coming back ain't easy. I went up to Waco to see Fromholz in the hospital, and though he was bedridden with pain and confusion, he still had on his game face.

"Did you bring me a drink?" he asked, trying to find some smile muscles on the side of his body that didn't seem to be working very well.

When you've played a jillion holes of golf with a guy and he needs a little help, there's not much doubt that you owe it to him, especially when he's a musician with insurance that's exhausted in a matter of days and a long road of no income ahead. Seemed like Fromholz was looking at the longest, hardest four-wood from a hardpan lie of his life.

So Willie, Lyle Lovett, Ray Benson, and I all put up a little seed money, and I went down to Liberty Bank and opened a medical-assistance account in Steven's name. After an e-mail to friends and a couple of radio spots, the donations started coming in from far and wide, some of them generous indeed, and a *lot* of it was from golfers. I'd look at the contribution list and could generally predict by the amount whether it was someone with whom Fromholz had broken tees.

As if to prove my point, one night after a Willie Nelson and Family concert at Stubb's Bar-B-Q in Austin, Willie slipped something fat into my pocket.

"This is for Fromholz," Willie said softly.

I felt the weight of the bills, peeked at the denomination and said, "That's too much for one guy."

"I'd just lose it playing poker," Willie told me.

A couple of months after the stroke, Fromholz was on loan from the VA hospital when he decided it was time to pick up the sticks again. After assuring us that his doctor had given approval, we met Steve one morning at Barton Creek. Bud Shrake and I drove up to the practice green where Fromholz was standing with former Texas Land Commissioner Bob Armstrong, who also suffered a severe stroke a few years back and defied all odds by recovering to the extent that he regained his pilot's license and twin-engine instrument rating.

"You owe us both a stroke," Fromholz quipped.

Shrake and I about spit up laughing, and when we'd recovered, the game was on. None of us, Fromholz included, knew if he'd be able to hit it, but he cracked one down the middle and life was good again, especially when he made that first par on number two. Fromholz was back.

Not too surprisingly, he ran out of steam before we finished nine, but we didn't care. What mattered was that his mind was growing keener and his body stronger. If he could play a few holes of golf—and he was already playing guitar—then in a few months, he'd be writing heartbreaking songs again and telling funny stories as he was always meant to.

After my father's stroke, there was never any question of his playing golf again. Swamped with confusion and unable to walk, only Pip's heart kept him going. Quitting the booze and eating healthy nursing home food made that heart even stronger, but he could not overcome the assault on his mind. Seven long years later, he finally began to lose his sense of decorum as well and began to revert to a more childlike spirit.

One day, a woman visiting the nursing home was "prancing around"—as my mother described it—and showing off her gaudy engagement ring.

"How long have you been sleeping together?" Pip asked the woman.

When my well-fed brother Marvin came to visit, Pip said, "That's quite a belly you've got there."

My next visit, Pip took in my shaggy hair and baggy clothes, and said, "You look like a bum."

He was right all three times. She *was* shacking up, Marvin *was* getting a little rotund, and I *do* look like a bum. I was filming *The Sopranos* at the time, and Pip's unwitting honesty reminded me of Tony Soprano's mother. "Between brain and mouth," it was said at her memorial, "there was no interlocutor."

Fromholz

Though he was not the Pip of old, he was still entertaining.

Twenty years ago, shortly after Pip waltzed with Christy at our wedding, I introduced him to Fromholz for the first and only time.

"He hits a mean four-wood," I told Pip.

The two of them stood there grinning, then both polished off a glass of Callaway wine.

"I always liked a four-wood. It's my favorite club," Pip said. "With a four-wood, all you have to do is hit it."

I think the only reason I remember this is that it was the only golf advice I'd heard from Pip since he told me to keep my head down when I was twelve.

After a little more wine, Fromholz got up in front of our families and friends, and started to play one of his songs for my bride and me—the one we still call "our song."

I'd have to be crazy
Plum out of my mind
To fall out of love with you

Let me tell you, it was perfect. Just like Fromholz's four-wood.

Donald Ross was right, Fromholz—golf will never fail you. Which is why I must say that, if you and I were the last two people on earth, and there was just one shot of tequila left between the two of us, I would drink a toast to you.

Cheers!

Fundamentals of Golf

Playing Through

As told by Steve Fromholz

Two guys are playing golf one day and they're stuck behind two women who are really playing slow.

Unable to take it anymore, one guy offers to speed things up and walks down the fairway. But halfway to the women, he turns around and comes back to his buddy.

"I couldn't say anything," he explains. "One is my wife and the other is my mistress."

"No problem," says his pal. "I'll handle it."

But after going halfway down the fairway, he also comes back, then says to his buddy, "Small world, isn't it?"

CHAPTER 28

Lord Byron

"Byron probably was the greatest striker of the ball, the greatest player the game has ever known. That's open to debate, of course—but my father said so."

—Tom Watson

For the past sixty years, various names have risen to the top of the list of Texas golf greats. Lloyd Mangrum, Lee Trevino, Ben Crenshaw, Tom Kite, and Justin Leonard have all spent their time as the best, but each has had to make room at the top for someone else.

But there are two players who never had to step aside to make room for someone new, even after they'd quit playing competitive golf. They are, of course, Ben Hogan and Byron Nelson, and it is likely that we will never again see two such champions with careers so completely in parallel, yet whose lives are so completely different.

I never met Ben Hogan and only saw him once in person, an occasion that did nothing to change his image in my mind as a silent and fierce competitor. In the summer of my thirteenth year, Pip, my brother Marvin, and I were invited to play a round of golf in Fort Worth at the famed Colonial Country Club.

As with the tournament at Pebble Beach, Pip and I had often

watched the Colonial on TV during tournament week, but I had no idea how tough the course was. It is only slightly longer than the San Angelo Country Club, where I'd learned to play, but the ball rolled a third as far on Colonial's lush fairways, and even hitting the ball straight often got you in trouble. To a kid from West Texas, playing Colonial was like going through the woods to Grandma's, with the wolf waiting to eat you at every turn.

When I first played the game, Pip would patiently let me hit as many shots as it took, as long as I didn't hold up the game for anyone else. That meant staying on my toes, watching my ball until it stopped, then getting to it fast, habits that later helped make me a good caddie. But if I fell behind, the ball had to go into my pocket until the next hole. That hadn't happened in a while, and my worst fear at Colonial was that I'd play so poorly that Pip would make me pick up. I was with the men now, and I didn't want to go back to being a kid.

One thing that kept me in the game was that Colonial felt so familiar to me, and not just the few closing holes I'd seen on TV. The feel of the holes and the shape of the greens seemed to put me at ease. It wasn't till later that I discovered that the father of Texas golf, John Bredemus, had designed Colonial in 1935, seven years after he designed the San Angelo Country Club. His hands were still evident on both courses, which is perhaps why I managed to stay in the game at Colonial and shoot a round in the nineties.

After the round, we feasted on great cheeseburgers in Colonial's Grill Room—where the burgers are just as incredible today—and I noticed a man sitting at a table by the window that overlooked the golf course. He was not a large man, but there was an imposing sense about him, nevertheless, despite the fact that he was paying no attention whatsoever to the others in the room. He was in one world, and we were in another.

Placing my hand on Pip's arm, I asked him softly, "Is that—"

As if I were about to invoke some holy or unholy name, Pip cut me off with a simple, "Yes."

"Can we say hello?" I asked.

"No."

The man at the window table, of course, was Ben Hogan, and the matter didn't need further explaining. While we finished our burgers, I kept waiting for Hogan to glance around the room so I could wave at him, but he never did. When we left, he was still there. That was it. I never spoke to Hogan, never shook his hand, never saw him hit a ball except on television. Despite that, I went to the library when we got home and checked out every book I could find about or by Hogan. Right or wrong, for the next thirty years, Hogan's instruction books would guide me in golf.

How different things might have been, I wonder, had the legendary Texas golfer having lunch across from me been Byron Nelson.

Though Hogan and my father both had a fondness for whiskey, it was clean-living, church-going Byron Nelson who was the Texas golfer Pip most admired. In his clothes, his manner, and his golf, Byron Nelson exhibited a casual, easygoing elegance. For some reason I remember that Pip really liked the hats that Byron wore. Though he clearly had not forgotten his humble Texas roots, Byron Nelson was a class act.

After amassing one of the most incredible competitive records in the history of the game, Byron had abruptly retired from competitive golf, all of this before I was even born. But Byron had gone on to become a television announcer—golf's first color commentator—and all through my early years in golf, he reminded me of Pip.

Pip liked to come home from the golf course on Sunday afternoon, put his feet up, and tune in to whatever golf coverage was on the tube. Usually that meant inviting Byron into our home. We'd watch a few holes, and then I'd notice Pip was sound asleep, the golf shots, galleries, and announcers' voices falling on his ears like a lullaby.

At some point, my mother would come into the room, and even if Pip was snoring, she'd ask, "Are you napping?"

Without moving any muscle except his lips, Pip would say, "I'm just resting my eyes," a tradition I carry on to this very day. There is no nap like a golf nap, and no voice more soothing than Byron's.

Ever since I'd started to remake my game the summer before, I'd fostered the hope that I could sit and talk golf with Lord Byron. Working through his friends at the Four Seasons Las Colinas, site of the Byron Nelson Invitational and the Byron Nelson Golf Academy, I'd been optimistic about my chances to see him in the fall, but Byron had needed hip replacement surgery and I had to wait.

Winter came and went, as did much of the spring, and then I got the call suggesting I come to Dallas to have lunch with Byron. A suggestion was all that I needed.

He was already seated when I came into the clubhouse restaurant at Las Colinas. I hadn't seen him for a few years, and was amazed at how good he looked.

"The thing is," Byron told me, "people who don't know me and who only see me when I'm seated, they think I'm seventy-one instead of ninety-one. But when I get up and move around, I've got back and hip problems and I do look like an old man. But I'm still driving around, doing the things I want to do."

"How do you explain that?" I asked. "Is it golf?"

"Not necessarily," he said. "The main thing is, I've lived an active life and I've never had a sitting-down job. I've always been moving, always on the go, always working. Even when I was a kid."

"A kid far from any golf course," I said.

"Yes, sir. When I was little, I was a country boy and rode a horse to school. When we moved to Fort Worth, I'd never heard the word 'golf.' I started caddying when I was thirteen. From then on, I never quit thinking about the game."

"And you perfected your game simply by trial and error, right?"

"When I was eighteen, I was a pretty good amateur, so I went to San

Antone and entered the pro-am. I was paired with Bobby Cruikshank—a fine old Scottish pro. I had a very strong grip and was kind of hanging around him. Finally he looked at me and he said, 'Laddie, if you don't learn to grip the club right, you'll never make a good player.' So I went back home—you couldn't go to a pro to learn then—and I finally found a little book that had some articles in it by various authors, and Harry Vardon had one small article about the grip. Right then, I changed to the Vardon grip [with the little finger of the right hand overlapping the index finger of the left hand], and I never changed it again."

"Tell me about the swing you developed," I asked. "The modern swing, everyone called it."

"I hit the ball too high for a while, then I shanked almost every shot for six months. I kept working on my game and finally realized I needed to move underneath and keep my head back. As I went through the ball, my knees flexed just a little, and I kept the clubhead through the ball longer in this area than anyone ever had. I called it a rocking-chair swing—back and through, back and through. I wasn't really long, but I could play a whole tournament and not have a tee ball I couldn't play well."

Though I could barely remember my shots from the round with Fromholz the week before, Byron could still recall every hole of the eleven straight PGA events he won in 1945, a record no one will ever come close to matching. So how did he do it?

"In 1944," Byron told me, "I kept a little diary of my time on tour. At the end of the year, the thing I saw in my diary more than anything else was careless shots and poor chipping. So I made up my mind I would practice my chipping and I would not play a careless golf shot in 1945. In 1944, I averaged 69.67 which was the lowest score at that time. In 1945 I did 68.33—a little over a stroke a round. That's five shots in a tournament, and that was the difference. And I did it by working on the weakest part of my game.

"Human nature is to like to do what you do better, but to improve your golf game, you have to work on the worst part of your game.

You have to be completely honest with yourself. And working on the worst part of your game will help the other parts, too."

With our time winding down, I told Byron about the loss of my father and about the work I'd done on my game to prepare for my final round at Pebble Beach. Like so many others I'd asked, I wanted to know if he had any advice for my final round at Pebble.

"I played the Crosby in 1951," he told me. "I was retired, but Bing called and wanted me to play, so I did. To get my feel back, I got there two days early, and I just practiced my short game from a hundred yards in because that was what was the worst of my game. And even though I hadn't been playing, I won the tournament."

"Any particular holes or shots I should watch out for?"

"It's an intimidating golf course. You have to accept that on certain holes there are places you just don't want to go. The third hole, you don't want to go left. The fourth hole, don't be long on the green. It's fast coming back."

And just like that, fifty-two years after winning at Pebble—as far as I know without having played the course since—Byron gave me a hole-by-hole, shot-by-shot rundown of Pebble Beach. I could scarcely believe my good fortune.

I was thanking Byron and he was placing his checked hat back on his head when he had one final thought for me.

"To work and develop a golf swing, you need to get a picture in your mind. I taught myself more about my swing when I was lying in bed and in the dark than anywhere else. Your eyes are closed, and you can see what you're trying to do."

"I do that, too," I told Byron. "I have for years. When I can't sleep, I just lie there playing the old San Angelo Country Club course in the my mind."

"Keep it up," he told me. "And good luck at Pebble Beach."

. . .

Lord Byron

Later that day, I strolled down from the Four Seasons clubhouse to the Byron Nelson Golf Academy for a lesson from the Academy's director, Paul Ernest.

Knowing that I'd already worked with a lot of different teachers, Paul was careful not to introduce any additional confusion into my overcrowded head. But with a little video feedback, and a few small observations about my swing, he soon had me hitting it great.

The most remarkable thing Paul showed me was a low-tech trick to get me swinging through the ball. All he wanted me to do was to make a loud "whoosh" sound with the shaft as I swung. An over-the-top swing, I discovered, does not "whoosh." A swing that you fail to finish does not "whoosh."

But an on-plane swing with good clubhead action through the ball and a great finish makes a wonderfully satisfying "whoosh." Try it, it works.

Remembering that Byron had told me it was essential to work on the weakest part of my game, I thought about the fact that the club I was most uncomfortable with was my four-iron. Since the club I trusted the most was my five-wood, the obvious solution was to switch to a seven-wood, but my ego didn't want an Old Man's club in my bag.

So I told Paul I was thinking about putting a seven-wood in my bag.

"Don't let pride stop you!" Paul said without a moment's hesitation.

Since pride was the only thing stopping me, I took his advice and never regretted it for a single shot. If I never mishit another four-iron in my life, that's okay with me. Even in my sleep, I hit the seven-wood better.

Fundamentals of Golf

The Modern Swing

In the words of Byron Nelson

"All I was trying to do was find a better way to swing so I could make a living at the game. I found a better way and, as a result, I've been credited by most experts with developing the modern way to play golf. But I sure wasn't thinking about that at the time."

"The best way to swing is the simplest way. Most players try to make the golf swing more difficult than it really is."

"I had proven to myself that the best way to ensure a well-timed swing was to start the clubhead, hands, and shoulders back in a single motion. It seemed that when I did this, my timing turned out to be okay throughout my swing."

"The key thought—and it's one of the most important you'll ever be given—is don't get too anxious to hit. Don't try to get the downswing started before the backswing is complete."

"If you don't think straight, you won't hit straight."

CHAPTER 29

Gear Head

"In all my years, I've never found the game too easy. The new clubs and balls are keeping a lot of us playing."

— Arnold Palmer

With my joust against Pebble Beach growing ever closer, I knew it was time to make more equipment decisions than simply putting a seven-wood in my bag. My game was coming back, and though I hadn't notched any more rounds in the midseventies, I'd broken 80 a couple of times, once at Falconhead, the PGA's new daily fee course in Austin, where I managed to get up and down for par on six straight holes.

"Dave Pelz!" I yelled every time I hit it close. The guys I was playing with couldn't decide whether to beat me over the head with a lob wedge or ask for a lesson.

While at the Pelz school, I'd tried his new Pelz wedges, which are forged to such tight specs that the grooves shave tiny bits of white fuzz off the balls as you practice. I had a better feel, though, for Ping's new Mid-Bounce wedges and ordered a set of three—a 52-degree gap wedge, a 56-degree sand wedge (bent to 55 degrees to give me even gaps between my clubs), and a 58-degree lob wedge. The first day I played with them, I knew they'd be going to Pebble with me.

The rest of my Callaway X-14 irons were treating me pretty good, so the only equipment questions remaining were my driver and ball.

After my club fitting, Callaway had sent me a 10-degree ERC II driver that I absolutely loved and never wanted to give up. Unfortunately, the United States Golf Association had different ideas about that. After flip-flopping on the issue, the USGA announced that my driver was permanently banned in the United States. Apparently they thought I was hitting the ball too far, which might be the funniest golf joke I ever heard.

In order to preserve the traditions of the game, American golf's ruling body adapted something called COR, or the coefficient of restitution. In layman's terms, COR is a measurement of the springlike effect that takes place when a ball rebounds from the face of a club. The newly established COR limit would be .830, which more or less means an 83 percent efficiency in the transfer of energy from the clubface to the ball.

Now I can appreciate the worry the USGA has over the possibility that some up-and-coming young pro is going to be reaching the longest par fours while he's still in diapers, but I also don't think there are many golfers whose main problem is that they hit the ball too far.

Let's face it, *trying* to hit it long is the single most fun part of the game. Hitting it long is the sex of golf, while coercing the ball into the cup is the golf equivalent of a single guy getting the girl out of his apartment.

What's next? Limiting the number of hours the pros can spend in the weight room? At least that wouldn't penalize the rest of us.

Come on, guys, loosen the knots in those USGA neckties, take a chill pill, and let's all have some fun. You've done great things for the game, so don't drop the ball now. If it's the traditions of the game you're trying to preserve, then why can I use a new long putter that doesn't even look like a golf club, but not the old croquet-style putter, which was once a mainstay of the game? When they banned my grandfather, Sam Snead, and everyone else from using that putter between their legs, Snead simply used the same putter alongside his body, so they banned that, too.

Maybe we should quit worrying about the impossible and start worrying how many hours it takes to play these seven-thousand-yard courses. If you Tiger-proof golf through restrictions on equipment and by making the courses longer and harder, it stands to reason that you're going to Joe Golf–proof the game a whole lot more.

The USGA says it's not in their charter to grow the game, and that philosophy seems to be working, because the past ten years has seen unprecedented growth in the popularity of the game, construction of God knows how many new courses, gigantic increases in equipment sales, and not one iota of growth in the total number of golfers in America. New players, we're learning, take up the game for a while, then a great number of them quit after discovering how hard it is and how much of an investment of time and money it takes to play.

Baseball—which was once the only true contender as America's Sport—has been on such a long decline that America's youngsters are now more likely to grow up running around a soccer field than a diamond. I don't want golf to start slipping backward, too. Let the game be fun again, in its purest and simplest form.

Further confusion—and slow play—arises from the handicap system, which now rivals the complexity of the IRS tax codes. If you don't believe me, take a weekend to read and decipher the Section 10 USGA Handicap Formulas, then calculate your own handicap. I happen to be fairly brilliant at math, and I simply couldn't do it. Why not use the flat tax approach? Calculate your average number of strokes over par: that's your handicap.

I'm not naive enough to think that will happen, but in one quick ruling, the USGA could speed up slow play, which is the largest single complaint about public golf. Why not encourage players to pick up their ball after reaching a certain score on a hole. Did you ever play a six-hour round because the players ahead of you were carefully reading that all-important eighth putt? Pick it up! Write down the maximum score you can take on the hole and better luck on the next one. We'll all be happier, and the world of golf healthier for it.

But that's just my opinion, as Dennis Miller says, and I could be wrong.

After taking a couple of pills myself, I replaced my illegal ERC II driver with a 10-degree Great Big Bertha II, which I felt had a good balance of distance and control. But as I struggled with my swing after working on *The Alamo,* I was still having trouble off the tee. One day after playing in the Crawfish Open in Llano, Texas (eighteen holes and all the crawfish you can eat for forty bucks), I stopped by the range where the Adams Golf rep let me try their gigantic new Redline driver. I swung it once and hit the longest drive of my life, then swung it again and put one ten yards past the first.

Drawn to the idea of hitting long, bombing drives, but uncertain about giving up the straight-hitting consistency of my Callaway driver, I decided to take the Pelz route and conduct a driver test, *mano a mano.*

"In this corner!" I announced to no one on the first tee at Barton Creek's Fazio Foothills Course, "From Carlsbad, California, we have the Great Big Bertha II, weighing in with a 10.5 degree loft and a firm-flex shaft!

"And the challenger! From Dallas, Texas, the Redline driver, tipping the ball with 10.5 degrees of loft and a stiff shaft! *Drivers, are you ready to rumble?*"

The drivers did not reply to my loud introductions, though an old man taking a walk nearby did pull out his cell phone and begin to dial furiously. Ten minutes later, security showed up, but all they wanted was to watch my test.

With the course closed for maintenance, my plan was to hit seven dozen drives, thirty-six with each weapon. Not only would I be able to determine which driver I hit the longest and straightest, but I also hoped to find out what ball was best for me.

"The proper ball," Richard Helmstetter had told me at Callaway, "is overlooked by a lot of middle and upper handicappers."

At Austin's giant Golfsmith store, I'd purchased seven dozen balls: the high bounce Maxfli Noodle and Precept Laddie, the Nike TA Longs, the Wilson Staff True balls (endorsed by Dave Pelz because they're perfectly balanced), the Callaway Hex Red (a three-piece ball played by lots of pros), and the new Titleist Pro V1x (at $50 a dozen, the most expensive ball on the market). Because I'd been told you need to be swinging at 115 mph or faster to enjoy the benefits of the X ball, I also bought a dozen Titleist Logo overruns for comparison.

Having marked half of each dozen balls with a red Sharpie, my plan was to hit the red-lined balls with the Redline driver, and the un-marked balls with the Great Big Bertha.

Though my plan was far from scientific, its biggest single flaw was the simple fact that I hadn't been hitting my driver well. In the past month, I'd missed more fairways than John Daly and lost more balls than Ray Charles. Of my first thirty drives, ten missed the fairway, with most of them coming to rest in the right rough maybe 225 yards from the tee.

"This will not stand!" I said.

The day before, my golf pro buddy, Dave Preisler, had given me a quick tune-up, which could be summarized as "Quit standing with your weight on your heels like an old man!" Preisler wanted my swing to be more athletic and less arthritic. For control and power, he wanted me to get my left shoulder back above my right foot. Think-ing back, I realized that this general idea in one form or another had also been given to me by Kip Puterbaugh, David Leadbetter, Chuck Cook, and Stefan Carlsmith. Finally, I'd found something that every-one agreed upon—even if it had taken awhile to sink in.

Doing as they all suggested, I put that left shoulder over my right foot, and it worked just fine. Alternating brands and balls every few shots, I swung away, banging ball after ball down the first fairway.

Two hours after I'd started, and pretty much soaked in sweat, I hit my eighty-fourth drive of the morning and came to one easy conclusion: I was tired. And I still had to pick them all up and record the results.

As to the results of my test, the worst 24 of my 84 drives were so bad that I felt sure they were the result of bad swings. Eliminating those, I was left me with 60 drives that were either in or close to the fairway and at least 250 yards from the tee (okay, the hole was downhill, though the wind was in my face).

Of those 60 good drives, 31 were hit with the Redline driver and 29 with the Callaway, practically a dead heat. But as I walked from ball to ball recording results, it became clear that the balls hit by the Redline driver were farther downfield.

While the average distance of the balls hit with the Callaway was 269 yards, the balls hit by the Redline averaged 280 yards. That's 11 yards more per drive, or one club closer to every par four.

As for the balls, over half of the Nike and discount Titleist balls were pretty much out of play. That could've been chance, but not one I was willing to take. The Precept Laddie had a dead-even mix of six balls in jail or not far from the tee, and six more that averaged an impressive 274 yards.

Four different brands had either eleven or twelve balls in my playable zone. Both the high-dollar balls—the Hex Reds and X Balls—averaged 264 yards. Not bad. On the other hand, the Noodle and the Wilson Staff, both of which sell for about half the price of the X, averaged 271 yards—a full 7 yards longer than their high-dollar competitors.

The winner for the longest, straightest drive was a Noodle, sitting 316 yards from the tee, hit there by the new driver in my bag, the Adams Redline.

And now for the punch line. After all my "scientific" testing, I went out to play the next day, bragging to my pals about my new Redline driver, and proceeded to miss almost every fairway. Two days later—the same thing. The club that worked great with my repeating, grooved swing on the practice tee didn't give me the same results on the course.

I had a different, more predictable problem with the Noodle. While it had been extremely long on the hard first fairway at Barton Creek, it showed almost no bounce at all when I played it on courses with softer or wetter fairways. Around the greens, it was just the opposite, for I found that the Noodle landed hard and bounced high.

Within two weeks of my test, I'd put the Great Big Bertha II back in my bag and had switched to the Callaway Hex Red ball, which seemed the perfect combination of long and soft.

Ultimately, my choice was a compromise of information and feel, which is a fairly good summary of everything I've learned about golf the past year.

Though far from greatness, I was getting better, and I was learning. And my fiftieth birthday at Pebble was right around the corner.

CHAPTER 30

Analyze This

"Jimmy Demaret and I had the best sports psychologist in the world. His name was Jack Daniels, and he was waiting for us after every round."
—Jackie Burke Jr.

Like so many players, I am a golfer of impressive skill and considerable talent on the practice tee. While practicing, I can launch long, straight drives, work my midirons both right and left, and clip my wedge shots from the turf with perfect divots.

Then I go out on the course and hit my drives O.B., my irons fat, and my wedges thin. By the turn, I'm kicking myself in the butt—no simple feat in itself—and as I walk up to jab that last putt in the hole, I'm often questioning my reasons to live. So much for the good days.

Despite ten straight months of lessons and hard work, I could still blow just about any shot in my bag. Just as vexing was my persistent inability to break 80. No matter how fine a round I put together, chances were that I'd choke on one of the last two holes and shoot 80 or 81 instead of the 78 or 79 I had so clearly in my sights.

My conclusion was that both of these problems might not have been the result of the club I held in my hands but the thoughts I held in my head.

The Westin La Cantera in San Antonio is the home to both the PGA Texas Open and the Golf Academy at La Cantera, one of the only schools to combine the mental and physical sides of the game.

The head man, so to speak, at the academy is Dr. David Cook, a sports psychologist who helps golfers put the dimpled ball in the hole and the San Antonio Spurs to put the round ball in the hoop.

By the time I got to David Cook, I'd scratched, clawed, and scrambled my handicap from 16 down to 9. After playing for forty years, it felt good to finally have a single-digit handicap, but would it be good enough? Nine over at Pebble is 81, and that's too high. Even worse, with handicaps calculated to represent potential, not averages, the USGA says a 9-handicap means I'm expected to shoot nine-over just one round in five.

That means with a little more than a month remaining, I needed more than ever to get my handicap down and my confidence up.

"I'm two-thirds of the way to my goal," I told the golf doctor. "Can you take me the rest of the way there?"

"That depends," Cook told me. "Sports psychology is not a cure-all. It doesn't do beans to be coolheaded and confident if you don't know how to hit the ball out of your shadow. But the better you play, the more the mental side comes into play."

Most of us have heard those clever quotes about golf being 90 percent mental, but Cook has a more balanced approach.

"Golf is a game of mechanics, course management, and fitness," he says. "And finally, golf is a mental game. Of those four areas, the mental side is clearly the least understood, and it can easily undermine the other three parts."

The trick to playing to your potential, Cook explained, is to eliminate interference—like the crowd at a basketball game or a lack of confidence in your swing—and reestablish control. If you have control, you know that you can do it. If you don't have control, you become fatalistic and start making excuses: It wasn't my day. I'm tired. I'm sore. We all have so many excuses.

"Our purpose today is to focus and get in control," Dr. Cook told me as we drove toward our opening tee shots on the Palmer Course at La Cantera. "You don't have to focus for five hours like Hogan, but you'd better be riveted for those last twelve seconds before each shot, because the thoughts you have just before the clubhead moves are going to make or break your shot."

"So what am I supposed to think during those twelve seconds?"

"I want you to see it, feel it, and trust it," Cook told me. "When I say, 'See the shot,' I mean choose a target and visualize how your ball is going to get there. When we 'see' the shot, we're going to paint a picture, visualize a shot, and then call it out loud by stating the target, the trajectory, and the shape of the shot. 'Feel,' means stepping up to the ball and literally feeling the shape of that shot. When I say, 'trust,' I mean let go of your mechanical control and have the courage to let the shot happen."

Seeing the shot, Cook explains, starts with a wide view—checking the yardage, the wind, and the lie. As we narrow that focus, we close in on our target, then create a strategy for how to get the ball there. And as that focus becomes internal, we reduce our thoughts to trusting what we've visualized and felt. That final single thought—trust—is the trigger that starts the club moving.

For eighteen holes, Cook and I played golf in a way that I'd never imagined. Before every shot, I went through Cook's twelve-second routine—visualizing and calling my shot, feeling it with a waggle at the ball, and trying my best to trust it.

"Ten feet right of the pin," I'd say. "A high, soft shot with a draw."

Stepping up to the ball, I'd "feel" that shot in a practice swing, move into the ball, come to what I hoped was "trust" . . . and then I'd fall apart. After all my lessons, I still didn't trust my swing. The reason I hit the ball perfectly on the range, but terribly on the course, is because I had nothing to fear on the range, and nothing I had to trust except the fun of hitting a shot.

Because he is a Ph.D., David Cook refers to what I call fear as "errors of trust." According to David, there are four errors of trust: pressing, guiding, overaiming, and jamming.

The first error, pressing, is when you create pressure on yourself by increasing the importance of a shot or by simply trying too hard. In many cases, the more you press, the more difficult it is to hit a good shot.

The yips are a classic example of pressing. In case you're unfamiliar with the term, the yips can be summarized as a disastrous failure of confidence, most usually on short putts. The yips are five to ten strokes on your score and five to ten years off your life. But the yips are all in your head. A short putt is no more important than any other stroke. Make or miss, you have to commit to a shot.

The second error, guiding, is playing *away* from trouble rather than playing *to* a target.

"You can shoot eighty by guiding the ball," Cook tells me, "but you'll never get to par."

Faced with a dangerous shot like the eighteenth tee at Pebble Beach, the last thing most of us say to ourself is "Do *not* hit it left into the ocean." Well, in doing that, we've just visualized the ball going into the ocean.

"You can say to yourself, *Don't think about the ocean; don't think about the ocean*," Cook tells me, "but you're still *thinking* about the ocean. You have to choose a target and play to it."

The third error of trust, overaiming, means you've created a target so tight that your body and mind become bound up in an effort to hit the ball perfectly. Overaiming often results in a tight body, tight grip pressure, and a bad result.

"Instead of overaiming," Cook tells me, "it's better to visualize a spot and allow yourself a 10 percent margin of error. On a 150-yard shot, 10 percent is a fifteen-yard wide target, or seven and a half yards on each side of the spot you've chosen. On a ten-foot putt, you're allowing six inches on each side. No longer bound by your precision, you're now free to make a good shot."

The final error of trust, jamming, occurs when your mind is cluttered with too many mechanical thoughts. That results in your jamming against all the good things that can happen in your swing.

By understanding that trust is not a lack of confidence but a matter of avoiding specific errors, I found myself free to just make a swing. It's a shot like any other shot, I reminded myself. I have a specific target and only have to get close to it to succeed. Knowing that reduces my need for fourteen swing thoughts. Knowing that lets me trust. Knowing that lets me finally start hitting good shots on the back nine at La Cantera.

"Be your own best friend," Cook tells me as we come to the eighteenth hole. "The conversations we have with ourselves on the course are usually a lot more negative than the conversation we'd have with a friend faced with the same shots."

"You mean calling myself an idiot and a moron isn't a confidence builder?"

"When you're on the eighteenth hole and you need to make a par to break 80, right before you hit that shot, it's up to you to be your coach and your friend. Think about the ways that you'd encourage someone else in that situation. You'd tell them they *have* that shot, that they can do it. And that's what you have to tell yourself. You've worked hard to build the right golf swing for you, and now you have to believe in your method. You have to trust yourself. That's what makes it a great game."

Believe in your method. I liked the sound of that.

I'd asked everyone else what they thought about my chances of success on my ten-stroke quest, so I put the same question to Dr. Cook.

"It's the same thing I'd say to Tim Duncan or Bruce Bowen when they're going to get fouled a lot in the NBA playoffs," Cook told me. "Let's quit *trying* to make free throws. Your job, Turk, is not to go shoot seventy-nine at Pebble Beach. You may think that's your goal, but it's not, and here's why. There's only one thing you have control over on the golf course. It isn't your score. It isn't fairways or greens hit or putts made. The one thing you have control over is placing your body and your mind in position to score. So the concept is to go to Pebble Beach and put your mind in position over every single shot. Then when it's done, you'll know that you played the best round of golf that your could that day. Then you add 'em up and see how you did. That's how you shoot seventy-nine or better."

As we walked back to our carts from the eighteenth green, Cook had one last thought for me.

"Remember, ten strokes is not your goal," he told me. "It's your motivation—the motivation for an adventure."

The way David Cook described it, my golf quest suddenly felt akin to my adventure on *The Alamo,* to my childhood dreams of swashbuckling quests around the world, to those hundreds of jump shots I'd fired toward the basket with an imaginary clock counting down to zero in the NBA finals, to the thousands of putts on the practice green we'd pretended were to win the Masters or the U.S. Open at Pebble Beach.

Through all my lessons and hard work, in all my mechanical thoughts and paralysis by analysis, I'd left out one essential thing: I'd forgotten the joy of simply being able to go out and play!

Golf has never been better than when I was young and swinging the club barefoot in the green grass, when we played till dark and lost every ball in our bag because we couldn't see them anymore, when we putted for hours with a pal for a dime a hole, when we simply walked up to the ball and hit it.

What my dad loved about my being on a golf course, I suddenly realized, was not the score that I shot, but the joy that I found there. In learning that, like a bolt from the blue, I suddenly found that joy again. The reason I can trust it now is the same reason I could trust it when I was young—because it's fun! That's what Pip knew about golf and life—all you need is the right attitude. No wonder everyone loved him.

Fundamentals of Golf

Seven Foundations of the Mental Game

As taught by Dr. David Cook

STEP 1. CHOOSE TO BELIEVE IN YOUR METHOD
Jim Furyk may have the most unconventional swing on tour, but it works, and he believes that it works.

STEP 2. CHOOSE POSITIVE INNER COACHING
The brain works by language. We are in constant communications with ourselves, so be your own best friend and choose your words carefully.

STEP 3. CHOOSE TO CALL YOUR SHOT
On every shot, choose your target, shape trajectory. Now you've visualized your shot.

STEP 4. CHOOSE TO TRUST YOUR INSTINCTS
Trust is the courage to let go of mechanical control and let it happen. Use trust to release your instincts instead of doubt, which locks them inside.

STEP 5. CHOOSE MENTAL TOUGHNESS
Don't gripe. Think! Be prepared for the reality of wayward shots. When you blow your drive right, stay with your positive mind-set and try to discover what you failed to do.

STEP 6. CHOOSE A PRESHOT MIND-SET
Concentrate to overcome distractions. See it, feel it, trust it.

STEP 7. CHOOSE AN EFFECTIVE PERSPECTIVE
There are no crucial shots. This is a game, not brain surgery. Enjoy it!

CHAPTER 31

The Grand Canyon

———

"The harder you work, the luckier you get."

—Gary Player

On the plane to San Jose, where I'd rent one more red convertible for the drive to the Monterey Peninsula, I closed my eyes and thought through my rounds of the previous month, calculating whether my play on any of those days would have been good enough for Pebble.

I'd teed it up with legendary Texas football coach Darrell Royal. Coach has shot his age every year since he turned sixty-eight, but only once a year. Going for 76 with Tinsley Penick, Bud Shrake, and me, Coach only missed that 76 by a couple of years, which was good enough to beat me handily.

I'd come close to beating my brother John for the first time, taking him by two strokes on the front nine at Lakecliff before he took me by three on the back to win the day.

After Dennis Quaid finished his work on *The Alamo,* the two of us teed it up at Barton Creek Canyons late one afternoon. Despite having played little or no golf in many months, Dennis gave me two strokes a side for a few bucks and bragging rights, but we were having so much fun we ended up giving each other a mulligan on the back nine to keep the game close. And just as each of us had done as kids, we played until it was too dark to see the ball. A great afternoon of golf, but there's no way my driver that day would've been up for Pebble.

Deciding I wanted to be the one golfer in the world who is better on the course than on the range, I returned to Canyons the next day and didn't take a single practice swing on the front nine. Instead, I simply visualized my shot, then gave myself a nice slow waggle or preview of my move away from the ball. Like Mike Weir, I was rehearsing the feel of how I'd take the club back.

Eight holes later, I'd played the most consistent golf of my life. How consistent? Well, as I stood on the ninth tee, I was looking at a scorecard that showed a four on every hole. That's right, I'd made eight fours in a row, including two bogeys on the par threes and two birdies on the par fives. A par on the ninth would give me nine straight fours and a 36, even par, on the side. Without a doubt, this was the greatest stretch of holes of my life; now I just had to finish the job.

Standing in the way of that ninth four were two problems: first, the long, uphill ninth at Canyons is practically a par five for me. The second problem was a joke I could not get out of my head.

A caddie goes out with a player who is just terrible. On the first hole, the golfer makes a nine. On the second hole, same thing, a nine. Third hole—you guessed it—another nine.

Standing on the ninth green, the golfer has a short putt for—that's right—another nine. He stabs at the putt, and the ball just lips out.

"Say," says the caddie, "if you'd made that putt, you would have scored nine nines in a row!"

And the golfer says indignantly, "What am I, a machine?"

On every shot of the ninth hole, that joke was my final swing thought, which might explain why I made a double bogey that gave me a 38 on the front nine—pretty good, but not a machine.

At the beginning of my year, I'd promised myself that I'd play a hundred rounds, so in my final weeks before my fiftieth birthday, I completed my quota by playing in a nearly constant procession of charity golf tournaments. My round with Dennis was our warm-up for the Dennis Quaid Celebrity Classic. Because Bill Murray was unable to make it to Austin for the event, I tried to fill his considerable shoes as the tournament clown. On the first tee, I was introduced to hometown applause. Someone yelled, "Juggle!" and I thought, what the heck. For about twenty throws, I juggled my driver, a golf ball, and a tee, which ain't too shabby.

I managed to shoot 79 on the first day of Quaid's tournament, but the combination of late-night partying, three days of golf in hundred-degree heat, plus clowning all over the course, put my other scores closer to 90 than 80.

In a benefit at Barton Creek's Crenshaw course, the hole-in-one prize on number eight was one of those hotshot BMW Z4 roadsters. I told my teammates—my brother John included—that the pin was cut short and out of sight on a green that sloped away from us.

"The only way to get it close," I explained, "is to hit a knockdown shot and roll it over the hill."

When I did exactly that, my teammates thought I'd hit a bad shot, but I knew better. As my ball bounded over the little mound in front of the green, I saw both marshals stand to get a better look, then start forward. I held my breath, but heard no victory yells. When we got to the green, we found my ball a foot short of the cup. As we walked away with our birdie, I could not help looking back longingly at the Z4.

All year I'd been hoping to make an ace as part of my journey. My father never made one, and I hadn't either until right after *Fast Greens* was published. Then, within a period of months, I made two aces, the first playing with most of my old foursome—Fromholz, Shrake, and *Austin City Limits* director Gary Menotti.

Less than a year after my first ace, I made a second one on another Austin course, but looking back on that unusual year, I'd have gladly given either of those aces to Pip. I'd give up *both* of them for one more par three with Pip, and know that I'd gotten the greatest deal in the history of the game.

Running out of chances to make an ace during my big year, the day after missing the Z4, I lipped one out on the eighth at Canyons and the ball stopped a foot *behind* the hole.

"If I could have averaged number eight yesterday and number eight today," I told my group, "I'd have made two aces and driven a Z4 home to my wife." Even after twenty years of marriage, I figured I could get some action out of that.

The biggest miracle of my year was that Christy hadn't simply given up on me. I'd spent endless hours at the range, countless entire days at the golf course, and weeks on the road. A lesser marriage might not have survived madness like mine, but Christy didn't even worry when I stayed out half the night during Dennis's tourney, partying in bars with the celebs, scads of beautiful women all around.

And *why* wasn't Christy worried? Because she knew the guys were all golfers, and instead of hitting on the lovely ladies, we were all standing at the bar talking about whether we had *two* or *three* knuckles showing on our left hands. We were talking about the advantages of the short and long thumb and theorizing about which pro had the best swing thought. In the meantime, the ladies were on the other side of the room having long conversations that can be summed up in one phrase, "These guys must be gay!"

But no, we're not gay. We're just golfers. We already know we're as good as we'll ever be at sex. It doesn't matter how many manuals we read; we've been practicing it since we were teenagers, and chances are we're not going to improve at this point.

But our golf games. Oh, our golf games offer infinite promise of taking us to new heights of ecstasy. Truly, golf is the ultimate mistress. Women break our hearts, and we walk away the wiser. But golf breaks our hearts, and the only wisdom we learn is that we're not yet worthy of her love. Someday, we dream, we'll master our strokes of affection, and she'll bestow upon us all her desirable favors.

In the meantime, all we're left with is bits of purloined wisdom.

"The best swing thought," I told everyone at the bar that night, "belongs to Ernie Els. His caddie told it to me one night in a bar in Hawaii, and you can see it when Ernie swings."

"What is it?" they all wanted to know.

"*One, two*. That's why Ernie's so good. His swing thought is so simple, *one, two*."

So there we were, putting our glasses down and swinging imaginary clubs in all directions while the ladies went off in search of some real fun. Who knows? Maybe we are gay.

Posting my scores for that final month of golf, I was almost dumbfounded to learn that my handicap index at Barton Creek had plummeted to 5.7. Ten strokes lower than where I'd started, that should've been cause for celebration, but I didn't *feel* like a 6. I was a 6 because I'd recently broken 80 a few times. I'd also posted some dreadful rounds in the upper eighties, but the handicap system automatically throws out the high scores and calculates from the ten best out of your last twenty. Does that make me a 6? The USGA says it does, but I wouldn't bet on my skills and six strokes in the U.S. Open.

Making some quick calculations, I figured that, over the course of my year, I'd taken seventy-five hours of professional instruction, hit every one of the ten thousand balls on the Canyons driving range an average of five times, holed somewhere in the vicinity of twenty thousand putts, played a hundred and five rounds in weather that ranged from a windchill in the teens to a heat index over 120, three-putted on three score and ten different golf courses, drunk several cases of beer while golfing (almost all of them in Mexico), ridden more than I'd walked (which should have been the other way around), won more money than I lost (unless it *was* the other way around), bought a couple of hundred golf balls and probably lost a hundred (no, that was definitely the other way around).

On my scorecard, I'd made a dozen eagles, a gross of birdies, more than a thousand pars and bogeys, too many doubles and triples, and one snowman that was recorded in the actual snow.

I'd told a hundred golf jokes without learning a single new one. I'd broken bread with Byron Nelson and was carrying his notes about Pebble in my pocket, and putted with Ben Crenshaw and was carrying his rhythm in my heart. I'd been insulted *and* complimented by Scottish caddies. I'd hit a drive 314 yards in Austin's new Championship Tour event, the Kinko's Classic, only to have tour pro and big-time gentlemen Jim Thorpe put it *way* past me. On a par three in that same tournament, I'd hit a six-iron inside of Tom Kite's fine tee shot, and every day of every round—as I had all year—I'd thought of my father.

The highlight of my year, even though my shaggy hair and *Alamo* mutton chops were probably a bit much for the King, was my conversation with Arnold Palmer at the opening of Lakecliff in Austin. Arnie was my father's favorite golfer—and is in truth still my favorite golfer. Receiving Arnie's affirmation of my ability to achieve my goal and fulfill my quest had been the turning point in my own confidence, but there was a lot more at play in my brief time with Arnold.

Winging to Pebble Beach, I remembered how I'd explained to the King of Golf that I was doing this for my father, that I was dealing— in the only way I could think of—with the loss of a father that had given me much and to whom I had not given nearly enough back. I had not spent enough time with my father, learned enough from him, or taken enough time to help him understand who I'd become.

I'd started my quest wanting the impossible—for the two of us to somehow play one more round of golf together. A year later, I would have settled for a final game of checkers, or a chance to sit by his wheelchair and tell him something about his granddaughters, who already can barely remember him.

Arnold Palmer—whom generations of young golfers have looked up to as a hero and a father figure—has also been dealing with loss. Look in his eyes and you can see how those losses weigh on him—his wife, Winnie, his friend Ely Callaway, no doubt many more. Choose to love and care for a lot of people, then live to be Arnie's age, and you can end up spending much of your life in mourning.

Or you can continue to drive yourself to excel at the things you love. You can continue to "Dance with who brung ya," as Ann Richards puts it, and occasionally take a few moments to remember that your loved ones who are gone are still with you, too.

You can take a minute of your life to listen to a tale of woe and wonder from an overgrown, middle-aged, floppy-eared kid from Texas, then stare him in the eye another minute and recognize that same look you see in your own mirror every morning and somehow know that your words of encouragement might mean more than all the lessons and practice balls and books and magazine tips put together.

"You can do it," Arnie told me. "I know you can."

We were flying over the Grand Canyon as I recalled that look, Arnie's words, and the feel of his hand as he placed it in mine. And looking down at the ribbon of muddy brown water surging at the base of the canyon's steep walls, for the first time in the entire year that I'd been chasing this crazy dream, I suddenly realized that Arnie was right.

I could do it. I *knew* I could.

When I stepped onto that first tee at Pebble, I'd be far from alone. My father would be stepping up to the ball with me, Harvey Penick would be slipping my left hand onto the club, and Arnold Palmer would be placing my right. A legion of great golfers and teachers— Byron Nelson, David Leadbetter, Sean Hogan, Paul Earnest, and many others would be helping me swing that club.

If my iron play was errant, Dave Pelz would be helping me chip. Ben Crenshaw would be reading the greens.

Looking ahead of the plane, I could just see Las Vegas—the city of dreams—but my dream had already been fulfilled. I'd regained my love of golf and life, and gotten them back tenfold over. I'd just broken 80 at Pebble Beach. The rest was just details.

Thanks to all of you who believed in me.

And thanks, Arnie, you really are the King.

CHAPTER 32

Straight Down the Middle

"It is better to be lucky. But I would rather be exact. Then when luck comes you are ready."

—Ernest Hemingway,
The Old Man and the Sea

It was eight A.M. as I drove down the big hill toward the course. The rising sun was painting halos on the tops of trees, and the scent of pine and sea air washed in on the morning's first breeze. Though it was cold, I had the top down on my red convertible. From the CD player, Bing Crosby was singing,

> *. . . straight down the middle*
> *Where it wound up is a riddle*
> *But it went straight down the middle, far away.*

Pip had loved Bing Crosby, both for his music, and because Bing liked to have fun. Late one night after a drunken party at the Clambake, Bing was in the chips in the backseat of his convertible while his young son drove him home. Pulling them over, a policeman asked Bing why a boy was driving.

"He's the best we got!" Bing quipped.

I'd received a lot of good advice about playing Pebble. Crenshaw had told me that the greens would roll truer and faster in the morning.

Richard Helmstetter from Callaway had cautioned me that I needed a ball that was long, could handle the wind, and would stop quickly on Pebble's small greens. I had a dozen Hex Reds in my bag.

Byron Nelson had told me that when he won the Crosby in '51, he'd arrived two days early and practiced nothing but his short game.

Sean Hogan had called to convey some final advice from him and Leadbetter. "Confront the course before you tee it up. Think about where you can be aggressive and where you need to be conservative."

Certainly the most memorable advice on how to break 80 at Pebble—given about a week earlier—was from golf's most colorful cat, David Feherty, who simply told me, "Start drinking now."

And finally, the folks at Pebble Beach, who seemed to have bought into their end of my dream, had an even better suggestion.

"What about a playing lesson with Laird Small?"

As director of golf at the Pebble Beach Golf Academy, Laird Small was in a unique position to teach me how to play the course. Starting at nearby Spyglass Golf Club when he was ten, on weekends and in the summer Laird had worked the driving range, put carts away, and caddied on the Peninsula. After college, he played golf professionally before deciding Pebble was the place to be.

I was pulling my clubs from the trunk with Bing still singing "Straight Down the Middle" when Laird and I met in the Pebble parking lot. To help me avoid another collapse on the back nine like I'd suffered a year earlier, Laird took me directly to number ten. Looking out at one of the hardest par fours in golf, with ocean and beach begging for my ball on the right, I threw myself on Laird's mercy.

"So I've got ocean on the right here, just like the five holes before this one. Despite a year of work, even my draw is a five-yard fade. What do I do, just aim way left?"

"Aim at nothing and you'll hit it every time," Laird tells me. "Pick a spot on the left—say the *left edge* of the bunker on the left. That takes the ocean out of play, but lets you fade the ball back into the fairway. If you hit it straight, the rough is heavy, so you probably won't reach the bunker anyway."

So that's what I did. I hit it straight and ended up in the left rough about a half mile from the green. From there I made bogey on the hole, which even Byron Nelson had told me was a good score on ten.

With Laird telling me not to go long on my approach to eleven, I chose one less club and made par.

"You can do this," he assured me.

As I surveyed the par-three twelfth without a clue as what to do, Laird got more specific on how I should approach the course.

"If I could only tell you one thing out here today," he said. "It would be S.A.T.—Strategy. Aim. Target."

"On every shot, I want you to complete your S.A.T. Look at the hole, formulate your strategy, and call your shot. Tell me your club, your trajectory, and the shape of the shot. That's Strategy. Then pick your line; that's Aim. Finally, acquire your Target. S.A.T."

"After your shot," Laird concluded, "I want you to review all three and see how you did—where you went right or wrong."

My strategy was a high, easy seven-wood straight at the pin. I made a good pass at the shot, but ended up long and right.

"Now review your S.A.T.," Laird told me as we moved to the green.

"Okay. I ignored the hill and the wind," I now realized, "so I had the wrong target and the wrong club."

"You made a good swing, but had a bad result. The lesson is that strategy and aim will often do more for you than a good swing."

Though I continue to work on my S.A.T., even with Laird's help, I once again find myself falling apart on the back nine at Pebble. Missing the fairways by just a few feet, I can barely advance the ball in the heavy kikuyu grass. "Bermuda on steroids," Gary McCord calls this stuff. It's easy to see why.

On the fifteenth tee, I take care to do everything I've been told.

Low takeaway, push down the handle, follow my thumbs into the slot . . . then I hit my worst drive in months.

If this is a practice round, I think, it's a rehearsal for disaster.

"You have to let go of the quart to get the gallon," Laird tells me.

"What!?" I ask. I'm thinking about mechanics, and he's talking in riddles.

"You're too focused on controlling your swing," Laird explains, making him the fourth instructor to point this out. How many times have I been told to let go—let it happen, trust it, enjoy the game? Too many.

Teeing up a second ball, this time I think about the one move I'm sure I can trust—a big shoulder turn. I make a huge cut at the ball and it sails high and right, landing in the yard of a fantastic house whose owner really doesn't need my Callaway balls.

"What were you thinking?" Laird asks.

"Shoulder turn."

"Why? You've made a great shoulder turn on every shot today, but your ball still went right. So what went wrong?"

After twelve months of lessons, a terrible moment of truth.

"I don't have a clue."

"Then think about this," Laird explains. "Who won the race to the ball—your body or your hands?

"If I hit it right," I say in self-analysis, "then my body won by a mile."

"Exactly! Your hands lagged behind, and you hit it right. I see this every single day of my life—when people try to make a big shoulder turn, where does the clubface go? Inside. And the ball goes right. Jim Flick helped me understand that. When you're on the range, what do you work on to keep from hitting it right?"

"I try to keep my clubface looking at the ball on the way back."

"Then why are you trying to make a shoulder turn?" Laird asks. "If your issue is clubface, then think about that. Otherwise, just let it go and hit it. But don't think about shoulder turn when you've already got a good one."

. . .

We come to seventeen, a hole that fills me with fear. I'd sat here, not far from Kevin Costner, and watched him miss this little hourglass-shaped green by farther than he'd like me to report. On final-round Sunday, Pip and I used to watch hard-charging pros make or break their chances on this tough shot toward the ocean. Now Laird wanted me to think about S.A.T., but I didn't have a strategy, aim, or target.

"Let's play it like the pros," he tells me, dropping a ball on the back tee—actually the back of the tee to number four—which makes the hole twenty yards longer and is never in play on seventeen except for tournament time.

"Call our shots!" Laird says. "It's two hundred yards, I've got a four-iron, I'm going to draw it into the back tier."

Not only does he do all this, he makes it look easy.

"Your turn to paint a picture," he says. "This hole is your canvas; what are you going to paint?"

"A high five-wood with a little cut."

"Then do it."

Thinking about nothing more than finishing my swing, I make my best move. As my ball soars up against the sky, for the first time all morning, the sun's rays stream through the clouds, casting a beautiful light that seems like an omen from above.

"Go in!" Laird yells.

Landing just in front of the hole, my ball barely misses the pin and bounces off the back of the green into Tom Watson land—big trouble in paradise.

"So close," Laird says wistfully.

Walking off the tee, I look to the sky.

"Come on, Pip," I whisper. "If you're up there, I could use a little help!"

Eighteen. The end of the lesson. After this hole, life gets serious again. But for now, we're having fun.

"A guy stands right here on the eighteenth tee at Pebble Beach," I tell Laird, "and sees nothing but ocean all down the left side. As he starts to tee up an old ball, he hears a commanding voice from the heavens: *'Use a new ball!'*

"So he pulls out a new ball and tees it up.

" *'Take a practice swing!'* the voice commands.

"He takes a practice swing, then the voice says, *'Get out the OLD ball!'*"

Teeing up a new Callaway, I line up at the tree in the fairway. Trying to aim at the tree and not think about the ocean—which is *still* thinking about the ocean—I hit a low screamer straight toward the water.

"Hale Irwin!" Laird yells, referring to Irwin's great stroke of luck in the last round of the '94 AT&T. Trailing by one shot, Hale banged his tee shot on eighteen straight into the ocean. All was lost. But then, in one of the greatest bounces in the history of the game, the ball hit a rock in the water and caromed into the fairway. From there Hale made birdie and ultimately won the tournament.

No sooner has Laird invoked the famous miracle, than my ball hits a rock and also bounds into the fairway.

Looking up to the sky, I say, "Thanks, Pip."

Hale Irwin. Cinderella story. It's good to be alive.

I haven't conquered Pebble, but I'm learning. And like my father, I'm lucky.

The last night before my fiftieth birthday and the final round of my yearlong quest, I've tried to follow all the advice I've received about Pebble with the exception of David Feherty's advice to start drinking now. Though I haven't planned to get half-soused before the big event, I'm nervous, I'm thirsty, and I figure it's what Pip would have done.

In downtown Monterey, I head to the Britannia Arms. My butt is soon parked on the same stool where I'd enjoyed a pint or two the evening before my emergency departure and my father's passing.

Not being tournament week, this time around the place is only slightly packed to the rafters. Over the thirsty shouts for cold drinks, I am struck by the realization that—despite our shared fondness for fun and cold beer—I can only remember one time in my life that I actually shared drinks in a bar with my father.

Until I was old enough, Pip just went in for a drink and left me in the car. When I was a young teen working at the store in San Angelo, I'd put in three hours after school, then we'd lock up and head home, stopping along the way at the local bowling alley, which had a seedy little bar attached on one side. While Pip dashed in for a couple of quick ones, I'd sit in the car and fall asleep with the radio playing—waking only when he returned a good bit happier than when he'd gone inside. I didn't know at the time that Pip was well along the way to a real drinking problem. It was just something he did, like most of the other adults I knew.

The only time I remember drinking *with* him in a bar was in Austin during a UT football game weekend. With my brother Marvin, I was taken along for a visit to a seedy local watering hole called the Pink Lizard—so named for a side room filled with ratty sofas and illuminated by black lights on a mural of a pink lizard with his tongue extending into a pitcher of beer.

Behind the bar—at least when we arrived—was Fast Enco Eddie Burke—a now-deceased but then legendary gentlemen of excess who could well have been the inspiration of John Belushi's Bluto in *Animal House*. Thrilled to have so many Pipkins in the house, Fast Eddie soon turned the bartending tasks over to Pip, who had a glow about him much brighter than the pink lizard as he filled pitcher after pitcher with cold Lone Star and handed them over to thirsty patrons at the happy hour rate of one dollar per pitcher. We were there about an hour, and I must say, it was a happy one, indeed.

Avoiding a late and drunken night in Monterey, I was out of the Britannia at a reasonable hour and soon in my bed at Carmel Valley Ranch with a heartwarming fire going in the fireplace. The fire reminded me of all the countless mornings that Pip had risen before five A.M. in the freezing cold cabin at our ranch and built a roaring fire in the fireplace. Just a few feet away, I'd lie in my bunk, more asleep than awake, but smiling anyway because I knew he must love us very much to get up so early after staying up so late just so we wouldn't have to climb out of bed into the same cold that didn't bother him a bit. It wasn't until he'd warmed the cabin and cooked up a couple of pans of venison sausage and scrambled eggs that he'd shake us out of bed with a "Rise and shine" or an "Up and at 'em." I was eight years old before I realized Up and Adam weren't some biblical names that had somehow escaped me at church.

If we weren't at the ranch when I was a kid, Sunday mornings found all the Pipkin family at church, though I didn't see why we couldn't just go to the golf course.

Pip's mother—my namesake Clyde Turk—had played the organ at her small-town Methodist church for fifty years, and Pip never lost his love of those old hymns, especially in his final years at the nursing home, where he loved to sing "In the Garden."

And He walks with me, and He talks with me,
And He tells me I am His own;
And the joy we share as we tarry there,
None other has ever known.

Lying there in front of the fire, I could still hear his deep voice. But hard as I tried, I could not picture his face as he sang. And then a slow panic started to come over me, for I suddenly found that I could not picture my father's face at all. I've never carried a photo of him, and for some reason don't have a single photo of just the two of us.

What I have is memories, and not much more than a year after Pip's death, I realized that my memories of his loving face were slowly fading into the past. On the wall of my office at home, I had recently hung a beautiful photo of my parents with Christy and me on our wedding night, framed with a proclamation from the Senate of the State of Texas commemorating Pip's life. Even so, a photo is not the same as a face, and I could not help wonder if my lapse was just a hint of things to come? I'd loved him too much to lose him again.

Closing my eyes, I searched for him until I fell into an uneasy sleep. When I awoke the next morning, the fire was out, and my room was cold.

CHAPTER 33

Final Round

"Every day is a new day."

—Ernest Hemingway,
The Old Man and the Sea

About to step onto the first tee at Pebble, I was suddenly struck by an even worse case of jitters than I'd had on the day I shot 89 a year before. Pulling a glove from my bag, I tried to get it on my left hand, but couldn't remember how. I mean that sucker just would not go on my fingers. As I tried to figure it out, the starter was staring at me with a look that seemed to say, "What's up with this clown?"

That's when I realized the glove was *right*-handed, one I'd worn in Scotland when the weather was so cold I had to wear golf gloves on both hands. Dumping a couple of hundred long tees on the ground, I found a proper glove, slipped it on, and stepped to the tee.

My heart was pounding, my face was itchy, and my hands were trembling enough to make me drop my ball, then my tee, then my ball again. Taking some long, deep breaths to calm myself, I got so much oxygen in my lungs I nearly passed out.

And why shouldn't I be nervous. I was the leader of my own U.S.

Open. To win the event, I needed a 79. To come in last, an 80. Either way, the only person who could beat me was me.

After my lesson with Laird, I'd played Carmel Valley Ranch with David Wood's brother, who'd recently moved back to the Monterey Peninsula from St. Andrews, where he'd played the Old Course over a hundred times.

"How long did it take you to get over your first tee jitters at the Old Course?" I asked.

"I never did," Patrick Wood told me. "I was just as nervous the last time as the first."

Now I knew what he meant. But nerves or not, I had to hit. The others in my group had played their drives, and I was up.

Gripping my three-wood, I aimed at the bunker on the left side of the dogleg and fired away. I'm not exactly sure where the ball stopped, because that swing was the last thing I remembered about the hole until I was stroking in a short putt at the green.

"Good bogey!" someone said.

Looking back at the hole I was barely able to remember playing it. That was weird I thought.

The rest of the front nine is a roller coaster of emotions and breaks, both good and bad. For starters, my lower back hurts like hell. I don't know if this is the result of the plane ride to California or simply too much golf, but this is the most important round of my life, and my body is betraying me as if I really am an old man.

My temporary solution is to grit my teeth and swing hard. Reaching the par-five second in two, I three-putt, partially because we're putting on a temp green, and feel as though I've been robbed of my birdie at gunpoint.

On three, my S.A.T. calls for an aggressive shot—a long, high hook around the corner. I hit it perfect, put an eight-iron on the green, then blast the putt way past the hole and blow an easy par.

"Your first and most important objective when you get to Pebble,"

Crenshaw had told me, "is to get a feel for the distance of the greens. To get a feel for the greens, get rid of direction, and focus on distance only."

What's the good of all this advice, I wonder, if I don't follow it?

On the other hand, I coach myself, I'm swinging great, and the wind is at our backs.

A year earlier, I'd sliced my drive from the fourth tee over the the bluff to the shores of Stillwater Cove. Playing smarter and better, this time I swing my five-wood, split the fairway, and make an easy par, then make another on the new Nicklaus-designed fifth.

From the left rough on six, I can almost hear Byron Nelson's syrupy Texas voice saying, "That hill is taller than you think, so use a lot of loft and aim left on that second shot. There's not much trouble on that side."

Another par. Thanks, Byron.

That leaves me just two over as I come to the hundred-yard seventh, a simple little shot if you can ignore the entire Pacific Ocean. Pulling my sand wedge, I look down at the little green thinking I can make anything from birdie to nine.

If ever there was ever a time I need to see it, feel it, and trust it, this is it. But all I see is ocean; all I feel is nerves. And the only thing I trust is the notion that I've put too much into this, laid too much on the line, risked too much. I've risked my family's financial footing on a costly yearlong lark. I've risked a solid string of work in L.A., and for what? To play golf. I've risked the trust my kids have in the idea that I am invincible, for what if I fail? I've driven my wife almost to madness with my obsession and, in doing so, risked our twenty-year relationship. All that and more, I've risked on a bet that even I had thought impossible. I've wagered a heartache, and on the twelfth tee at Pebble, I'm terrified that I'm about to come up snake eyes.

While I'm telling myself to hit in the hole, I hear my mind ticking through other possibilities: so easy to fan it right into the ocean, blade it into the waves behind the green, or simply top a dribbler down the hill.

Then I hear what may have been the best golf advice of my life. I hear my dad say, "Keep your head down."

Sure, I know what Kip and David and all the other great golf pros think of that advice. But that's the way Pip played golf, and right now it's exactly the advice I need.

So I keep my head down, and take a swing. Right away I hear my playing partners say, "Good shot!"

Here's the problem. Other than a terrible drive on eight, I'm hitting the ball pretty good, I'm playing with purpose, and I'm fairly satisfied with nearly every shot I hit. And still the bogeys come. It's the nature of Pebble. Miss the green by three feet and I dare you to make par.

When I lip out a five-foot putt for par on eleven, I check my card and realize that I'm already six over par. Six over after eleven holes—and I need to be seven over after eighteen. To do that, I have to play all the way home, against the wind, and give up only one more stroke to par.

Add in a sore back and tender wrist from playing too dang much golf, and I'll be lucky to *bogey* every hole.

Poke a fork in me, I'm done.

A thought flashes through my mind: What would it cost to postpone my departure and play another round the next day? It wouldn't be on my fiftieth birthday, but who cares about that? I'd miss my birthday party in Austin with family and friends, but what other option do I have?

At the end of my rope, as I wait with my playing partners for the group in front of us to clear the twelfth green, I realized I've ignored a secret weapon I've been holding in reserve. Digging deep in my bag, my fingers feel the smooth glass, then I pull out a small bottle containing one large shot of Turnberry twelve-year-old scotch.

For six months, I've carried this little bottle in my bag, for this is the same magic elixir that soothed my shin splints, warmed my chilled bones, and brought me home from the Ailsa halfway house in fine form. Opening the bottle, I drink it down in two gulps, sending a jolt of fire from my chest to every inch of my body. Within seconds, my back is fine, my nerves are calm, and my scorecard pretty much forgotten. I'm pulling the seven-wood from my bag when I remember that Laird Small told me not to go long here.

What I need is five-iron, but it's not in my bag, for a week earlier, I finally admitted that—like the four-iron before it—I had zero confidence in my five. Since I had every confidence in my seven-wood, the obvious solution was to make one last switch to my fourteen clubs and replace the five-iron with a Great Big Bertha II nine-wood.

A nine-wood! Man, I think as I pull it out, I really am old!

After two or three chips each, the group in front of us is just lining up their putts, so while the scotch turns my ears a brilliant red, I pull out a beer coaster from the Britannia Arms on which, late the night before, I'd written my game plan for this fateful round. That I've thus far neglected to consult my own advice even once will give you some indication of how keyed up I've been.

And so it comes to pass that twelve holes into the final round of my year, I finally get around to the essence of what I've learned.

And while the sources of these thoughts may be obvious, what also needs pointing out is that for all my efforts to "swing the handle" and "make a world-class finish," nothing on my list deals with golf mechanics.

For what I've finally concluded is that, if I can't be a good golfer, I'll have to be a wise one. That's why I titled my beer-coaster list:

The Seven Pillars of Golf Wisdom

1. *Every shot counts.*
2. *Pull the right club.*
3. *Call your shot.*
4. *Take dead aim.*

5. *Believe in yourself.*
6. *Complete your swing.*
7. *Never give up.*

Those are the words—no more, no less—that I'd written on the cardboard coaster. My guess is that almost any golfer reading this book could make a list that suits his or her game just as well as this list suits mine. Why should I make it a point to complete my swing? Because—like a lot of golfers—I tend not to and leave a lot of shots short and right. Who knows, you may need to complete your *backswing.*

But perhaps, if you made your own list, a few of my pillars would also appear on yours. See something there you like? That'd make me as happy as it did Harvey Penick when people connected to his simple idea to take dead aim. Having known Harvey—and having benefited firsthand from his knowledge of golf—it's no surprise that "Take dead aim" lies at the exact center of all that I know about the game.

The one definite thing I can say about my list is that it worked for me, because one swing after reading through it a second time on the twelfth tee at Pebble, my ball is sitting eight feet from the hole. And one putt later, I've made my first birdie of the day. With six holes to go, I am five over par.

Never give up, I read again as I walk to the thirteenth tee.

Now I'm having fun. Suddenly I have the kind of feel for the game that I knew in those early years in West Texas—like those first times I actually got the ball airborne. Like teeing off at dawn, then walking down the middle of the fairway making the first footprints in the wet dew. Like my father's hand on my shoulder as he said, "Good shot."

Two pars and two bogeys later, I come to seventeen, seven over par. In order to break 80, I need to finish with back-to-back pars. How many pros, I wonder, have come to seventeen needing just two pars to win the Crosby or the U.S. Open, and walked away in second place? Nine strokes in a year? It just doesn't have the same ring to it. And I haven't done that yet, either.

Final Round

But I have good things going for me. Hitting from farther back during the practice round with Laird Small, I'd played a high seven-wood and struck it well. But the tee is closer now, and the pin is in the *front-right* part of the hourglass green. Seven-wood is too much, and I'd known that before I even came to Pebble.

It was for this hole—for this exact shot—that I put the nine-wood in my bag. So let's see what the Old Man and his Old Man Club can do.

Calling my shot (high from the right), I take dead aim, trust it, and make damn sure to complete my swing. There are no miraculous shafts of sunlight through the clouds this time, but flying high, then diving home, the ball lands in the front fringe, hops forward and rolls to three feet from the cup.

One putt later, I've birdied seventeen, and I'm almost home.

Six over par, I stand on eighteen and do my best not to think about my last two tee shots from this spot. A year earlier, a watery grave. With Laird, the same, saved only by a one-in-a-million lucky break. I'll bet even Hale Irwin hasn't bounced two in a row out of the ocean.

Placing tee and ball in the grass, I line up, not at the tree in the fairway, but twenty yards right of it. If my nerves on this shot give me half of a backswing and all of a hook, then by God I'll hook it. What I don't want to do, I think, is turn into Jean Van der Velde at the Open. I don't want to walk away from this round saying, "What if?"

Anywhere on the right is better than the ocean. And that's where I hit it. From the right side, I hit another safe shot down the right, but with the ball in the air, I realize the right isn't as safe as it appears, for the out-of-bounds stakes are close by the cart path.

"No!" I yell.

But yes, my ball lands hard and bounces out of bounds into someone's yard. Then just as suddenly, the ball bounces again and rolls back into play. Shades of Crenshaw at the Masters, I think.

As I walk forward, I say it again, "Thanks, Pip. I couldn't have gotten here without you."

The Old Man and the Tee

From the heavy rough, I advance the ball once more down the right side, leaving myself fifty yards from the green. It's not until I arrive at the ball that I realize I'm blocked by Pebble's famous Monterey pine. Two years before, after the original tree that protected this approach angle succumbed to lightning and disease, the Pebble Beach Company moved a gigantic, sixty-seven-foot tree from the first hole to this spot, digging up and binding a thirty-foot-wide, five-foot-high root ball, then moving the half-a-million-pound tree along a one-mile route with an eighty-wheel trailer.

The result is spectacular, but all I can think is, what an incredible amount of expense and trouble just to block my shot. Perhaps one of Pelz's distance wedge shots with my lob wedge would make it over, but the potential for disaster is high.

What to do? What to do? I mutter. Next to the green, a course employee, waiting to hand us our souvenir Pebble Beach bag tags, watches me with interest. No doubt, he's seen a lot of golfers eat it big-time from here.

The only logical choice is to hit *under* the overhanging branches, but *over* the bunker between me and the pin. Pulling my pitching wedge, I move my hands forward and rehearse the feel of pulling the clubhead through the shot. Then I pitch my ball under the tree limbs, over the bunker, and onto the green.

A year ago, I think, I could not have done that.

The guys in my group, knowing I have a chance to break 80, are watching me closely now. We've all played well, but I'm the one with something on the line.

Thirty feet remain between my ball and the hole, and all I have to do is two-putt. Walking the line, I'm thinking, this is it! Two little putts and I've accomplished what I set out to do. I'll have taken ten strokes off my handicap *and* ten strokes off my score. This putt is everything.

But as soon as I think it, I know it's a lie. As I mark my ball, I still know it's a lie. This putt isn't everything. This putt doesn't mean anything at all. It simply doesn't matter. What matters is that my father took me out to the golf course, put a golf club in my hands, dropped a ball, and said, "Hit it in the hole."

What matters is that I joyfully spent a large part of my childhood trying to knock that ball in the hole. I've grown up and traveled the world in a variety of pursuits, yet over and over I've made the choice to continue with a game I love. I've made and missed a million putts, and this is just one more.

What matters, I think as I replace my ball on my marker, is that I made a promise to myself and to my father and vowed that I'd fulfill it. In my mind, I made this putt well over a year ago. Shoot, I made this putt when I was ten years old. Twenty feet, right to left, slightly uphill. I can see it, I can feel it, and I can trust it. I can trust it because golf has never failed me.

In all my life, I can't remember a single shot in which I was smiling when I hit it. Perhaps there were many, but not once was I in the frame of mind to remember it. But as I stand over that putt on the eighteenth green at Pebble Beach, my eye above the ball and my arms hanging beneath my shoulders, my whole body is smiling.

I am still smiling when the ball falls into the cup.

After buying a round of beers for my group in the Tap Room, I headed out to see what the second fifty years of my life would be like. With my quest at an end, I was once again a wanderer and literally did not know where to go. Next to the pro shop in Cambridge Golf Antiquities, I looked at old golf books and fine memorabilia, and gave the owner a copy of *Fast Greens*. Back at eighteen, I simply stared at the magnificent tree.

Finally, I had to admit that it was time to leave. Picking up my bag from next to the putting green where my journey began, I slung it on my shoulder and started back to my car. As I passed the first tee, the same course employee I'd seen earlier stepped over and said, "I was watching you down on eighteen; that was a nice pitch you hit under the tree. Did you make the putt?"

"I made it," I told him. "I saved my par. I saved my round. I saved my life."

And he said, "Thanks for coming out."

But what had I really done? I wondered. I hadn't brought my father back to life, and I hadn't seen a rainbow in the sky that told me he was watching. But the truth is, I hadn't expected a miracle. I'd never know whether Pip was watching me from above, but I did know that if he was watching, and if he is watching me still, he is as proud of me in heaven as he was on earth.

I'd begun my life without him, feeling as if I hadn't done enough with him or for him, that I'd been a disappointment for too much of his life. I'd also started my year trying to hide from the opposite feelings, that he hadn't given me what I needed at times when my whole future seemed to hang in the balance. Somehow, in my year, I'd managed to trade in all that useless baggage and finally accepted and come to love who we were and what we thought of each other, for we were a father and a son who loved each other, and I suddenly knew that I would always wear his precious gold watch with pride.

With my clubs in the trunk, I put the top down on my red convertible. The night before, I'd lain awake worrying that I was forgetting my father's face, but now I can see him clearly.

I see him walking down the fairway just ahead of me at the San Angelo Country Club. With his heavy bag over my shoulder, I'm trying to keep up, but my legs aren't long yet, and I'm falling behind. Then he stops, looks back at me with a smile, and waits for me to catch up.

I see him years later on the only day Christy and our oldest girl, Katie, ever saw him play golf. Pip and I are coming up the eighteenth fairway in San Angelo, it's about 105 degrees and we're half-fried. But we haven't played together in a couple of years, and I can see how happy he is that we're together. We don't know it at the time, but it's the last round we'll ever play together, and the last round of his life. And both of us have played well.

I see him in the nursing home, pushing a checker to the back row, turning it into a king and hopping my pieces all over the board with a triumphant grin. I see that same smile as my daughters climb into his lap in his wheelchair and give their grandfather a kiss.

I see him in the hospital on that last afternoon, the tournament broadcast showing number eighteen fairway from the tee.

"That's a beautiful place," he tells me.

In all of these memories and a thousand more, I can see him now in glorious detail. There in my red convertible, he is with me—not some apparition in the sky or a ghost riding shotgun, but with me in a more real way—in my head and in my heart—right where he belongs. Right where he will always be. Forever.

I start the car and Bing starts to sing.

> *. . . straight down the middle*
> *Where it wound up is a riddle*
> *But it went straight down the middle, far away.*

AFTERWORD

There is an much-abused notion in the literature of our sport that golf is a metaphor for life. Sounds lovely, but is it? Even if you're a professional golfer, golf is still golf, and life is life. If you confuse the two, you're likely to not be very good at either one.

On the other hand, if you lose your love of one, it may also cause you to lose your passion for the other. When I read about the struggles of formerly great golfers like Sandy Lyle or Seve Ballesteros, I don't wonder what happened to their swings, I always wonder what happened to their lives.

A few days after my birthday, I could not help but wonder what happened to the first fifty years of mine. Life's universal truism is that the days and hours pass slowly, but your life as a whole passes like a flash. One day, you're young and carefree, and the next, only your memories are free of cares.

The only cure to the speed at which life passes is to open your eyes and look around you. Our lives are a never-ending cycle of birth, joy, learning, love, loss, and sorrow—all without purpose except for one simple goal—the celebration, the exaltation, of life itself.

With a lot of help from others, I was able to achieve my ten-stroke goal because—as David Cook advised—I managed to put myself in the best possible place to accomplish my goal. And *that* is the way in which golf is most like life.

If your goal is to write, I've learned daily for the last thirty years, there's only one way to do it. Every day you have to sit down and write. People who know my work often come up to me and say, "I want to be a writer." My reply is simple to the point that people sometimes think me rude. "Then write," I say. Write your story or your screenplay or your book. When you've done that, you *are* a writer.

If your goal is to have a wonderful family, then you must devote yourself to them the way my parents did. The effort may come at the expense of other things you hope to accomplish, but you'll be rewarded a thousandfold for the love you give your spouse and children.

Are you a person of dreams? Of course you are. We are made of dreams. That commitment to your family doesn't have to come at the expense of your dreams. Do you dream—while working your tail off to pay the bills and save money for college educations—of playing the Old Course or Pebble Beach? Then find a way to make it happen, even if it's just once in your life. Enlist the support of those you love in your dream, and you'll be amazed at what may happen.

Don't grow old with regret in your eyes, but with a smile on your face. Though my father was dealt a crummy hand in the last years of his life, his choice to play out that hand with a light in his eyes was my final lesson from him.

Having started with "Keep your head down," we progressed to "Keep your head up."

For if you hold your head high, and walk proudly with your club at your side, you will never regret it.

ACKNOWLEDGMENTS

Thanks to all of you who stopped what you were doing to help push a 220-pound guy up a ladder with no rungs. I couldn't have gotten here without each and every one of you.

MY TEACHERS

David Leadbetter and Sean Hogan from the David Leadbetter Golf Academy; Dave Pelz, Eddie Pelz, Dennis Close, and Stefan Carlsmith at the Dave Pelz Scoring School; Byron Nelson, Paul Ernest, and Kenny Huff at the Byron Nelson Golf School; Chris Brown and Colin Montgomerie at the Colin Montgomerie Links Golf Academy; Kip Puterbaugh at the Kip Puterbaugh School of Golf; Dr. David Cook at La Cantera Golf Academy; Laird Small at the Pebble Beach Golf Academy; Tom Bennett and all the pros and staff at Barton Creek Resort and Country Club; Larry Goswehr and Jim Hopkins at the Harvey

Acknowledgments

Penick Golf Academy; Willie Nelson at the Zen-Cowboy School of Golf; Bill Murray at the Golf School of Cool; and particular thanks to Chuck Cook, Ben Crenshaw, Chip Gist, Tom Kite, Bill Murray, Willie Nelson, Arnold Palmer, Tinsley Penick, Dave Preisler, Curt Sampson, Bud Shrake, Jim Thorpe, and Brad Wheatley.

MY HOSTS

Particular thanks go to Valerie Ramsey and everyone at the Pebble Beach Company. Likewise to Sam Baker at Haversham and Baker Golf Tours; Martha Heagany at Barton Creek Resort & Spa; Rachel Williamson at Troon Golf; Nicola Blazier at Four Seasons Hotels and Resorts; Angela Enright at the Four Seasons Las Colinas; Phil Weidinger for Reno and Tahoe golf; Tony Cerone at the Westin La Cantera. Also to Carmel Valley Ranch, Cordevalle; the Four Seasons Aviara; the Four Seasons Las Colinas; the Inn at Spanish Bay, Lajitas; the Ultimate Hideout, La Quinta Resort & Spa; and the Westin Monarch Beach.

In Scotland: Ewen Bowmat Turnberry Resort; Grant Sword at the Royal Golf Hotel in Dornoch; the Old Course Hotel; and the Sheraton Grand Hotel & Spa in Edinburgh.

In Mexico: Esperanza, the Four Seasons Punta Mita, the One & Only Palmilla, and El Tamarindo.

MY GEAR

Special thanks to Larry Dorman and Richard Helmstetter at Callaway Golf; to Gary Poole and Putting Greens Direct; to Ping Golf; and Adams Golf.

THE COURSES

Barton Creek Fazio Canyons, Fazio Foothills, Crenshaw Cliffside, and Palmer Lakeside courses. Also in Austin: Avery Ranch Golf Club, Cimarron Hills Country Club, Circle C Ranch Golf Course, Colovista

Acknowledgments

Golf Course, Falconhead Golf Club, Flint Rock Falls & The Hills Country Club, Forest Creek Golf Club, Lions Municipal Golf Course, Pedernales Country Club, Lakecliff Country Club, Star Ranch Golf Club, Terravista Golf Club, and Twin Creeks Country Club.

In Dallas: Cowboys Club, Four Seasons TPC at Las Colinas, Heritage Ranch Golf Club, and the Tribute at the Colony. In Fort Worth: Colonial Country Club and Z-Boaz Golf Course. In San Antonio: La Cantera Palmer and Resort Courses, La Quinta Golf Course, Pecan Valley Golf Course, Quarry Golf Club, and Republic Golf Club. Also the Ambush at Lajitas, Llano Golf Course, Rockport Country Club.

In California: Atwater Golf Course, Carmel Valley Ranch, Cordevalle Golf Course, Coyote Moon, the Dragon at Graeagle, Four Seasons Aviara, the Links at Spanish Bay, Monarch Beach Golf Links, Pebble Beach Golf Club, Riviera Country Club, Robinson Ranch, Squaw Creek, and the Golf Club at Whitehawk Ranch. In Nevada: Edgewood Tahoe, the Golf Club at Genoa Lakes, and Sierra Nevada Golf Ranch. In Arizona: the Monument and the Pinnacle at Troon North. In Tennessee: the Golf Club of Tennessee and the President's Reserve. In Nebraska: Arthur Golf Course, Big Springs Golf Course, Hemingford Golf Course, and Sand Hills Golf Club. In Wyoming: Salt Creek Country Club. In Florida: the New Course at Grand Cypress.

In Hawaii: Four Seasons Hualalai, Mauna Kea, Mauna Lani, and Waikaloa Golf Club. In Mexico: Cabo del Sol Ocean and Desert Courses, El Dorado Golf Course, El Tigre Golf Course, Four Seasons Punta Mita, Palmilla Golf Club, Querencia Golf Club, Tamarindo Golf Club, and Vista Vallarta Nicklaus and Weiskopf Courses.

In Scotland: Kingsbarns Golf Course, Muirfield Golf Course, Nairn Golf Club, North Berwick Golf Course, Royal Dornoch Golf Club, Turnberry Ailsa, Kintyre and Academy Courses, and Western Gailes Golf Club.

Acknowledgments

THE MAGAZINES

Golf Magazine, Golf Digest, Private Clubs Magazine, Travel and Leisure Golf, and the *Austin Chronicle.*

AND FINALLY

Shortly after my final round at Pebble Creek, Bob Hope died at age 100, followed by George Plimpton who passed away at age 76. Thanks for the jokes and the stories. I wish there were more.

To the staff of Meadow Creek nursing home, thanks for all of your loving care.

Rest in peace, Pip. We love you.